THE PERSONALITY COLOR MATRIX

The Personality Color Matrix

The Transformative Tool to Unlock Joy, Upgrade Your Awareness, & Reconnect

Dawn L. Billings and

Corbin B. Billings

Copyright © 2025 by Dawn L. Billings and Corbin B. Billings

Printed in the United States of America. All rights reserved under International Copyright Law. Contents and/or cover may not be reproduced in whole or in part in any form without the express written consent of the publisher.

Phone: (918) 605-1492

Web site: www.DawnBillingsConsultations.com

E-mail: connect@thecolormatrix.com

Published by: Game Changer Publishing

Paperback ISBN: 978-1-966659-86-0

Hardcover ISBN: 978-1-966659-87-7

Digital ISBN: 978-1-966659-88-4

DEDICATIONS

DAWN:
For my sons, Anthony C. Billings II and Corbin B. Billings,
to whom my life is dedicated.

To my dearest heart connections:
Anthony C. Billings I, Alison Billings,
JuliAnne Smith, Kerry Press, Rachel Hall,
and Yan Hughes.

To my now heavenly connections,
Sue Ellis and Larry Crain.

And my eternal gratitude to Dr. Scott Stanley and Jim Stovall, whose brilliance and patience have no bounds. Because of your contributions, each breath I take is one of enormous gratitude.

CORBIN:
To my son, Atlas Basil Billings,
For whom I am dedicated to leaving a better world.

And to my mother,
I love you a googolplex times a googolplex
to the googolplexth power.

READ THIS FIRST

Thank you for purchasing a copy of our book! We're thrilled to have you join our growing community of centered relationship seekers on this journey of self-discovery and understanding. As a token of our sincere appreciation, we're excited to offer you the opportunity to take the full online six-test series for **FREE**.

These tests are designed to provide deep insights into your personality and help you navigate life's challenges with greater clarity.

Scan the QR Code and use code: ReconnectNow

Thank you once again for your support and curiosity.
We hope you enjoy discovering your primary colors and
embracing a more centered and fulfilling path!

THE PERSONALITY COLOR MATRIX

THE TRANSFORMATIVE TOOL TO UNLOCK JOY,
UPGRADE YOUR AWARENESS, & RECONNECT

DAWN L. BILLINGS
AND
CORBIN B. BILLINGS

FOREWORD
BY JIM STOVALL

Dear Reader,

First and foremost, I want to congratulate you for the investment of time, money, and effort you have placed in this book. I believe the concepts contained within these pages will reap countless benefits in your personal and professional life. There have been many studies done on self-made millionaires, corporate CEOs, and other high-level achievers to determine what characteristics they share that create extraordinary results. Study after study has revealed that regularly reading motivational, inspirational, and instructional books is a trait that virtually all top achievers have in common.

I met Dawn Billings through the National Speakers Association. She is a driving force within the field of personal development and success. Dawn remains one of the great influences on my career as an author, speaker, columnist, and movie producer. Her concept of contrasting entitlement and endowment remains a pivotal part of my work and home life. Whenever I'm feeling challenged or things are out of sync, I simply ask myself, *Are you feeling entitled or endowed?* Entitlement presumes we deserve something or success is somehow owed to us, while endowment calls us to look at everything as a blessing for which we should be grateful.

I met Corbin when he was an elementary school student. My enduring memory of him is of the day they were having show and tell in his class, and he asked me to come and bring a copy of my book, *You Don't Have to be Blind to See*. That book was autobiographical in that it shared my

Foreword

journey of having to set aside my goal of being an NFL football player when I was diagnosed with a condition that would cause me to lose my sight. It then recounts my journey of becoming an Olympic weightlifting champion, founding the Emmy Award-winning Narrative Television Network, which makes TV and movies accessible for 13 million blind and visually impaired people and their families, and learning to live my life as a blind person. When I arrived at Corbin's class, he greeted me wearing an impeccable three-piece suit with a stylish tie. He told me to stand at the front of the class while he talked, and he addressed his classmates utilizing a wooden pointer his teacher had on hand. I will never forget his opening as he strategically used the pointer explaining, "This is Jim Stovall, and this is his book." Not what you would expect from a grade school student, but Corbin has always exceeded expectations.

As a blind person myself, I am always intrigued with the way that sighted people get or fail to get from point A to point B. It is fascinating to me that people who can see perfectly spend a great deal of their time being lost.

Recently, I made one of my rare trips to a giant shopping mall. As usual, I was listening to all the conversations going on around me. I discovered that most people spend a great deal of effort during their shopping experience trying to figure out where they are in relation to where they wish they were.

I discovered that throughout the mall, there are a number of maps showing the locations of the various shops and restaurants in the building. These maps are identical at every location throughout the facility, with one very critical exception. In each map location, there is one unique piece of information—that is the large arrow pointing to a spot on the map with the explanation reading, "You are here."

This points out a vital link in the chain of personal achievement. That is, quite simply, that the single most vital piece of information necessary in order to get where you are going is to know where you are. There are millions of people who want to have a certain bank balance, weigh a certain amount, or achieve any other business or personal goal. These people fantasize about where they want to be, but they have not taken the practical step of determining where they are.

A dream turns into a goal when you get specific. The ancient Chinese proverb says, "A journey of a thousand miles begins with a single step." This is only true if you take that first step in the right direction. That is only possible when you know where you are. Think about all the things you want in the personal and professional areas of your life. Then take

Foreword

account of where you are today. You may find that you're closer than you think. But, in any event, you will have taken the first step in the right direction, and you will have reduced an ethereal dream into a practical goal that can begin now.

Once you have determined where you are, an even more critical discovery waiting to be revealed is *who you are*. This book and the matrix that is the foundation of Dawn and Corbin's transformational work will help you understand yourself and those around you as you begin your journey to success. Any master craftsman fully understands his tools. A virtuoso musician has an elemental connection to her instrument. In much the same way, your personality and psychological makeup will be an integral part of success in your personal and professional life.

Too often, people mistakenly look outside of themselves at prevailing conditions or other people as they contemplate their strategy to success. If you want to be the person of your dreams and live your best life, it begins by looking within. Dawn and Corbin Billings will be your guides, your cheerleaders, and your coaches as you move toward success.

—Jim Stovall, bestselling author

CONTENTS

Preface   xvii
Introduction   xxiii

1. Blinded by Enmity   1
2. Understanding Entitlement   15
3. Strength and Warmth: Angry Opponents or Imperative Partners   29
4. The Growing Wrath of Extremes   43
5. What Is the Help Paradox?   65
6. Humans Being Right   85
7. Do We Teach Capability or Victimhood?   107
8. Rights Without Responsibility   123
9. Who Has the Real Power?   139
10. In Conclusion: You Choose   163

Glossary   181
About the Authors   189
Thank You For Reading Our Book!   191

The things that will destroy us are:
Politics without principle;
pleasure without conscience;
wealth without work;
knowledge without character;
business without morality;
science without humanity;
and worship without sacrifice.

– Mahatma Gandhi

PREFACE
CHOOSING COLLABORATION

DAWN'S WELCOME

This book is the revised version of *Entitled to Fail, Endowed to Succeed*, which I penned twenty years ago. Corbin and I have not only revised my original book, but we have augmented and expanded it in substantial ways. We are not limiting this version to the wrath of entitlement and the subsequent enmity it creates. We have updated it to include fascinating and enlightening behavioral insights using a unique personality technology called The Personality Color Matrix (once known only as the Primary Colors Personality Insight Tool) that expands your understanding of yourself and others. The book also contains strategies to battle the destruction of entitlement in your life and community.

I am the architect and author of the original Primary Colors Personality Insight Tool, which uses the artist's color wheel as its base. I wanted this technology to be both profoundly impactful and *simple to understand*, hence the name Primary Colors. When people are in distress, they do not need more complications in their lives. They need a simple way to understand the roots of their distress. For over three decades, I licensed the test series to therapists and organizations across North America who were dedicated, as I was, to the cause of reducing conflict in personal relationships. My youngest son, Corbin, grew to see tremendous value in the Primary Colors Personality Insight Tool and dedicated himself to upgrading and updating the original paper test into a gamified digital experience, making it an absolute joy to take. Together, we have continued to update the technology, usability, and depth of these powerful insight tools. It has been a challenging but truly wonderful experience that has left my heart full of gratitude for Corbin's brilliant capacities to carry on my life's legacy. Any parent understands the powerful gift that comes from a child having a strong desire to ensure your life's work lives on.

As a counselor, I focused this technology on helping couples and families heal the inevitable rifts that can tear relationships apart. Going forward, Corbin's dream is to increase the accessibility and depth of these tools. In fact, The Personality Color Matrix goes as deep as you can imagine, reflecting the complexity of the human psyche. That being said, it has remained easy to understand and apply. Our goal is to greatly expand the use of our insight tools to help people who are feeling lost, hopeless, and overwhelmed. While my focus was on healing the great misery caused by misunderstanding and heartbreak in the lives of couples, we now realize it is time to take this technology to the masses to help people understand more about their unique gifts and talents, as well as the misery and distress caused by attitudes, behaviors, and tendencies that sabotage their happiness, security, and dreams.

As we were brainstorming the title of this book, Corbin proposed ***The Personality Color Matrix: The Transformative Tool To Unlock Joy, Upgrade Your Awareness, & Reconnect.*** I loved it immediately. We will explain later in this book how the movie *The Matrix* impacted both of us deeply. However, that is not why I loved the name "Personality Color Matrix." For me, the meaning goes much deeper. The word "matrix" is defined as "an environment or material in which something develops; a surrounding medium or structure."[1] In other words, free choices become the matrix of human life. This is the core belief upon which the original Primary Colors Personality Insight Tool was created.

My affinity for the word "matrix" grew even deeper when I discovered that it comes from the Latin word "mater," which means "mother." The original meaning of "matrix" was "uterus or womb," but today, it usually refers to a situation or set of conditions in which something develops or forms.[2] This is a powerful word to describe our insight technology because Corbin, my son, is the one expanding and developing the Primary Colors Personality Insight Tool into The Personality Color Matrix. I am excited

---

1. Encyclopedia.com, s.v. "Matrix," accessed 2024, https://www.encyclopedia.com/science-and-technology/mathematics/mathematics/matrix.
2. Etymonline, s.v. "Matrix," accessed 2024, https://www.etymonline.com/word/matrix

Preface

about this new evolution. We will continue to use Primary Colors Personality Insight Tools in our work with families, schools, churches, and nonprofits. At the same time, The Personality Color Matrix offers valuable insights for those looking to understand themselves, their reality, and the key personality elements that shape relationships. It provides tools for developing skills and awareness to recognize how these core traits influence interpersonal dynamics. Pursuing either path will ultimately lead to more joy, meaning, and purpose.

The antithesis of joy, meaning, and purpose is entitlement. In the 20 years since the first version of this book was published, entitlement has mushroomed into a feverish monster of enmity. Entitlement causes us to morph into extreme and ugly versions of ourselves. Entitlement's extremes of bitterness, loathing, disrespect, and rage have flooded our streets, pummeling compassion, cooperation, and collaboration, which used to be the bedrock of community. We cry out for tolerance but have conflicted and dissenting directions as to how to heal, nurture, and strengthen it in our hearts. People cannot be shamed into tolerance. Tolerance, like love, cannot be demanded, mandated, or forced. Our society must learn how to foster the connections born out of amity to nurture healthy compassion. Therefore, Corbin and I will focus on ways to help you recognize the virus of entitlement that corrupts and inhibits tolerance.

In the original version of this book, I warned of the devastation that entitlement would bring. This book will not only reinforce my cautionary prognostication but will also focus on ways to heal this devastating *disease* and expose how our thoughts and choices create contentment and peace or conflict and discontent. The reality is that perceiving one's world through an entitled versus endowed lens determines the quality of one's life.

I was born in 1953 to an extremely poor family with little education and even fewer resources. My son, born in 1988, grew up in a very educated family with many resources. The zeitgeist (the defining spirit or mood of a particular period of history as shown by the ideas and beliefs of the time) in my early years was: "You can accomplish anything if you have a strong enough desire and are willing to work hard enough." My parents loved me as best they could, but my home was very dysfunctional. My father was an alcoholic, and my mother was a valium addict. Both had childhoods that I would not wish on my worst enemy, so my childhood, however rough, was gentle compared to theirs.

Corbin's dad and I were both workaholics. Corbin's father's parents were Italian immigrants who wanted nothing more than to be Americans and for their children to live the American dream. They believed in the value of hard work and education. What little money they did earn, they spent on their son's and daughter's education. They were the immigrants so often spoken about with reverence that built this nation.

Twenty years ago, I had no political affiliation. I did not care for "politics as usual" on either side. Politics seemed to me to be a game where cheating and deception were accepted. It simply felt like a breeding ground for corruption. In hindsight, I think I would describe myself as a very liberal conservative or a conservative liberal. To attempt to be either in today's political environment has proven to be as difficult as keeping your balance while riding two wild stallions with a foot on the back of each as they run in opposite directions. The enmity between the two major parties is so violent that it makes it impossible to get the horses to charge forward together. Politics are ubiquitous and are a perfect example of entitled, toxic mindsets that are used to divide, dissemble, and destroy functional relationships. Today, I still intensely dislike politics, maybe even more than I did back then. However, our political system is so infected by the cancer of entitlement that I do, on occasion, find myself stepping into that sewage.

Back then, my youngest son, Corbin, was an adolescent. I have watched him develop into a student of life, a man, a husband, and a father. Life experiences have given him deeper insight and understanding. He, too, is an author—a quite good one, I might add—and because he is 35 years younger than I am, he has grown up in a time and culture very different from my own.

I felt strongly that this newest update of the book would be enhanced if I invited Corbin to join me in hopes that you, the reader, could gain an expanded view into generational and ideological differences that you, too, might face in your lives. Corbin and I view life through very different lenses and have nearly come to blows over our differing views of the world, especially when it comes to politics. Of course, I'm being hyperbolic, but only a little. I want to stress how much Corbin and I tend to see the world differently. Throughout the book, he will join me with his unique perspectives as we address how to recognize the root of the misery and toxicity that corrupt the system we live in.

CORBIN'S WELCOME

I was ten years old when I first saw *The Matrix* in a modest eight-screen cineplex in Tulsa, Oklahoma. The movie tells the story of characters coming to realize the world in which they lived was an artificial simulation created by sentient machines to subjugate humanity. Watching the film was a foundational experience that forever changed how I perceived the world and interpreted reality. Besides seeing myself as part of a grand design, I also questioned my programming. Why did I believe what I believed? Like Neo, the protagonist of *The Matrix* film franchise, I yearned to free my mind, untether myself from limiting beliefs, and reshape my world into a better place.

After being diagnosed with restrictive air disease the previous year, I launched a clean-air campaign in my home state, raising money and garnering commitments to plant trees to purify the air. I made it my mission to plant a thousand trees in Oklahoma by the end of 1998. To reach that goal, I spoke to anyone that would listen. By the year's end, I had spoken to churches, schools, and organizations across the state, met with the governor and the mayor of my hometown, and partnered with organizations like Up With Trees and American Forests to plant 169,105 trees in Oklahoma.

Needless to say, when I first saw *The Matrix*, I had already been conditioned to believe in my capacity to push the limits, defy expectations, and turn my dreams into reality. However, after leaving the theater, I became fascinated by concepts like how to expand human consciousness and see the unseen. In my opinion, awareness is equivalent to empowerment. I have always wanted to awaken and comprehend the intricate internal workings of reality on a physical, spiritual, and emotional level.

Seeing *The Matrix* also inspired my fascination with movie-making and storytelling. Although I was born and raised in a conservative environment in Oklahoma, at the age of 17, I moved to California to study film production at USC. While living on the coast, I was exposed to a diverse and liberal culture. As a result, many of my pre-existing beliefs about reality were challenged, and my mind was opened to more socially progressive ideals. While I was proud to outgrow beliefs that I inherited from my upbringing that I considered to be fear-based, I also grew judgmental and resentful of those I perceived to be intolerant. In essence, I became intolerant of intolerance. My judgmental, righteous attitude justified my contempt for "unenlightened" opposing views. For many years, this caused my mother and I to consistently butt heads on hot-button issues.

Although I've been labeled a contrarian, I prefer to see myself as someone who speaks up as an impartial observer to point out the assumptions or projections that both sides are making (usually about the other)

Preface

and that serve as the foundation for their mutual enmity. It has always been my goal to encourage people to awaken from the "programmed narratives" that divide our population. Like Morpheus, the wise mentor who helps Neo awaken from *The Matrix*, I want everyone to be free of the bondage they were born into, transcend these prisons of thought, and move toward reconciliation.

However, recently, I've wondered, what if the entire time I convinced myself that I'd been focused on reconciliation, I was actually feeding the flames of agitation and conflict by trying to force what I believed was my "correct" interpretation of reality upon others? You cannot force others to see the truth. You can only make that choice for yourself. Using the Primary Colors Personality Insight Tools that my mother created, I began to learn more about my personality color blend in different contexts (as well as the difference between centered and extreme tendencies). As a result, I became aware of my own blind spots instead of simply focusing on what I believed to be the blind spots of others.

I accepted my mother's invitation to collaborate in writing this book with the hope that the stories and information included in these pages might inspire others to choose to gain insight into themselves and the unconscious personality extremes that fuel conflict in relationships. In addition to being separated by a significant generational divide, my mother and I have differing personality color blends that cause us to view the world through different lenses. What unites us is a passionate desire to see humanity grow more conscious, compassionate, and capable of managing extreme personality tendencies that will always attempt to divide and destroy us.

> *"I can only show you the door.*
> *You're the one that has to walk through it."*
> – Morpheus

INTRODUCTION
WHY BOTHER TO REWRITE THIS BOOK?

"We cannot direct the wind, but we can adjust the sails."
– Dolly Parton

We wrote this book for you, especially if your life isn't unfolding as you would like. Do you find yourself living in a world that frightens and frustrates you? Do you find yourself repeating patterns of behavior that make you miserable? The fact that you are reading this book says a great deal about you. Maybe it speaks to your brilliance, curiosity, or even desperation to discover the answers you have been searching for.

As I mentioned earlier, entitlement (and the extreme emotional reactions it fuels) is more ingrained in our society and dangerous than it was twenty years ago. Self-deception, caused by the subterfuge of a toxic, entitled mindset, determines our experience in every aspect of our lives. When self-deception takes hold, centered tolerance and compassion morph into dark and twisted versions of themselves. We begin to justify attitudes, actions, and behaviors that are judgmental and exclusionary. This is where enmity takes its first hideous breath.

With the information in this book, we want to help you understand what causes you to feel out of control, enraged, confused, frustrated, or even hopeless. In today's world, we are inundated with conflicting information. This bombardment is relentless and comes from every direction. Too often, we find ourselves drowning in a barrage of data that serves primarily to frighten and restrict us, leaving us to frantically fight to keep our heads above water in an ocean of deception.

We live in an opposition-driven society that is extremely conflicted. Opposition is defined as resistance, hostility, obstruction, enmity, and dissent. In my practice, people have told me that they feel abhorrence, revulsion, loathing, and even hatred for those they oppose and feel opposed to. Arguments and conjectures regarding what is right or wrong, what is good or evil, what is kind or cruel, what is good or bad for humanity, or what is helpful or destructive in our relationships are boundless. In reality, we spend more time gazing at the pretend lives of others on social media than we do attempting to carve out our purpose, understand who we are, and pave a path toward a future of confidence, tranquility, and joy.

You are undoubtedly familiar with the intense social opposition that I am addressing. Consider the heated dispute about whether the COVID-19 virus originated from a wet market or a laboratory. Many regarded Dr. Anthony Fauci as a trusted voice of science to lead us through the pandemic, while his opposition saw him as a corrupt public health official who was complicit in funding the gain-of-function research that created the global health crisis. Enmity ensued. There are certainly people who believe that Donald Trump or Joe Biden are evil personified, while others believe them to be the average citizen's champion. Some people fear the rise and implementation of artificial intelligence, and others believe it will propel humanity to new heights of creativity and productivity. Some believe in the legalization of psychotropic drugs, while others view the possession or use of such substances as criminal or incredibly destructive. There are enormous opposing camps that argue, scream, hate, and judge, all the while feeling enraged. Enmity grows. Again, we are left to choose who is right and who is wrong.

Some people believe that people are wretched at their core, while others believe just as strongly that people are innately good at heart. People spout conflicting, *irrefutable* science and *verifiable* statistics from opposite hilltops. Both sides vilify, dehumanize, and wage war against one another under the righteous belief that they are morally superior. The consequences of man's self-deceived, entitled mindsets are horrendous, hateful, and destructive.

People need answers. "What is happening to humanity? Are we all simply going crazy? Can our mutual animosity be healed or redirected? Is there any hope of waking up from this nightmare?" Like ghosts, these questions haunt our lives as we come face to face with the misery, fear, confusion, and unhappiness that we allow to rule us. At its heart, the

Introduction

mission of The Personality Color Matrix is to encourage people to find the safety, connection, and genuine peace that we innately long for. I am confident that the information in this book will enhance your understanding of the world and empower your ability to choose what is best for you and your relationships. Instead of attempting to justify a particular side in political or relational arguments, this book will ask you to reconsider your perceptions, investigate alternate points of view, and understand your opposition.

People find themselves entrenched in conflict because they do not yet understand that the human population is innately divided between two different (but complimentary) value systems: strength and warmth. We have dedicated an entire chapter to elucidating the differences between people who base their values on the concept of strength and those who base their values on warmth. This information will help you discover how YOU can balance these different values to nurture the heart of human kindness.

As you begin your journey of self-discovery, we invite you to enjoy The Personality Color Matrix Test Series. (*Take* The Personality Color Matrix Test Series *online as a gift with the purchase of this book.*) We want to help you understand YOU. Besides identifying the strengths, gifts, and talents associated with your centered personality color tendencies, we also encourage you to explore your extreme color personality tendencies. This technology empowers people with the insight to recognize when they have moved into extreme personality tendencies that always damage success and relationships, so they can choose to return to the best of themselves, their center. Let us take a moment to consider extremes.

We live in a world of extremes. Extremes push us to vastly opposing ends of ideological spectrums and attempt to convince us that we are not only separate from those who have a different opinion, view, or understanding of the world, but we are enemies. In our extremes, we seek to eliminate differing perspectives. Extreme thoughts, feelings, attitudes and fervent attachments to social and political causes have always created the division that leads to the downfall of relationships, communities, countries, and civilizations. Extremes negatively affect education, politics, and government and profoundly impact our legal system. The effects are devastating and global.

The damage is most evident in places where your life simply doesn't work, the places where your relationships are falling apart—areas where you are dissatisfied, depressed, anxious, miserable, and angry. By shining a light on personality extremes, our intention is to enable you to recognize

Introduction

when they are affecting your thoughts and behavior and why it is vital that we all do everything we can to diminish the time we choose to spend in our extremes and reclaim peace and joy.

> *The extreme self-centered attitude*
> *is the source of suffering.*
> – Dalai Lama

We want you to understand, love, and honor your extraordinary, centered color personality tendencies. In these pages, we hope to expand your emotional intelligence, embolden your accountability, magnify your insight into yourself and others, and help you reduce feelings of anger, rage, and discontent. We will examine what gives relationships life and enables them to thrive and, maybe more importantly, what destroys and mangles them. For most people, life is discovered through relationships—with yourself and others and with your community, country, and planet. It is defined by your ability to relate and be related to in compassionate and positive ways.

In the chapters ahead, we will also introduce you to the cause of all dis-*ease* in your life. We want to help you understand what chokes life out of communication, hinders compassion, squelches equity, tramples dignity, and crushes respect. The stories and examples provided in these pages reveal the root of all misery, dissatisfaction, and unhappiness and explain how the cancer called entitlement poisons our lives and feeds deceptive, oppositional, and destructive extremes. We will discuss the negative impact that entitlement has on marriages, parent-child relationships, business partnerships, friendships, political rivalries, and global power dynamics. We encourage you to use The Personality Color Matrix as a tool to evaluate your life, examine the entitled and extreme beliefs that deceive you, and choose the behaviors and attitudes that will bless your personal or professional relationships rather than tear them apart.

The goal of this journey is not to chase happiness but to cultivate a meaningful experience of joy. Most people would agree that happiness is a feeling. Feelings ebb and flow, come and go. A feeling of happiness is often based on our thoughts about or perception of some external circumstance. Often, we feel that our happiness is outside of our control, but joy comes from within. It exists in our center. Therefore, the focus of this book will be to awaken, understand, and nurture an internal sense of peace and joy. To ensure that you experience the joy that inspires compassion and strengthens resilience, even in challenging times, we will examine what

Introduction

conditions create feelings of connection, compassion, and delight. We hope that after reading this book, you will unlock an enhanced ability to cherish, treasure, and appreciate the moments you spend with the people you care about.

CORBIN'S THOUGHTS

Considering I wasn't involved in writing the first version of this book, I'll keep my contribution to this introduction relatively brief. Let me begin by expressing my appreciation to my mother (the original author) and you (the reader). I am grateful to share these pages with you. Hopefully, you will find my unique perspective to be inspiring or insightful. At the very least, I hope you find it to be entertaining.

As a Millennial, I grew up in a culture heavily influenced by video games. In particular, I have always been an avid fan of the epic adventure franchise known as The Legend of Zelda. In 2023, I purchased the latest installment in the series, *The Tears of the Kingdom*, to play as a way to unwind at the end of the day. As a new dad, I hoped to find solace and respite by squeezing in a few hours of gaming after my wife and baby went to sleep.

In addition to the sprawling surface world, the game included an equally vast subterranean tier called "the Depths," which was completely shrouded in shadow. To enter the underworld, one had to dive headfirst into a gaping hole in the countryside and plunge a terrifying distance into the chasm below, at which point the music would bellow ominously. The darkness at the bottom was smothering. Using whatever resources I could gather to light my way, I wandered anxiously through the depths in search of scattered beacons called "lightroots" that, when activated, lit up a small portion of the map. As if the experience wasn't eerie and stressful enough, a variety of monsters and environmental hazards infected with toxic "gloom" lurked in the shadows, ready to attack the moment I strayed into their path.

Unsurprisingly, it's hard to relax while being chased by monsters in the dark. For a time, I avoided the Depths at all costs. Just the thought of the massive, uncharted territory terrified me, not to mention the many enemies hidden in the dark. However, there came a time when I amassed the courage to make it my mission to journey to all 120 lightroots in the depths and eradicate the darkness. To my surprise, bringing light to the shadows was highly gratifying.

After activating all 120 lightroots, I was rewarded with a medal for "dispelling the darkness." It was hardly fair compensation for the time and effort it had taken to accomplish the feat. However, the far greater reward was the eradication of the fear and dis-*ease* that I felt in my body as a player. Interestingly, the best way to relieve my fear of the Depths was to dive into the unknown and explore it. The moment that light was fully restored, I realized there was nothing left to fear. The divisive shadows dispersed to reveal a single, unified territory. At last, rather than fear the Depths, I was grateful to have a whole other arena in which to play and explore.

It is my firm belief that the awareness provided by The Personality Color Matrix has the power to dispel the darkness of discontent in our society and help our polarized population restore communication and reconcile our differences. The key to mending the division and restoring unity is to learn to find wisdom and value in perspectives that we are inclined to reject. Reprogramming how we interpret reality (and its many challenges) takes practice, but the insight gained from The Personality Color Matrix makes it possible. The widespread adoption of this technology can help our society change course from violence, enmity, and despair to kindness, love, and understanding.

As a new father, I want my son to inherit a country where the rule of law is respected, and each person's sovereignty is protected. I want him to grow up feeling safe. I do not wish for him to live in constant fear of gun violence, terrorism, or nuclear war. I want him to feel accepted, not judged based on his appearance. For the sake of future generations, we must fulfill our promise to leave this world in better shape than we found it. For that to be possible, we must hold on to hope that we can all make a difference, both individually and collectively. The best way to do this is by raising our consciousness to see ourselves as one with humanity. This feat can only be accomplished in our center. By embodying love, gratitude, and grace, we each possess the potential to transcend the dualistic illusions of our existence and experience the remembrance of joy and unity.

The history of America is a flawed human story. It has never been a tale of perfection. It is a story of progress and growth despite adversity. I still believe we have the potential to walk hand in hand toward the promised land that Dr. Martin Luther King Jr. envisioned. In fact, I'd argue that the America we currently inhabit (corrupt and polarized as it may be) is far closer to the realization of Dr. Martin Luther King Jr.'s dream than it was 60 years ago during the civil rights era. That is not to say that our society can't be improved. However, our advancement up to this point should be celebrated rather than admonished for not being enough. Evolution is a

Introduction

natural phenomenon, but it takes place over generations, not individual lifetimes.

I understand the progressive push to "be better." I believe we should strive to provide equal opportunity to all and abandon any lingering illusions of superiority, hate, and prejudice between groups of people. As we begin this book, I'd like us to imagine that America is not a lost cause; it is a place where progress is possible. The United States' history of reform provides ample evidence to give us hope that our country's best days still lie ahead.

However, to move forward as a society, culture warriors must sharpen their awareness instead of their swords. Those who wish to see the truth must remove the lenses that cover their eyes and open themselves up to experiencing reality through other paradigms. Having the ability to interpret the world from different perspectives helps us transcend conflict and break free from the cold, mechanical grasp of predatory technologies programmed to exploit our biases, pit us against each other, and farm outrage for profit.

I accepted my mother's invitation to chime in chapter by chapter because I sincerely admire her call to shine a light on our unconscious personality extremes. I must commend her for writing (and rewriting) this book to dispel the darkness. Now, I am ready to leap into the depths beside her to illuminate the way forward. May this book be a beacon for you in the darkness to help enlighten your mind, reveal your extreme personality tendencies, and expose the toxic "gloom" in your path.

1

BLINDED BY ENMITY

For readers who are unfamiliar with the term, enmity is the state or feeling of being actively hostile toward someone or something. Enmity is defined as deep-rooted hatred and refers to the hostility, anger, and resentment two people or two parties have toward each other. Reading those words conjures up the intensity of that extremely negative feeling. In short, a bitter foe is a person who feels enmity, hatred, or malice toward someone or something.

Let's look more deeply into how an entitled mindset leads to enmity:

- *An entitled mindset causes us to perceive others as threats:* This perception of threat can trigger defensive reactions, leading to hostility or enmity toward those perceived as obstacles or competitors.
- *An entitled mindset makes it difficult to accept differing opinions and perspectives:* This resistance to acknowledging others' viewpoints contributes to communication breakdowns.
- *An entitled mindset limits and restricts empathy:* When people prioritize their needs and desires over those of others, their lack of empathy contributes to a disregard for others' feelings and experiences.
- *An entitled mindset fuels a sense of superiority:* Entitlement leads to superiority complexes that manifest as disrespect or

dismissiveness toward individuals who are perceived as inferior.
- *An entitled mindset negatively impacts interpersonal relationships:* The disappointment associated with unmet expectations leads to resentment. When people believe they deserve more than they are getting, it most often leads to enmity in their personal and professional relationships.
- *An entitled mindset causes us to see others as adversaries:* Entitled "rights" lead to rivalries, bitterness, and opposition.
- *Entitled mindsets resist cooperation and collaboration, especially when it involves compromise:* People with entitled mindsets believe that compromise is for suckers, which creates an atmosphere of contempt.
- *An entitled mindset morphs critical feedback into affronts:* Entitled people struggle to handle feedback, viewing any kind of criticism as a put-down and affront.
- *An entitled mindset causes individuals or groups to isolate:* Entitled people may isolate themselves from those who think differently than they do.
- *Entitlement negatively impacts group dynamics:* Entitled people prioritize their interests over the group's well-being, leading to conflicts, divisions, and the emergence of enmity among group members.

Narcissistic entitlement poisons our thoughts, choices, and actions, leading us to hate anyone whose point of view does not align with our beliefs. Some people feel enmity for corrupt unions or big corporations. Others feel enmity for the fossil fuel industry or self-consumed, materialistic billionaires. While we are swimming in an ocean polluted by entitlement, feeling righteously exhausted from the battle of keeping our heads above the raging waves of destruction, we might not even realize that the actual bitter foe wreaking havoc in our world is the enmity demanding that we continue the fight, no matter the costs.

Human beings are always creating. Every intense thought or feeling, whether filled with hope or disgust, dramatically affects our attitudes and subsequent actions. As we grow in our understanding of how powerful our thoughts and feelings are in creating reality, we realize it is the feeling or state of being actively opposed to something that actually helps to create more of it.

Entitlement's most destructive purpose is to blind each of us to enmity's opposite—amity. Amity is defined as a respectful relationship filled with goodwill and cooperation. Entitlement destroys amity and tells us that if someone has differing beliefs and values from our group identity, they *deserve* to be obliterated. We yell, riot, scream, and destroy in the name of the justice we desperately long for, and in the process, we create enmity's chaos, which keeps us hating, judging, fighting, demeaning, terrorizing, pillaging, screaming, burning, and destroying.

Many people have lost sight of the amity they need to be fighting **for**. Instead, they are consumed with fighting **against** their many perceived foes. Entitlement is humanity's true enemy and inhibits us from feeling anything but frustration, disdain, and rage. In the extreme, we no longer support and encourage a tolerance for differences. Instead, we develop a tolerance for cruelty, dissent, destruction, and opposition.

Conflict has always been a reality between human beings. I have worked most of my life as a relationship expert, helping people heal the wounds that tear them apart. Healing entitled mindsets involves fostering self-awareness and empathy. It cultivates a more humble and inclusive approach that can help reduce enmity and contribute to healthier relationships and social interactions. That is why, in the early 1980s, I created my relationship personality tests and insight tools.

I saw so many people experiencing enmity toward a person they once loved. Instead of being friends, partners, or confidants, they had become adversaries. They had lost what the famous Righteous Brothers song referred to as "that lovin' feeling." My life's work has been to help people reconcile their differences. In that vein, I created a relationship personality tool that helps people understand one another by teaching them to see the world through the colored lenses of differing personality tendencies.

Our personality inventory, The Personality Color Matrix, is unique because it was built using the artist's color wheel. Sir Isaac Newton developed the first circular diagram of colors in 1666. I used the artist's color wheel as a base upon which to build my series of personality insight tools because painters have used it for thousands of years. By blending colors in various hues, they recreated what they could see, as well as all they could imagine. A person's blend of color personality tendencies determines the lenses through which they see and interact with the world. Therefore, it seemed the perfect metaphorical base to explain human behavior.

Each of the six colors represents unique personality attributes or tendencies that we witness and interact with every day. Each color has both centered and extreme tendencies. All that is wonderful and attractive about each of us resides in our color personality centers. These centered tendencies fuel our success. It is by using the gifts, strengths, and talents of our centered color personality tendencies that we develop our worth, live out our purpose, and expand our joy.

Along with centered tendencies, we also have extreme personality tendencies, which represent the worst of what human beings are capable of. Our extreme color personality tendencies sabotage and derail our centered positives. They are the source of all relational misery and conflict.

Over the last four decades of using these tools with clients, corporations, churches, and universities, I discovered that if people had access to a tool that enabled them to understand themselves by looking carefully at their strengths and blind spots, the understanding they gained would enable them to make more positive and purposeful choices. The understanding they gained about themselves and others through these insight tools had the power to completely alter their narrative about the motives of people in their lives. The insight provided by The Personality Color Matrix strengthened and nurtured their tolerance for the differences in others. It gave them a way to move people from the "You are such a dumbsh*t!" category to an "Oh, now I at least see how that made sense to you" category. These new insights lead to an understanding that allows people to move from disgusted enmity to the beginnings of empathy. The process is exciting, healing, and fun and can literally revive a toxic, nearly-dead relationship.

The researcher I respect the most in psychology is an Austrian-American psychologist named Walter Mischel. Dr. Mischel's work influenced the development of my personality tests tremendously. Mischel, in his book *Personality and Assessment (1968)*, explained that study after study failed to support the fundamental traditional assumption of personality theory that an individual's behavior regarding a trait (e.g., conscientiousness, sociability) is highly consistent across diverse situations. Instead, Mischel's analyses revealed that an individual's behavior, when closely examined, depended highly upon context or situational cues rather than expressed consistently across diverse situations that differed in meaning. Mischel maintained that behavior is shaped largely by the exigencies of a given situation—in other words, ***context***.

I realized a frozen snapshot cannot adequately define our personality tendencies. Personality tendencies behave more like a movie that changes sets and emotional intensity as we change contexts. For example, when we are happy and excited, we usually do not behave the same as when we are angry, stressed, and depressed. We probably use different skills and ways of interacting with others when we are at work than we do when we are at home with our loved ones. People are not stagnant but have complex, fluid "if, then" responses to situations.

Walter Mischel's theory of personality states that an individual's behavior is influenced by the specific attributes of a given situation and the manner in which one perceives the situation. He emphasized that we have individual differences, so our values and expectancies must be considered to successfully predict our behavior and personalities.

Dr. Robert Hogan was another highly respected mentor of mine whose ideas and research greatly influenced me. He was the chair of the psychology department at the University of Tulsa, where I attended. Drs. Robert and Joyce Hogan published the Hogan Personality Inventory, the first measure of normal personality, based on the (Big) Five-Factor Model, designed to predict effectiveness in the workplace. He coined the terms "bright side" and "dark side" of personality. He believes dark-side behaviors are extreme versions of bright-side behaviors, as when self-assertion gives way to bullying or charm becomes duplicity. When I developed my personality insight tools, I wanted my tests to help people understand and recognize their bright and dark behaviors, but I refer to them as centered color personality tendencies versus extreme color personality tendencies.

Dr. Hogan's socio-analytic theory asks three questions.[1] My goal in creating The Personality Color Matrix was to answer these important questions in ways that were easy to understand and implement:

1: In what meaningful ways are people alike—human universals?

According to The Personality Color Matrix: We are meaning-making machines who love to create narratives that allow us to experience and perceive the world through either centered or extreme versions of our color personality blends in different contexts in our lives.

2: In what meaningful ways are people different—individual differences?

According to The Personality Color Matrix: We each have color blends that can influence how we perceive and experience the world. Our color blends can change according to the needs of different life and emotional contexts.

3: How can we best explain anomalous or self-defeating behavior?

According to The Personality Color Matrix: Self-defeating, destructive behavior is always born out of our extreme color personality tendencies, fueled by feelings of entitlement. I believe our extreme color personality tendencies sabotage our potential, happiness, and success.

---

1. Hogan Assessments, *Socioanalytic Theory*, accessed 2024, https://www.hoganassessments.com/sites/default/files/Socioanalytic%20Theory%20%282%29.pdf.

The assessment was also designed to help people understand where they draw their values from—strength or warmth. The concepts of strength and warmth values and their impact on how we relate to others cannot be overstated. For that reason, we have dedicated Chapter 4 to discussing strength and warmth in detail.

My goal was to create a series of jargon-free, universal, easy-to-understand-and-implement *contextual* personality insight tools. I wanted to help people gain awareness of their default ways of viewing and interacting with the world as they experienced it in varying *life and emotional contexts*. I used the term personality "tendencies" versus "traits" or "types" to describe personality attributes. I believe the word "tendencies" is a clearer way of describing the fluidity of how the actions, thoughts, and behaviors we choose vary in combination, depending on the context.

The Personality Color Matrix was not created to typify or categorize anyone according to traits, like "outgoing" or "agreeable," nor to define someone as a single color or set of initials. Instead, the goal is to encourage individuals to define *themselves* through the use of the insights gained through analyzing their test results. Because I believe that personality is more like EQ (emotional intelligence) versus IQ, which is innate, I believe one can enhance their default personality tendencies as well as strengthen less-dominant color tendencies, which will augment their skills in interacting with the world around them. I believe human beings can make conscious psychological adjustments that enable them to use more centered color personality tendencies, which will bring them more peace, joy, and success. Most importantly, I believe that the insights they gain through our technology can better equip them to manage and diminish extreme personality tendencies that subvert and sabotage their potential.

Leadership professionals, professors of leadership and communication, success coaches, and the most respected relationship researchers on the planet have all licensed the Personality Color Matrix insight tools. These experts have used my personality inventory widely in schools, churches, the military, corporations, government programs, etc., with incredibly positive results. As I mentioned, I have also used these personality insight tools for almost 40 years, working with individuals, couples, and families with outstanding results.

Moving away from our personality color extremes and from entitlement's enmity toward an expanded, centered, endowed feeling of respect and appreciation is always the first step back to our center. We will delve into the importance of our centers in great detail throughout this book. The first step requires us to learn to recognize when we are thinking and behaving out of our personality extremes. It is impossible to choose to manage or let go of something we don't realize we are unconsciously gripping with all of our might.

This journey will be fun, even fascinating. You will learn about your personality color tendencies and those of the people you care about. Corbin and I will also help you recognize the extreme color personality tendencies that sabotage joy, tranquility, and the health of our relationships. We'll also help you develop an appreciation of differing points of view, including political and religious beliefs, and open your mind to the possibility of benefiting from other people's wisdom and experience.

CORBIN'S THOUGHTS

Enmity not only tears apart the great tapestry of our nation, but it also devastates our relationships at home. In the fall of 2020, amidst the hysteria of the COVID-19 pandemic, mass protests, and the U.S. presidential election, I attacked my mother's Facebook page. At the time, I believed the memes and videos that she shared were misrepresentations of critical issues facing our country. I responded to her posts with total intolerance of her opinions in an angry attempt to dismantle and alter her worldview. I wanted her (and her many friends on social media) to know how much her son disapproved of her outdated views. My fingertips stung with righteous energy as I typed, unleashing a barrage of dismissive, disrespectful, and scathing comments that accused her of spreading misinformation, harboring prejudice, and being manipulated by the mainstream media.

They say hindsight is 2020... Looking back, I now see that my actions were misinformed, haughty, highly emotional, and entirely devoid of grace and compassion. Although the language I used wasn't necessarily hateful, the act itself was. A desire to make my mother feel small and ashamed because of her differing political beliefs took over me. At the same time, I felt good about myself for correcting her. As I saw it, someone needed to wake her up. Since I was her son, I not only felt entitled to call her out, but I believed my comments would carry a highly damaging emotional blow that would force her to listen. Instead of changing her mind, however, my righteous, disrespectful display resulted in severe negative consequences.

I expected my mother to delete the posts. I expected her to unfriend me or block me on social media. That would have been a relief. I was prepared for those outcomes. However, I did not expect her to arrive at my door days later and tell me that although she loved me, she would be taking a step back from our relationship. She struggled to believe that I could behave with such enmity, especially in public, in full view of her friends, who had great respect for her. My tendency to harshly judge her beliefs, combined with my sharp, condescending language, had wounded her too many times for her to feel safe communicating with me or sharing space. To protect her peace, she needed distance.

Although my mother did not explicitly disown me, at the time, I felt very much as if she had. For a short period in my early 30s, I feared I had irrevocably damaged our precious relationship. And for what? Smug satisfaction and political points on an imaginary scoreboard in my mind? Those prizes were meaningless compared to the price I had paid! My entitled attempt to be right (and righteous) had ripped holes in the canvas of our mother-son portrait.

The regret I experienced afterward forced me to not only take accountability for my extreme, destructive behavior but to seek reconciliation by any means. The first step in that process was acknowledging the problem: a difference in political ideologies had driven a wedge between my mother and me. Unfortunately, we are not the only family torn apart by political discord. On the contrary, the breakdown of relationships over ideological disagreements is becoming more and more prevalent as the polarization between political spheres continues to grow in the USA. Increasingly, Americans are struggling to tolerate differences in opinion and communicate respectfully to find common ground. Instead, we resort to name-calling, shame, and violence.

Most of the conflict between my mother and me boiled down to our differing generational perspectives. In my extreme, I would call her "willfully blind" for not seeing my side. My mother would reply that she was 35 years older than me and that had a great impact on how she experienced and observed the world. She had a completely different upbringing, filled with poverty and hardship, and thus possessed an entirely different outlook and set of values. To invalidate her opinions was to discount all of her education, time spent in a counseling chair, and the books that she had read (and written).

Although I was somewhat familiar with the Primary Colors Personality Insight Tools that my mother had spent her life developing, at the time, I was by no means an "expert" in her psycho-technology. My mother insisted that if I simply studied more of her work, I would understand that she had different personality tendencies than me, which caused her to see the world through different colored lenses than I did. Although she appreciated how differently we saw the world, she made it clear that she did not appreciate my judgmental attitude. All she wanted was for me to show her the same grace and respect that she was willing to extend my way. Because I wanted to heal our relationship, I accepted her offer to become more familiar with her personality insight tools so that we could better understand how the dynamic between us had become so toxic and change it.

The conflict between us took conscious effort and diligent communication to resolve. The awareness provided by the Primary Colors Insight Tools made it possible. The more I explored the material, the more I developed a deep respect for my mother's work. When I began learning about my personality color blend, as well as the differing personality tendencies of the people close to me, I was impressed by the simplicity of the concepts and the depth of insight they provided. After years of searching for answers online and in books to improve my life, I was astonished to discover the cheat codes for hacking personality and improving interpersonal relationships could be found on a four-page pamphlet in a drawer in my mother's study.

For me, discovering this psycho-technology was like awakening from *The Matrix*. In the movie, those who seek to discover the unseen, true nature of reality are offered a choice between a blue pill, which keeps them asleep, and a red pill, which awakens them from the illusion. After discovering The Primary Colors Insight Tools, I felt like I had taken the red pill *and* the blue pill, not to mention the purple, green, yellow, and orange pills. I became fascinated with learning as much as I could about all six different colors and how they behaved differently in centered versus extreme states of mind. The experience was like learning emotional kung fu. I developed techniques to defend myself from my extreme personality tendencies, as well as the discipline to resist the impulse to pass judgment and attack others.

At a certain point, I began to feel like a character from *The Matrix* franchise, dodging relational bullets in super-slow motion whenever I encountered conflict in my marriage, family, or friendships. That is not to say that I dodged every shot or resisted the temptation to take shots of my own. To this day, I still get hit. In all honesty, I've been hit by far more bullets than I ever dodged. However, I used my understanding of the system to extract the bullet from myself or someone that I loved and found a way to heal.

I began to see people's colors when I listened to them speak. Recognizing their color blends helped me understand their outlooks and empathize with their views and beliefs. Being able to decipher a stranger's personality helped me optimize the enjoyableness and effectiveness of our interaction. This skill has benefited me greatly in forming new connections and resolving conflict at home, in business, and within myself. This is why, when conceiving the title of this book, I approached my mother with a new name for the Primary Colors Personality Insight Tool that she had created: The Personality Color Matrix. I believe this name reflects the potential awakening that awaits everyone who uses this technology. With insight comes awareness and the opportunity to make an informed choice. Through informed choice, we can intentionally transform our reality.

Before we proceed, allow me to share a brief description of each personality color tendency in their center and extreme. This information will be referenced repeatedly moving forward, so I encourage everyone who reads this book to familiarize themselves with these six core constructs.

i. **Red** (Motivated by Winning)
   - Centered: Direct, competitive, courageous, self-confident leaders
   - Extreme: Pushy, impatient, high-tempered, dominating, seen as bullies
ii. **Blue** (Motivated by Being Right)
   - Centered: Intelligent, focused, intense, problem-solving, seen as geniuses
   - Extreme: Condescending, demeaning, seen as arrogant know-it-alls
iii. **Purple** (Motivated by Results)
   - Centered: Responsible, organized, careful, follow through, seen as capable managers
   - Extreme: Task enforcers, micro-managers, seen as self-appointed behavior-rule police
iv. **Green** (Motivated by Fairness)
   - Centered: Hopeful, tolerant, respectful, honoring, just, seen as big-picture visionaries
   - Extreme: Dogmatic, radicalized, intolerant, seen as zealous extremists
v. **Yellow** (Motivated by Love)
   - Centered: Kind, caring, serving, inclusive, loyal, seen as heart-centered listeners
   - Extreme: Anxious, whiny, complaining, overly emotional, seen as passive-aggressive victims

THE PERSONALITY COLOR MATRIX

  i. **Orange** (Motivated by Fun)
     - Centered: Entertaining, full of life, inspiring, center of attention, seen as fun-loving
     - Extreme: Impulsive, irresponsible, sarcastic, manipulative, prone to addiction

(NOTE: The glossary at the back of this book includes breakdowns of how various color personality tendencies combine and complement each other).

Let me stress that no one is solely defined by a single color. Everyone's personality consists of a blend of three colors. Differing color blends can show up in different life and emotional contexts. We have created several levels of insight when taking the tests. Level 1 consists of taking a single test in one context of your life. We recommend beginning with a personal context. This means thinking about who you are at home, in relationships with your beloved, family, children, pets, etc.

Level 2 consists of retaking the tests in two additional contexts. The second test is to be taken in a professional mindset. This means who you are at work. The third test asks you to imagine your ideal self and take the test as the person you aspire to be. If you really want to understand where you sabotage yourself and where you find yourself in conflict, we highly recommend that you advance to the third level of the test series.

Level 3 consists of an assessment that reveals the strategies you use to deal with stress, an examination of how you express rage in your extreme, and a strength-warmth evaluation that helps you identify your value system. Of course, we highly recommend taking the six-test series in its entirety because of the depth of insight you will receive. However, you will benefit greatly from completing any level of the test series. To take the online assessment and discover more in-depth information about The Personality Color Matrix, visit www.thecolormatrix.com.

One of the first things one comes to realize after working with The Personality Color Matrix is that every person's beliefs are justified relative to their point of view. The same event, experienced from different angles and through different lenses, yields completely different outlooks. Consider this drawing of three concentric circles in three-dimensional space. Although the circles never move, approaching them from different angles leads to contradictory interpretations. All of these outlooks are simultaneously *true*. One is not more valid than the others. Even though each perspective is different, they all depict the same thing.

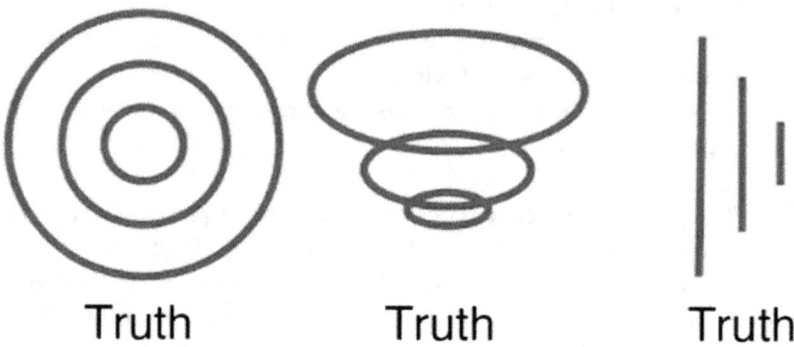

Truth   Truth   Truth

The ability to imagine and briefly adopt another person's perspective to better understand their mental and emotional experience is called empathy. We can only feel and express empathy in our center. When a person is trained in The Personality Color Matrix technology and understands the tendencies of each of the six personality colors (as well as the personality color blend combinations), their empathetic capacity multiplies exponentially.

From my strength-minded perspective, my attempts to "correct" my mother came from my extreme blue need to be right. However, from her warmth-minded perspective, I was behaving as her haughty superior. When I closed my eyes to go to sleep that night, I imagined waking up in confusion to a bombardment of demeaning and judgmental Facebook comments. I allowed myself to feel the sting of hurt and humiliation as I read the rebuke of my moral character. As a new father, I can't even conceive how devastated I would be if my son grew up to display such public enmity for me. It would make me feel hopeless and even betrayed to feel as if he possessed so little respect or appreciation for the years that I invested in loving and raising him. Understanding my mother's feelings through the lens of strong green and yellow personality influences helped me see the validity of her point of view and adjust my behavior accordingly.

Rather than continuing to judge or correct my mother, I centered myself in gratitude. Just because we viewed the world differently, it did not mean we needed to treat each other as enemies. Although it took time and effort to rebuild trust and communication, our relationship meant enough to me to put in the hard work. Personally, I believe that the reason relationships require so much work is the same reason that they are so rewarding: they help us grow. The only downside is that the process of growth is often uncomfortable. Experiencing discomfort in our relationships challenges us to resist our extreme personality tendencies, repeatedly choose our center, and offer others grace when we might prefer judgment.

The first step toward increasing our understanding is to identify the color of the lenses through which we see the world. The next step is to determine if those colors are centered or extreme. The final challenge is to see reality through the colored lenses of another person. Imagining how other people view and experience the world requires not only patience and compassion but education and direction.

Being able to recognize the six core behavioral constructs that combine to create The Personality Color Matrix expanded my capacity to empathetically interpret reality and integrate contradictory points of view. Many times, I have witnessed its power to change hearts, open minds, and inspire forgiveness. I have also experienced firsthand its capacity to save relationships. As I see it now, the value of this technology is priceless, and I couldn't be more excited for you to experience the value for yourself.

2

UNDERSTANDING ENTITLEMENT

"As an enemy of joy, satisfaction, and delight, entitlement is a subjective and emotional reaction that justifies, and even defends, dissatisfaction."
– Dawn Billings
Entitled to Fail, Endowed to Succeed

Thousands of books have been written explaining how to achieve happiness and success, yet attaining them remains baffling. Many hundreds of books have been written about personality and how it impacts the way we see and interact with the world. This book delves into both but with unique and interesting new perspectives. One of the best ways to understand how to bring more joy into your life is to begin by understanding what limits and destroys it. The culprit is entitlement and the extreme personality tendencies that accompany an entitled mindset.

As we continue, we will make our case as to how the attitudes, perceptions, and beliefs that surround entitled mindsets are damaging, even psychologically destructive. Entitled mindsets engulf us in self-deception, damage and destroy relationships, and feed disorders, such as narcissism and antisocial personality disorder.

For this introduction to the *entitlement mentality* or *entitled mindset*, we will use the definition as it relates to *narcissistic entitlement: a belief that one's importance, superiority, past trauma, uniqueness, or perceived needs should result in getting special treatment and receiving more resources than others.* When we feel entitled, most often, we feel justified and righteous about those feelings and attitudes. Entitlement fuels self-deception.

> *"Self-deception blinds us to the true cause of problems, and once blind, all the "solutions" we can think of will actually make matters worse."*
> – The Arbinger Institute
> *Leadership and Self Deception*

When we use the word "entitlement" or speak in terms of a "sense of entitlement" or an "entitled mindset," we will not be referring to the political form of entitlements. Such "entitlements" are real or assumed contracts between entities like governments and citizens, such as Social Security in the U.S. We will leave those government entitlements for politicians to argue about.

Twenty years ago, when I first penned this book, narcissistic entitlement was rearing its ugly head in every direction. There was much confusion about the concept of entitlement. Americans were not completely sure what to call it, but we knew we wanted to get away from it and do all we could to avoid it. We hoped it would go away if we ignored it or just didn't make eye contact with it. However, we began to witness it in strangers, the people we worked with, the people we watched on television, and the people we interacted with online. Entitlement is a relational plague of the worst kind.

Entitlement inveigles us to believe we *have the right to* or *deserve* something. This ends up backfiring on us. Let me explain. An entitled mindset can convince us that we have a *right to demand* or receive. Why is that a negative? It is a negative because it is an incredibly sly way of shutting down our ability to feel gratitude. After all, when you believe something is your *right,* you also begin to believe you *deserve* it.

When we believe we *deserve* something, that mindset leads us toward disappointment and frustration while simultaneously smothering our feelings of compassion and understanding. I believe the rampant entitlement poisoning our nation can be traced back to a misunderstanding of the pure intent held by our country's founding documents. Many wrongly believe that the Declaration of Independence *entitles* its citizens to three things: life, liberty, and the pursuit of happiness. So, let's begin by looking at what the Declaration of Independence actually states:

THE PERSONALITY COLOR MATRIX

We hold these truths to be self-evident,
that all men are created equal,
*that they are **endowed** by their Creator*
with certain inalienable rights,
that among these are life, liberty, and the pursuit of happiness.

Notice that the word "entitled" does not appear, nor is it implied. It is purported that the founding fathers fought over every word in these documents. Some of the greatest minds of those times authored these impactful pages. So, the fact that the words "entitled" and "entitlement" are never used is not an accident. Instead, this revered statement tells us that we are "endowed" by our Creator with certain inalienable rights. According to vocabulary.com, "If you've been *endowed* with something, it means you've been given a gift."[1] With this definition in mind, let's look at this important paragraph once again.

We hold these things to be true,
that everyone is created equal.
They are generously provided by their Creator
with inalienable qualities and talents
(that we refer to as your centered personality tendencies)
that cannot be legally or justly taken away or transferred to another.
It is your right as a citizen to develop
and use these talents and qualities
in the pursuit of liberty and happiness.

Clearly, our forefathers wanted to create a nation that would encourage people to be free to be whatever they dreamed of being.

The word "endowment" connotes a precious *gift*, which actually invites gratitude to attend the party. With this powerful distinction, we discover the secret to experiencing satisfaction and true joy versus misery, greed, and enmity. When feelings of gratitude are suppressed, we forfeit all the psychological and physical benefits they bring to our lives. Instead, we begin to believe that the world we live in owes us something *more*. Sadly, however, the payment is never enough.

---

1. Vocabulary.com, s.v. "Endow," accessed 2024, https://www.vocabulary.com/dictionary/endow.

> *"Don't complain about what you don't have.*
> *Use what you've got.*
> *To do less than your best is a sin.*
> *Every single one of us has the power for greatness,*
> *because greatness is determined*
> *by service -- to yourself and to others."*
> – Oprah Winfrey

As I have mentioned, we are currently living in a world where attitudes of entitlement are not only dominant but pervasive. Through lenses of "NOT enough" or "I am owed MORE," our view of the world becomes restricted, distorted, and self-absorbed. This distorted view creates fertile soil for the weeds of selfishness and greed to grow, choking out the lovely blossoms of reverence and gratitude.

When we feel we are not getting what we deserve or are owed, we convince ourselves that we are being neglected and even cheated. We convince ourselves that we deserve what others have without putting in the effort required to earn it. It is then that entitlement grows even stronger as it encourages us to justify feeling dissatisfied and miserable, all while blaming these feelings on others. After all, people around us, life circumstances, and even societal norms are *cheating* us.

When we believe we aren't getting what we're due, time, attention, money, affection, recognition, appreciation—the list can be endless—an entitled mindset takes over. Feeling entitled, and the disappointment that follows when we don't get what we want, actually reinforces destructive, entitled attitudes. This typically follows a vicious three-step cycle:

- When feeling entitled, we're vulnerable to the negative and extreme feelings that surround unmet expectations.
- When our expectations aren't met, it leads to dissatisfaction and feelings like anger and a sense of being cheated.
- When we're distressed, we attempt to validate and assure ourselves that we *deserve* what we want and to get it when we want it. This can cause people to see themselves through one of two lenses: as entitled to feel superior to others or, on the other end of the spectrum, entitled to feel like a victim. Both identities reinforce and fuel deeper feelings of entitlement.

THE PERSONALITY COLOR MATRIX

A few of the consequences of an entitled mindset are:

- Conflicted and broken relationships
- Disappointment, resentment, and bitterness
- Anger and rage
- Loneliness
- Hopelessness and depression

*"A sense of entitlement is a cancerous thought process
that is void of gratitude
and can be deadly to our relationships."*
– Steve Maraboli,
*Unapologetically You:
Reflection of Life and the Human Experience*

Entitlement kills your joy by blinding you to the value of all you have to be grateful for. An entitled mindset filters out abundant data while leaving perceived scarcity and a lack in bright focus. Therefore, an *entitled perspective* pollutes satisfaction and destroys our opportunity for genuine joy.

*"Gratitude unlocks the fullness of life.
It turns what we have into enough, and more.
It turns denial into acceptance, chaos to order,
confusion to clarity.
Gratitude makes sense of our past, brings peace for today,
and creates a vision for tomorrow."*
– Melody Beattie

Let me share a simple, personal story that I believe helps describe the difference between an endowed mindset versus a sense of entitlement. When Corbin was five years old, he collected Teenage Mutant Ninja Turtles. There were a great number of them, and after a while, he had accumulated approximately 60. One morning, he came to me with a picture showing all the turtles, complaining sadly, "I don't have three." He had realized there were three turtles pictured that he did not have. The many turtles he owned did not seem to matter, and they certainly were not bringing him joy. Instead, focusing only on his perceived lack was causing him to feel discontent and sad.

Perceived lack is one of entitlement's favorite weapons. I asked my son to wheel out the bin that held all of his turtle characters and tell me the names of each and if they were good guys or bad guys. He thought this was going to be a fun game, and it was until about turtle 37. As he was tiring of naming his turtles, he became aware and remembered how many turtles he actually had.

"Whew," he said, wiping his forehead. "I got a lot of turtles. I didn't know how many I had until I remembered them."

Think about the power in his statement. His "not enough" perspective changed dramatically with the simple opportunity to count how many turtles he already owned. In doing so, he suddenly *remembered* or, in reality, reminded himself of how fortunate he was to own his many action figures. The term "count your blessings" reminds us to *remember* what we already possess simply by taking the time to take inventory.

> *"Gratitude is born in hearts*
> *That take the time to count up past mercies."*
> – Charles E. Jefferson

As this simple story illustrates, when we choose to see the world through lenses of *endowment* (remembering the gifts we have), we feel blessed, fortunate, favored, and even lucky. This perspective, or *sense of endowment,* ignites gratitude and invites us to acknowledge all that is good in our lives. When we feel abundant and fortunate, we are much more likely to behave in kind, respectful, and generous ways.

An endowed view of the world creates a vastly different internal experience for us than when we choose to view the world through lenses of perceived lack. When we feel there is *not enough* or *we deserve more*, it cripples our ability to feel gratitude. Feeling gratitude is associated with a wide range of positive psychological benefits that differ vastly from the miserable psychological effects born out of an entitled mindset.

As Corbin and I were reading through one of the last rewrites of this book, he laughingly teased me about my very green tendency to make use of long-winded, highly descriptive sentences. I realized he was absolutely correct. Therefore, I have also included for people with a strong purple color influence in their color blends, who much prefer bullet points, a list of some of the key *psychological benefits* of cultivating an attitude of gratitude:

- ***Improved Mood:*** Grateful individuals often report higher levels of positive emotions and lower levels of negative emotions. Regularly recognizing and appreciating positive aspects of life can lead to an overall improvement in mood.
- ***Reduced Depression and Anxiety:*** Practicing gratitude may act as a protective factor against the development of depressive symptoms and anxious thoughts.
- ***Enhanced Life Satisfaction:*** People who frequently experience and express gratitude tend to report higher levels of contentment and fulfillment in life.
- ***Increased Resilience:*** Grateful individuals often exhibit greater resilience in the face of life's challenges. The ability to find and appreciate positive aspects of one's circumstances can contribute to coping skills and adaptive responses to stress.
- ***Improved Relationships:*** Expressing gratitude can strengthen social bonds and relationships. Grateful people are more likely to engage in pro-social behaviors, leading to positive interactions and a sense of connection with others.
- ***Greater Empathy:*** Gratitude is associated with an increased capacity for empathy. When people are grateful, they may be more attuned to the experiences and feelings of others, fostering understanding and compassion.
- ***Positive Changes in Perspective:*** Gratitude encourages a shift in focus from negative aspects to positive ones. This change in perspective can lead to a more optimistic outlook on life and a greater appreciation for the present moment.
- ***Enhanced Mental Health:*** Regularly practicing gratitude has been linked to better mental health outcomes, including improved psychological well-being and a reduced risk of mental health disorders.
- ***Increased Generosity:*** Grateful people often show higher levels of generosity and a willingness to help others. The experience of gratitude may motivate people to contribute positively to their communities.
- ***Enhanced Self-Esteem:*** Recognizing and appreciating one's own accomplishments and the support of others can contribute to a positive self-image and higher self-esteem.

Entitlement's psychological effects are the antithesis of gratitude's. An entitled attitude increases depression and anxiety, lowers one's ability to feel empathy, contorts one's perceptions, creates conflict in relationships, dramatically decreases satisfaction in all areas of life, reduces and inhibits positive feelings, cripples personal resilience, and dramatically increases the risk of mental health disorders.

While research is ongoing, many existing studies suggest that practicing gratitude can also contribute to various health benefits. I may be getting carried away with these bullet points, but people with a strong purple influence in their color blend will greatly appreciate my efforts. Here are a few of those potential positive physical outcomes:

- *Improved Heart Health:* Gratitude may be linked to cardiovascular health. Studies have suggested that individuals who practice gratitude may experience lower blood pressure, reduced heart rate, and improved heart rate variability.
- *Strengthened Immune System:* Some research indicates that expressing gratitude may have a positive impact on the immune system. Grateful people may show increased immune function, which can help the body defend against illnesses.
- *Better Sleep Quality:* Gratitude practices have been associated with improved sleep quality. Expressing gratitude before bedtime may contribute to increased sleep duration and efficiency, as well as reduced insomnia.
- *Reduced Inflammation:* Chronic inflammation is associated with various health conditions. Gratitude may have anti-inflammatory effects, potentially contributing to a healthier inflammatory response in the body.
- *Stress Reduction:* Gratitude practices have been linked to reduced stress levels. Lower stress is associated with various health benefits, including improved mental well-being and a positive impact on overall physical health.
- *Pain Relief:* Some studies suggest that gratitude may have analgesic effects, meaning it could contribute to pain relief. Grateful people may exhibit reduced sensitivity to pain.
- *Improved Hormonal Balance:* Gratitude has been associated with changes in hormonal balance. For example, it may lead to increased levels of oxytocin, the "love hormone," which is linked to social bonding and well-being.

Enhancing and incorporating gratitude into daily life through practices such as keeping a gratitude journal, expressing thankfulness, saying grace, or reflecting on positive experiences can benefit both psychological and physical well-being. This simple yet powerful way to cultivate a positive mindset and foster a sense of appreciation for life is one of the greatest weapons you can use against entitlement's attempts to make your life miserable.

Even when we examine the lives of great people who have suffered terrible injustices, battled severe illness, or lived every day with a disability, we find that those who inspire us most are eager to share all the ways they feel they have been blessed and have found happiness despite their challenges and disadvantages—and often because of them.

> *"Yes, there is a "secret to happiness"—and it is gratitude.*
> *All happy people are grateful,*
> *and ungrateful people cannot be happy.*
> *We tend to think that it is being unhappy*
> *that leads people to complain,*
> *but it is truer to say that it is complaining*
> *that leads to people becoming unhappy."*
> – Dennis Prager,
> *Happiness Is a Serious Problem*

CORBIN'S THOUGHTS

I first learned about the concept of entitlement when I was in middle school, and my mother was writing the first version of this book. While I came to understand the general thesis of her writing, I must confess, as a teenager, I wasn't too eager to set aside my latest Harry Potter tome to dive into a pseudo-political diatribe on relationships written by one of my parents. That's a nice way of saying I didn't read my mother's book in its entirety until I was an adult (sorry, Mom). Nevertheless, my early introduction to the concept of entitlement has always led me to associate the word with destructive narcissistic personality traits as opposed to well-intentioned government programs.

Narcissistic entitlement refers to a narrative that we tell ourselves in response to feelings of scarcity to justify the fulfillment of our desires by any means necessary. It's important to stress that this state of mind is a fear-based response to perceived lack. It is the antithesis of the gratitude we experience when we feel surrounded by abundance. It's also crucial to reiterate that the fear of lack that fosters entitlement doesn't have to be based on "facts;" it only needs to be perceived. The lack may or may not be observable to others.

The moral of entitlement's insidious story is that what we currently have isn't enough, and we deserve more. Believing one's self to be superior allows a person to justify prioritizing their desires over others to ensure their expectations are met. In other words, people who believe they are special or insist that they deserve to be treated as the exception have no problems infringing on others' rights to get whatever they want.

No one is immune to feeling entitled. I must confess, as the co-author of this book, I struggle every day with my feelings that I deserve more time, money, or attention. As a Millennial, I honestly feel like I have been stuck with a bill for a party that I did not get to attend. I'm not only referring to the outrageous debt our country has accumulated; I'm speaking about the wars that we have waged, the water supply we have poisoned, and the mass extinction of animal life we have presided over. I'm speaking of endemic institutional and financial corruption, crumbling civil infrastructure, and a failing education system. In short, sometimes, I still feel like I don't have enough turtles.

I have learned that the more I focus on that lack, the more dis-*ease* and stress I feel. Entitlement is a confining, stifling, insecure state that creates stress, frustration, anger, apathy, and depression. Whenever it grips us, we feel as if the walls are slowly closing in around us while the target we are aiming for drifts farther and farther away. In effect, it blinds and immobilizes us. In our state of doom and gloom, entitlement chokes appreciation. Therefore, we value little.

Feeling entitled, we neglect to invest in our relationships, our communities, and ourselves. After all, what's the point? If society is already broken beyond repair and corrupt beyond salvation, is there any hope of preventing the inevitable collapse? A growing sense of nihilism, the belief that life is inherently meaningless, excuses and fuels our inaction. Appreciation, entitlement's antidote, is informed by our focus, which is determined by our level of awareness. The more insight we possess, the better we are at consciously evaluating our blessings.

Entitlement strangles our capacity to experience joy and gratitude. Our challenge is to break free of the chokehold. Allow me to share a personal story of how I learned this the hard way. I had just graduated high school and was fortunate enough to visit the Hawaiian islands with my girlfriend and her mother. Before we left, I went shopping for the trip and purchased a pair of white sneakers. It was a risky buy, considering how hard white shoes are to keep clean, but I had recently observed my brother sporting a pair of white kicks and was amazed by how pristine he managed to keep them.

At 17 years old, I decided I could handle the responsibility of owning my own pair of white sneakers and keeping them immaculate. I made a covenant with myself to clean them after each wearing. When other people saw my pristine white sneakers, I wanted them to shout, "Yo! What are those?" and mean it. I wanted to be seen as stylish and responsible. I realize how absurd this sounds in retrospect. However, the narratives that we write for ourselves are powerful (especially as adolescents).

My new white shoes were the first thing I packed in my suitcase; however, once we landed on Kauai, I found little opportunity to wear them. I spent my first several days in flip-flops at the beach. On the fourth day, we took an excursion to go horseback riding to a waterfall. I decided this would be the perfect opportunity to wear my white sneakers. I imagined that since I would be riding a horse, I wouldn't even have to worry about getting them dirty. I envisioned taking a picture in front of the waterfall in my new shoes, and when my friends saw the picture on Facebook, they would think, *Wow! Look how white his shoes are. This guy's really got life figured out.* Again, the narratives we come up with in our heads can be quite funny in retrospect.

To my dismay, my expectations differed greatly from reality. The horses did not deliver us conveniently to the foot of the waterfall as I had imagined. At the end of our horseback ride, I was informed that we had to hike through the jungle to reach our destination. It had rained the night before, and the ground had turned to mud. Disembarking from my horse, I winced as my white shoes sank into the sticky muck. I tried my best to tread lightly, but with each step forward, the soft, slick earth nearly swallowed my sneakers. I moaned and cursed as I struggled uphill, my eyes focused on my precious shoes the entire climb.

By the time we reached the waterfall, my perfect white shoes were stained brown. Pulling the travel toothbrush from my backpack, I squatted beside the water and spent the next 30 minutes attempting to scrub away the mud. Tears welled in my eyes as I tried futilely to solve the problem. I was so preoccupied with my silly materialistic obsession that I completely failed to recognize that I was in paradise! Instead of feeling gratitude and joy to be standing, muddy shoes and all, in a tropical oasis, my extremes caused me to disregard the beauty that surrounded me. I didn't even swim in the water! While my girlfriend basked and explored, I fixated on scrubbing my stupid shoes, ruminating on my "failure" to keep them clean. Looking back, it is easy to recognize that I allowed my unmet, entitled expectations to create my suffering.

I wish I could say that I snapped out of my obsessive blue extreme personality tendencies in time to enjoy the excursion. Unfortunately, that wasn't the case. When only minutes remained before we had to leave, I finally abandoned my muddy sneakers and joined my girlfriend for one quick photo in front of the waterfall. Once I returned to my center, I realized the obvious: I could always buy another pair of white sneakers. How many opportunities would I have to experience the unique, exotic beauty of Kauai? Considering I have yet to return to the Garden Isle, the answer is not many. Unfortunately, that realization arrived too late; I had already allowed my extremes to steal a priceless experience from me.

The reason I shared this story over more profound examples is that it perfectly illustrates how our extreme color personality tendencies steal joy from our lives. Extreme behavior is not always a reaction to a large challenge. Sometimes, small, trivial, even nonsensical self-narratives blind us to the big-picture beauty and blessings that surround us.

Months later, I realized my mistake while watching the movie *American Beauty*. The film concludes with a monologue by the main character as he reflects on his life. To this day, when I revisit these words, they impact me greatly. They remind me to reflect on my blessings and remember how much beauty there is to be grateful for.

> *"I guess I could be pretty pissed off about what happened to me... but it's hard to stay mad when there's so much beauty in the world. Sometimes I feel like I'm seeing it all at once, and it's too much; my heart fills up like a balloon that's about to burst... And then I remember to relax and stop trying to hold on to it, and then it flows through me like rain, and I can't feel anything but gratitude for every single moment of my stupid little life... You have no idea what I'm talking about, I'm sure. But don't worry... you will someday."*
> – Alan Ball
> *American Beauty*

Gratitude is the one emotion that enables you to transcend a gloom-and-doom mindset and experience meaningful fulfillment and joy. When we appreciate things, we give them value; we invest ourselves in them. To cherish and value something means to tend to it like a garden. We spend the time and energy necessary to nurture and maintain our relationships and communities because they are meaningful to us, and we wish to see them bloom.

Every day, we are invited to experience the beauty around us. Instead of fixating on the lack, reflect on the blessings. Don't allow entitlement to use the insignificant "white shoes" in your life to distract you from life's beauty and steal your moment in paradise.

3

STRENGTH AND WARMTH: ANGRY OPPONENTS OR IMPERATIVE PARTNERS

"If we could but recognize our common humanity,
that we do belong together,
that our destinies are bound up in one another's,
that we can be free only together,
that we can be human only together,
then a glorious world would come into being
where all of us lived harmoniously together."
– Desmond Tutu

The unfortunate truth is that most people do not recognize our common humanity. Instead of living harmoniously, we find ourselves living in a "choose your side" society filled with either/or choices loaded with bitterness, rage, and disrespect. To feel enraged by another's ideas, actions, or views, we must first find ourselves in some version of disgusted opposition to them. An entitled mindset invites people to move into their extreme personality tendencies, where misunderstanding and division thrive. This opposition is the basis of all personal and societal conflict.

Imagine what could be possible if we replaced either/or thinking with the synthesis of a both/and mindset. Such a mindset requires an evolved understanding that enhances one's ability to find a middle ground instead of driving people to the extreme ends of any given spectrum. Both/and thinking have the potential to reconcile the conflict brought about by perceived opposites.

Dr. Martin Luther King Jr. believed that it is neither common nor easy for a person to hold perceived opposites in a living blend. In his sermon "A Tough Mind and Tender Heart," he shared:

> **Life at its best is a creative synthesis of opposites in fruitful harmony.** *The philosopher Hegel said that truth is found neither in the thesis nor the antithesis, but in an emergent synthesis that reconciles the two.*

Dr. King often spoke of the importance of creating a synthesis out of the two perceived opposites: power and love. He had a brilliant understanding that if we could not amalgamate power and love ideals, which, together, make the best of each other, we would be left with weak and reckless versions of both.

> *"Power without love is reckless and abusive,*
> *and love without power is sentimental and anemic.*
> *Power at its best is love implementing the demands of justice.*
> *Justice at its best is love correcting everything*
> *that stands against love."*
> – Dr. Martin Luther King, Jr.

In this chapter, along with either/or versus both/and mindsets, we will contemplate the tension and division created by extreme versions of power and love ideals that succeed at thwarting unity and harmony. Going forward, we will refer to power and love ideals using the terms "strength" and "warmth." This chapter will also help you consider whether your values are based more on strength or warmth ideals.

In their book *Compelling People*, Matthew Kohut and John Neffinger purport that strength and warmth are key attributes that define the quality of our relationships with others. Although most of us admire both strength and warmth values, we usually lean toward one more than the other. The ultimate goal is to understand the incredible value that comes from blending the two. We will discuss in detail how strength and warmth ideals, in their extremes, play a significant role in impeding any kind of fruitful harmony with those who believe differently than we do.

People who value strength get things done. Those who value warmth nurture and care for people. These values broadly influence how we judge ourselves and others. For this reason, I made it a vital component of The Personality Color Matrix's six-test series. The person taking this particular test is asked to repeatedly select from two sets of descriptions to determine which values matter most to them. After tallying the results, the test analyzes whether the person scored higher in strength or warmth. On The Personality Color Matrix Wheel, a preference for strength is often found in people with strong red, blue, and purple color influences. This, of course, is not absolute. When it comes to people, there are few absolutes. However, it can be a helpful guide.

Warmth is associated with friendliness, approachability, and likability. People who base their values on warmth hold kindness, collaboration, care, inclusion, consideration, empathy, fairness, and sympathy in high regard. Strength is associated with intelligence, capability, and reliability. People who base their values on strength hold steadfastness, discipline, competence, and confidence in high regard. They value integrity, individual effort, merit, honor, and duty.

People who rely on strength values have a high regard for tradition, respect, and personal fortitude. They admire hard work and action. They gravitate to leadership positions, wield influence, and inspire us to follow them. They value ingenuity, outspokenness, and determination and have little tolerance for laziness. They pride themselves on their precision, persistence, and achievement. They seek solutions and avoid emotional reactions. To them, "crying over spilled milk" is a waste of time and mental resources. Because they are response-oriented instead of emotion-oriented, they usually keep a cool head during disasters. They like the fact that they don't feel compelled to cry over things most people shed tears about. Their ability to restrain their emotions aligns with and fortifies their ideal of what it means to be strong. Because of that, they encourage others to inhibit their emotional responses as well. This becomes an issue when dealing with interpersonal relationships, especially listening to other human beings and their problems.

When a person relies more heavily on strength tendencies, they respond with less sympathy and compassion, causing people who value warmth to imagine people who value strength as being emotionally stunted or heartless. We distrust the motives of people who lack warmth because we don't believe they actually care. People without warmth put us on guard. We want to keep our distance and try to avoid them. However, the foundation of centered strength is honor and respect. When one feels honored and respected, tears are unnecessary to prove the depth of one's dedication.

People who draw their values from warmth tend to value people, attention, affection, and relationships more than they value productivity or achievement. Warmth refers to a sense of belonging or being cared for. It's what people feel when they recognize they share interests or concerns. Therefore, people who draw their values from warmth see tears, or, at a minimum, moist eyes, as evidence that one understands the depth of another's feelings, loss, or sadness. Warmth people want to know if you can relate, care, and will help if possible. To them, emotional expression feels like a more genuine way of sharing. They prize what they define as authenticity over duty or honor.

So, asking who is right and who is wrong about showing or restricting emotions isn't the most relevant question. A more impactful question regarding nurturing relationships and improving communication could be, "How can I better understand the people I care about so that I can more effectively communicate with them?" Effective communication is greatly enhanced if you learn to recognize whether warmth or strength values influence the way others see the world.

People who value warmth say, "Follow your dreams," while strength-minded individuals are much more interested in following through. The warmth side says, "Let your heart lead you." The strength side says, "Use your head." People on the strength side will tell you that you are your own worst enemy, while people on the warmth side will remind you to never forget that you are a miracle. Some people speak and think with their hearts. Others use their heads. Those who favor warmth are usually dreamers. Those who value strength are realists. Because these two sides experience and evaluate the world in different ways, it can sometimes be extremely difficult to communicate, collaborate, or compromise. In truth, relating to others with warmth is an emotionally intelligent strength.

There is a vast difference between *centered* "both/and" strength and warmth versus the *extreme* "either/or" strength and warmth. Although they are different conceptual ideas, in their center, strength and warmth are two sides of the same coin, complementing one another. In their extremes, they behave in hostile opposition.

Entitlement does not live in a both/and center. Entitlement's goal is to always move us toward the extreme ends of any given spectrum. In their extremes, centered feelings, such as hope, duty, love, honor, compassion, and gratitude, are ground down into their opposites. One thing that extreme warmth and strength have in common is that they both become rigid, angry, and horribly disfigured versions of their centered truths.

THE PERSONALITY COLOR MATRIX

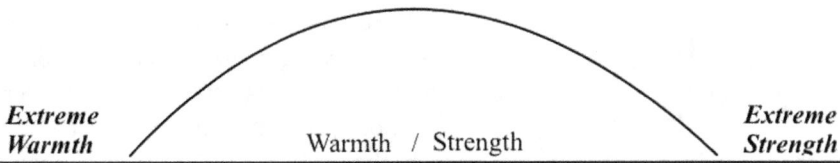

| Extreme Warmth | Warmth / Strength | Extreme Strength |

*I invite you to visit TheColorMatrix.com to gain a much deeper understanding of the strength and warm personality color tendencies.

In the center, strength feels safe because it is honorable, capable, substantial, firm, and fortified. Strength gets things done, even the difficult things. Strength stands tall, rarely falters, and is easy to respect. But when strength moves to its extremes, it becomes anything but honorable and far from respectable. Extreme strength morphs into domination and control. Obsessed with power, it becomes dictatorial, authoritarian, even brutal. It becomes an out-of-control bully who believes it can force those around them to succumb.

Centered warmth feels safe because it is caring, considerate, and empathetic. But extreme warmth causes us to lose our ability to remain centered and instead declares war against those we believe to be perpetrators of injustice. This rage can morph a warmth personality into the very thing they despise: an oppressor. In the center, warmth takes a stand *for* something it believes in. In the extreme, warmth takes a stand *against* what it despises.

Extreme feelings of hatred, bitterness, and rage desecrate the very definition of heart-centered warmth. Extreme warmth loses what is most wonderful about warmth: compassion, understanding, and heart. Extreme strength loses what is most wonderful about strength: its honor and dignity.

Now let's augment the linear continuum example I used previously and consider instead the metaphor of an upright tree to better understand how important the synthesis is between strength and warmth. (I use the term "upright" for both its literal and metaphorical implications.)

I have included an illustration of a tree with both a living and a dying side. This symbolizes the difference between the lush growth and beauty associated with endowed, centered thoughts and behaviors and the death and destruction associated with extreme, entitled thoughts and behaviors. It is a simple, logical, and practical fact that the crown, trunk, and roots must work together as a whole to ensure the health and survival of the tree.

When we picture a tree in our mind, we rarely imagine the elaborate network of roots that reaches underground, sprawling out in a vast nodal web that reflects the branches above. Although they resemble each other and are technically part of the same tree, the roots and branches behave differently. The roots form the sturdy foundation of the tree. They do not dance in the wind like the branches but are unmoving and provide stability. They hold their ground. The roots must be strong for the tree to endure the storm.

When we find ourselves lost in extremes of entitled opposition, we begin to imagine ourselves as superior. If we are "root" people with power/strength-oriented root beliefs and values, we can convince ourselves that we work harder, are more deserving, and have more importance. If we are "branch" people with love/warmth-oriented branch beliefs and values, we can convince ourselves that we are all that is truly beautiful about the tree. After all, the branches produce the fruit. Isn't that the purpose of a fruit tree?

In either extreme state of mind, we lose sight of the important and valuable views, ideals, duties, and skill sets that differ from our own. Once the vital parts of a system begin to loathe, distrust, and disrespect one another, we are heading toward the inevitable death of the tree.

In the last decade, opposition has greatly intensified. It is not only the metaphorical tree that is at war with itself. The entire forest is cutting itself down. The apricot trees choose to disdain the apple trees, the prickly pines bully the weeping willows, and the elm trees oppose the pecan trees. You get the picture. Rather than existing harmoniously in nature, we have planted ourselves on separate plots of land and built fences to protect us from the influence of opposing trees' seeds (values and beliefs).

Extreme behavior is so dangerous because it vastly overshadows any kind of reasoned, compassionate, centered behavior. Extremes are more atrocious, outrageous, and media-worthy. Once warmth- or strength-leaning people begin to define the other *only* according to their extreme behaviors, they lose sight of the centered possibilities. Compassionate people who value diversity and fairness get lumped in with their radical contemporaries, and anyone who values tradition and free speech gets accused of bigotry and oppression. It is impossible for people locked into the fallacies of their extreme warmth or strength misconceptions to respect or even consider listening to those they vehemently oppose. They begin to believe that they can "better" things by diminishing or destroying the other side.

However, those extreme drives and desires never work. They can't. The tree is a whole that thrives when its parts do what they were created to do in harmony. Entitled extremes require segregation. Once understanding and mutual respect are poisoned by entitlement, the differing parts of the system find themselves in opposition. But in the center, strength and warmth qualities operate as extraordinary complements.

It is in the trunk where the differing attributes connect to enable the tree to thrive. The trunk plays a crucial role, serving both the roots and branches. Our current political system has it backward. Each side argues that they know what is best for middle America, but the extremes at either end do *not* hold the answers to health, unity, and mutual respect.

In *The Suppliants*, a drama first performed about 423 BCE, Euripides tells us:

> *There are three groups of people. There are the rich who are never satisfied because their wealth is never enough for them—these citizens are totally useless for the city. Then there are the poor who, because their daily bread is never enough, are dangerous because they are deceived by the tongues of crooked politicians and by their own envy and so they aim the arrows of their hatred toward the rich. And then, between these two, there is a third. This one is between them. It's there to keep the order, it's there to keep the city safe.*

Aristotle also envisioned the middle class as not only morally superior to the elite but more stable and reliable than the poor. Middle citizens were thought of as the glue holding the two extreme ends together and preventing either from dominating.

In his book *The Dying Citizen*, Victor Davis Hanson—professor emeritus of classics at California State University, Fresno, and the Martin and Illie Anderson Senior Fellow in classics and military history at the Hoover Institution—discusses the significance of the middle class, which he describes as the heart of a democratic republic. The original American model was to own and farm a plot of ground—the more farmers there were, the better things were for all. Over 90 percent of American colonists were self-sufficient small farmers. Basically, the middle class literally built this nation from the ground up.

Hanson explains:

Citizens of the Greek city-state also reflected the empowerment of the middle class. The mesoi (middle ones) of the city-states were neither noble by birth nor condemned to poverty by either circumstance or lack of inheritance. "Middleness" (to meson) in thought and practice at the very beginning of the West was an innate ideal of citizenship.

What makes the United States unique is that it began as an experiment on the importance of the trunk. The trunk carries water and minerals from the roots up through the outer layers of the tree, just below the bark. The trunk doesn't just transport water and minerals; it also carries sugars from the leaves down to the roots to support and feed the root system. The trunk is the central support system for everything that happens in the tree. The central wood inside the tree is known as "heartwood." The heartwood is a hard core of old xylem layers of the trunk that have died and become compressed by the newer outer layers. Heartwood gives the trunk the strength to hold the tree upright.

Our two basic political parties are motivated by opposite sets of values. As a result, our political system is no longer centered. It has been operating out of its extremes for many decades. Political leaders from both sides are rigid in their ideas and extreme in their beliefs. Their extreme talking points declare, "If you don't vote for our political side, it will be *the end of democracy or America as we know it!*" Extremes create a toxic soil that kills all potential positive, unified strategies and policies.

If fellow Americans, in their extremes, denounce and demean one another as "pigs," hypocrites, and moral monsters, how can we possibly get anything done? In earlier times, there was some overlap in the two major parties: responsible, capable, conservative Democrats and compassionate, caring, liberal Republicans. These people were the center of their parties. They made room for conversation and compromise. Now, it often appears that both sides can barely tolerate sharing the same space.

We create safe spaces to protect us from thoughts that oppose ours. Today, both political parties are fiercely divided by ideology. The present crisis of our diminishing center may have less to do with what and how regular American citizens think and much more to do with the way media and political institutions endorse, reinforce, and encourage conflict rather than mediate it.

THE PERSONALITY COLOR MATRIX

Partisan polarization remains the dominant, seemingly unalterable condition of American politics. Republicans and Democrats agree on very little. When they do, it is often in the shared belief that they have little in common. Despite these challenges, the center may not yet be an entirely lost cause. Imagine America functioning as a mighty tree with roots representing centered strength/power and branches representing centered warmth/love. Between them, the trunk serves as the heart of the tree; its purpose is to keep the system alive and thriving by connecting both sides. What if, instead of seeing the other side as angry opponents, we realized that our destinies are bound together? To survive, the roots and branches must grow together.

It doesn't matter if we are talking about political ideals, generational biases, or familial or interpersonal relationships. Every time opposing ends wield their righteous axes, they only succeed at viciously hacking away at everything wonderful about the center. Entitlement blinds us to the devastating reality that the destruction caused and perpetuated by extreme opposition is ultimately fatal.

When will we lay down our righteous axes? When will we recognize that forgoing conversation and connection is foolish, as it only succeeds at hewing us in two? The damage that we do as individuals, i.e., severing ties or refusing to communicate over differences of opinion, is not only harmful to society at large but is also self-destructive. Whether we see ourselves as the roots or the branches, the trunk we share makes us inseparable from one another. Because both sides belong to one body, dealing damage to the opposition is the equivalent of hurting ourselves.

Warmth values embody the emotional heart of a human being, while strength values represent the logical brain. Attempting to remove either vital organ is no way to heal. Our survival depends on both working together harmoniously.

"Unity can only be manifested by the binary.
Unity itself and the idea of unity are already two."
– Buddha

CORBIN'S THOUGHTS

Acknowledging the distinction between strength and warmth allows us to more positively interpret and respect alternate, potentially conflicting perspectives instead of attempting to invalidate them. Having said that, it is also important to remember that our identification with either side does not actually divide us. The far left and far right exist as opposites, but they remain two points on a single spectrum. As my mother has illustrated, the branches and the roots belong to one tree.

Although we may initially find that we identify with one set of values over the other, each of us has the capacity to honor and embody strength and warmth values simultaneously, in a balanced state, regardless of our personality color blend. If one's personality is composed of a mixture of warmth- and strength-related colors, it may be easier to access and draw from both value sets. However, even if one's personality happens to align fully with strength or with warmth, it is still possible to lean into the alternative paradigm, even if only a little, to benefit from the wisdom of the other side. The fact that we are proficient in strength does not mean we must be deficient in warmth, and vice versa.

Where you derive your values from is not an excuse to inhibit growth or justify exclusionary behavior. It is a call to find balance. However, that potential can only be realized when we operate from our centered personality tendencies. Our extremes will always insist on pushing us to one side or the other. The best way to resist the forces attempting to sway us in either direction is to remain mindful that, in their center, strength and warmth both offer unique and beneficial perspectives. Neither side is superior, separate, or defined by their extremes.

According to author Stephen M. R. Covey, the four C's of creating trust are commitment, caring, consistency, and competence. While commitment and caring reflect the values of centered warmth, consistency and competence are ideals upheld by centered strength. Strength builds off of intellect. Warmth builds off of emotion. There is virtue behind both approaches, as well as shortcomings to consider. While our intellect helps us define and rule over the material world, it cannot rationally explain the wonders of spirit or the transformative, transcendent power of love. Though our emotions help us intuitively navigate toward a sense of meaning and purpose, giving in to their volatile whims can overwhelm, disempower, and immobilize us. Valuing one approach over the other essentially leaves us stuck with only half of the pieces necessary to complete the puzzle of existence.

While those who value warmth know how to let go, they can benefit from learning the value of accountability. And while those who value strength know how to take responsibility, they can benefit from learning how to let go. If those who value warmth reject strength, they will never understand that living as a victim denies us the opportunity to experience the triumph and confidence of becoming a victor. When we train to surpass our limits and surprise ourselves, we can experience the immense and rejuvenating pride and achievement that gives life meaning. If those who value strength reject warmth, they will never understand that others do not have to lose, be excluded, or sacrifice for them to win or excel. When we train ourselves to be mindful of other people's needs as opposed to simply satisfying our desires, we can discover win-win strategies that benefit everyone and make our lives meaningful.

Once we come to understand whether we value strength or warmth more, the challenge is not to lean into what is comfortable and box ourselves inside that categorization in an attempt to be "authentic." Identifying which side we draw our values from can help explain why we are the way we are. However, it does not validate our tendency to dismiss the other side. Knowing where we are strong also reveals where we are weak and in need of growth. For example, the revelation that one values strength over warmth does not justify being uncompromising and unsympathetic to others' emotions. It is an invitation to live more from the heart and develop empathy. By the same coin, knowing that one values warmth over strength is not an excuse to act like a victim and emotionally manipulate people. It is an invitation to increase one's capacity to take accountability and approach life with reason and practicality.

To grow into more effective, well-rounded versions of ourselves, our focus should be on expanding our capacity to embody and relate to whichever value set doesn't come naturally to us. If you tend to value strength, that means pushing yourself to reject superiority, nurture intimacy, practice empathy, offer grace, and take life less seriously to make the most of the time that is given to you. If you tend to value warmth, that means assuming responsibility, not taking things personally, being impeccable with your word, and taking life more seriously to make the most of the time given to you.

We should all strive to be proficient in understanding and speaking the language of both sides to expand our capacity to effectively relate to others. This allows us to serve as bridges of consciousness between strength and warmth. Being able to speak into the listening of both value sets makes us very effective communicators.

Whether we identify with strength or warmth values, we must learn to accept the other side, which means resisting our extreme color personality tendencies. The differences between us are not for us to judge. They present opportunities for us to be compassionate and learn from one another or, at the very least, learn to look away and let other people live their lives. Not everyone sees the world through the same lenses that we do.

That doesn't mean we need to defend ourselves from their differing beliefs, nor does it mean we need to exclude them. For either side to grow, we must incorporate wisdom from the values that don't come naturally. Strength is at its best when it acts in the service of others. Those who value strength possess the fortitude and expertise to handle real-world challenges that others may not be equipped to handle. Their sense of duty is their superpower. Warmth is at its best when it is supportive and resilient. Those who value warmth possess enhanced empathy. Their feelings of compassion are their superpower.

When both sides live to serve, we experience a greater feeling of connection and fulfillment. Throughout history, our most revered leaders are remembered for their ability to demonstrate a persuasive balance between warmth and strength. One such leader was Nelson Mandela, the former president of South Africa. Earlier in his life, Mandela was a key figure in the African National Congress (ANC), an armed resistance force fighting for justice against apartheid, a system of institutionalized racial segregation. For his involvement in conspiracies to overthrow the government, he was arrested and sentenced to life in prison. During his 27 years behind bars, Mandela underwent a transformation and embraced the principles of reconciliation and forgiveness. In his autobiography, *Long Walk to Freedom*, he wrote: "No one is born hating another person because of his skin, or his background, or his religion. People must learn to hate, and if they can learn to hate, they can be taught to love, for love comes more naturally to the human heart than the opposite." Mandela's centered strength was apparent in his resilience and persistence in his pursuit of equality.

However, upon his release from prison, Mandela also demonstrated tremendous, centered warmth in his advocacy for forgiveness and inclusivity, reaching out to his former oppressors and engaging in public and private discourse with them. Instead of seeking revenge for the injustice he experienced (as a person in their extreme green might typically react), he chose to respond from his center and promote empathy and understanding. Mandela was aware that for South Africa to move forward and unite as a nation, it was necessary to let go of the anger and resentment of the past. He encouraged his fellow countrymen to embrace unity as a way to heal and played a crucial role in the negotiations that led to the end of apartheid. A few years later, Mandela became the first black president of South Africa and helped build a more democratic, inclusive society founded on mutual respect and understanding.

Nelson Mandela explained that his decision to show grace to the opposition was inspired by the African principle of "ubuntu," a term that emphasizes the importance of recognizing the self in others. There is no corresponding word for this concept in English; however, learning this virtue is crucial to healing the enmity and violence between strength and warmth extremes. To better understand the meaning of ubuntu, consider this definition from Desmond Tutu:

Ubuntu is the essence of being human. It says a solitary human being is a contradiction in terms. I can't be a human being on my lonesome. I wouldn't know how to speak as a human being. I wouldn't know how to think as a human being. I wouldn't know how to walk as a human being. I have to learn from other human beings how to be human. Ubuntu says my humanity is bound up in yours. I am only because you are. A person becomes a person through other persons. We need this communal harmony if we are going to survive at all. Anger and revenge and bitterness are corrosive of this harmony.[1]

Exhibiting tolerance requires both strength and warmth. We must take responsibility for developing ourselves into more compassionate people. As we become more conscious, individually and collectively, we recognize that we are on a journey with others at all times, and we are co-creating, no matter where we are.

All of life is breathing, moving, and happening together. That is what it means to be one. We are all connected, and right now, we need each other. More specifically, we need to let go of our entitled extremes, return to our compassionate centers, and choose to reconcile. That means passing far fewer judgments and showing far more understanding and forgiveness. Although we are not the same, we are one. This means we are not only equal, but we should all strive to serve one another, just as individual cells cooperate to ensure the health and functioning of the greater body.

---

1. "Ubuntu: The Essence of Being Human," YouTube video, 2:48, posted by *DesmondTutu PeaceFoundation*, August 30, 2013, accessed 2024, https://www.youtube.com/watch?v=44xb-Z8MN1uk.

4

THE GROWING WRATH OF EXTREMES

*"I'm owed nothing, but I've been gifted with everything.
As such, I owe everything the commitment that I will never
find myself treating 'everything' as 'nothing.'"*
– Craig D. Lounsbrough

Today, we witness enormous amounts of opposition, greed, dysfunction, rage, and a near zero tolerance for tolerance. When I wrote the first version of this book, I felt a common question in the hearts of many: "We live in America, the land of plenty. We have more opportunities for wealth, education, success, and happiness than ever before. Yet dissatisfaction and despair surround us. Why?"

No longer a question, it has become an accusation filled with bitterness and enmity that sounds more like:

We live in America, the evil land of control, oppression, racism, and greed. F*ck your opportunities for wealth, education, and success. Forget the positives. Only failures deserve our attention. It is time to admit how despicable the history of this country truly is. Obey and give us what we want, even if we don't work for it. Our traumatic history, whether it be personal or societal, entitles us to more than what we have. Because of whatever excuse or narrative we use to justify our beliefs, YOU (the horrid ubiquitous you) owe us. So, shut the f*ck up and give us what we believe is our right. NOW!

The virus of entitlement fills our hearts with hate. As in the movie *The Matrix*, we discover that the machines are harvesting the energy of human beings as a power source. Similarly, people greedy for more power create and feed off the energy of enmity. The hatred, bitterness, and groupthink we experience are all mechanisms of control. Human beings are much easier to manipulate and distract when they feel threatened. They will surrender their freedoms in exchange for a feeling of security. Are wars fought to defeat evil and defend the sacred rights of innocent people, or are they a distraction that allows people behind the curtain to move chess pieces around a board to increase their power and wealth?

> "What do all men with power want?
> More power."
> – The Oracle
> *The Matrix Reloaded*

Twenty years ago, entitlement disguised itself as a friend. It no longer hides its ugly head and pretends to be a good friend to those in need. Now, entitlement needs no disguise. Since I wrote the original version of this book, entitlement has deceived many with the bald-faced lie that living with an entitled mindset can be fair, necessary, empowering, and even noble. In reality, nothing could be further from the truth.

Entitled extremes tell us it is our right to protest in the middle of a busy road, purposefully obstructing traffic, even if it puts other's lives in danger, to make a political point. It prowls the streets in the form of petty criminals and violent thugs who indiscriminately rob and assault strangers. It putrefies on sidewalks where people relieve themselves in public. People on the street think nothing of shooting up drugs and leaving the paraphernalia on the sidewalk for others to step over. Social services provide drug addicts with clean needles because they believe it is a loving and caring action to take. In their minds, drug addicts are entitled to anything necessary to help them use safely. It is all too obvious that programs built with a narrowly focused sense of entitlement rarely make sense. We will address this kind of entitled mindset in the upcoming Help Paradox chapter.

During the last 45 years of private practice as a family counselor and personality expert, I have witnessed entitled, poisoned mindsets devastate relationships, destroy hope, cripple possibility, and make everyone afflicted with it feel miserable, confused, and hateful. As I was revising this chapter, a news report popped up on my computer screen about a 53-year-old from Long Island, New York, named Paul Kutz, who was shot in the lobby of his hotel while he was visiting his son at college.

According to reports, two men got into a dispute, resulting in gunshots being sprayed throughout the lobby. What the media hesitated to tell us (it came to light a few days later) was that both men had prior arrests and histories of violence. However, they were released with no bail to potentially harm more people because the prosecutors for their case believed that they were entitled to leniency and grace that many would argue they did nothing to earn.

People who knew Kutz—who was a father, husband, Little League coach, accountant, and reliable neighbor—are trying to cope with his loss. Joseph Farrell, who lived next door to the Kutz family for 20 years, said, "His family is destroyed for no reason." As I see it, the reason was the evil of entitlement.

This story, as well as other numerous reports of mass shootings in America, will cause some to immediately launch into a condemnation of guns and others to defend the Second Amendment. Commentators will rant on the ineffectiveness of lenient judicial and legal programs, while those skilled in political persuasion will pontificate on the overarching dynamics that explain, even justify, such destructive behavior. Although people get sidetracked by ideals, dogmas, and political stances, the bottom line is that those men who had been given a generous chance to alter their destructive criminal tendencies felt entitled to shoot at one another with no care or caution about who might end up in the crossfire. Their entitled rage and complete lack of concern left Paul Kutz murdered.

Maybe the two young men were suffering psychologically. Many people hurt others when they are suffering from psychological illnesses. That is a tremendously sad fact. But enmity, fueled by toxic, entitled political beliefs, demands that instead of dealing with real and present psychological struggles and deficits, the only heart-centered and truly caring approach is to understand that they *deserve* to feel their bitterness and loathing and perpetrate their oppositional, defiant, and criminal behavior. Consequently, they believe criminals should be released back into society where they are free to lose control and assault, shoot, and kill innocent people like Paul Kutz, who certainly did not *deserve* to die.

No matter what cultural or political side entitled enmity infects, the sickness destroys everyone. Entitlement ensures that there are NO winners, NO successes, and NO positive outcomes, only guarantees of bitterness, heartbreak, frustration, rage, and loss.

> *"To be ignorant of the sacrifices of others*
> *that yielded the blessings I enjoy*
> *leaves me exchanging the reality of 'blessing'*
> *for the assumption of 'entitlement.'*
> *And once that happens, I will forfeit the reality of the former*
> *which will destroy the assumption of the latter.*
> *And in what terribly dark place will that now leave me?"*
> – Craig D. Lounsbrough

Whether your political leanings are red, blue, or a kaleidoscope of frustration, there is no argument about the fact that enmity is on the rise. When people do not feel safe, fear becomes the motivating factor for how we choose to relate to others. As I mentioned above, the norm is for psychological illnesses to go undiagnosed and remain untreated. An analysis conducted by the American Institute of Stress found the total economic impact of stress on U.S. employers was estimated to be $300 billion.[1] Fear has become ubiquitous. Enmity, fueled by entitlement, motivates people to harm each other without provocation. It has become accepted for many of our youth to make a game out of hurting or even killing each other. People run up behind others and cold-cock them. Teens are killing the elderly and each other for no apparent reason except that, in some very demented way, they feel entitled to do it. Although criminals are arrested, they are also immediately released without bail.

Burglaries have risen dramatically. However, the statistics for burglaries have decreased because it has become accepted that you can steal up to $950 a day in states like California and pay no consequences. If a crime is not seen as illegal, it cannot be counted or recorded as a burglary in city or state records. As a result, political leaders can pontificate about how crime has dramatically decreased under their watch when, in fact, everyone knows that what they are saying is a lie.

Convenience stores, drugstores, and neighborhood stores have closed because they cannot tolerate the terrorizing loss of merchandise. For example, in 2022, Starbucks closed at least 16 stores across five different states

---

1. American Institute of Stress, "Workplace Stress," accessed 2024, https://www.stress.org/workplace-stress/.

due to various issues concerning the safety of employees and the surrounding public.[2]

Suicide has also increased dramatically in the last two decades. In fact, more people die from suicide than from homicide. Suicide was the second leading cause of death for people ages 10– 14 and 20– 34. More teenagers and young adults fall victim to suicide than all natural causes combined. Between 2020 and 2021, suicide was responsible for 48,183 deaths, 36% greater than in years prior. For perspective, when I originally wrote this book, it was estimated that 20,000 Americans took their own lives every year. Now it's estimated that a suicide attempt occurs once a minute. Every 11 minutes, one of those attempts is successful, equating to an average of 130 suicides per day.

Are you in a crisis? Call or text 988 or text TALK to 741741.

Why are suicide rates spiking? Because entitled mindsets cause misery and distress. Entitled beliefs convince us that what we have, our gifts, our talents, our homes, our relationships, our freedoms, our opportunities, and our material blessings, are meaningless. As a result, we lose the ability to feel the joy that appreciation brings. Consequently, misery, frustration, and bitterness grow. An entitled mindset does not enrich or enhance our lives. In actuality, it steals our hope, enrages our hearts, motivates hateful actions, and kills trust. When entitled extreme beliefs take over, we not only damage ourselves, but we hurt each other.

The most recent estimate of approximately 850,000 gang members represents an 8.6 percent increase over the previous year. Gang members who shoot to kill or injure members of a rival gang are motivated by the feeling of entitlement. In addition to gang violence, each year, two million injuries and 1,300 deaths are caused as a result of domestic violence. Three women are murdered every day by an intimate partner whose entitlement convinced them that because they were not getting what they wanted when and how they wanted it, the people they once professed to love deserved to be beaten. Every nine seconds, a woman in the U.S. is the victim of domestic abuse. Entitled feelings and beliefs motivate all violence.

---

2. Joseph Lamour, "Starbucks Is Closing 16 Stores Over Safety Concerns," *Today*, July 12, 2022, accessed 2024, https://www.today.com/food/news/starbucks-closing-16-stores-safety-concerns-rcna38043.

> *"I think that there's something in the American psyche,*
> *it's almost this kind of right or privilege, this sense of entitlement,*
> *to resolve our conflicts with violence. There's an arrogance to*
> *that concept if you think about it. To actually have to*
> *sit down and talk, to listen, to compromise,*
> *that's hard work."*
> – Michael Moore

Entitlement corrupts through power, political gain, status, and money. Today, political factions are some of the worst examples of extreme entitlement. Politicians feel entitled to spend taxpayer money with no accountability. They feel entitled to print money without accepting responsibility for the inflationary consequences. Politicians forget they are political servants and become entitled pieces of parsley. They promote ideas and causes that they believe will preserve their power versus truly making a difference in the lives of their constituents. Enmity, created by toxic entitlement, doesn't care if you lean red, blue, or purple. It hates and destroys all colors. When we keep enmity at bay politically, there is hope that we can work across political aisles.

It is a politician's job to take a stand for what is in the best interests of the citizens they represent. Those who value duty and honor must loosen their entitled chokehold on feeling or believing that there is only one "right" way, and it is "their" way. Centered choices that strengthen amity and bless and benefit the whole require collaboration, compromise, and consideration of each other's ideas.

Wherever we witness the destruction and ruin of our cities, relationships, and families, wherever we feel overwhelmed by anxiety, fear, and misery, it results from the wrath of extremes caused by noxious entitlement. Whether it is corporate entitlement, union entitlement, rich entitlement, poor entitlement, political entitlement, abusive entitlement, or criminal entitlement, it all leads to the same horrible destination: fear, loathing, and misery.

CORBIN'S THOUGHTS

Extreme, entitled behavior will always seek to justify itself. That's why it can be so difficult to recognize within ourselves. However, the traits are glaringly obvious when we look at other people. It is apparent in the concerning surplus of videos of 40-plus-year-old American adults (not to mention teenagers) throwing temper tantrums in public spaces.

THE PERSONALITY COLOR MATRIX

When I'm in a public space in America, I can never be too sure that there won't be a sudden outbreak of violence. If a disagreement sparks between a thoughtless customer and a thoughtless employee in a fast-food restaurant, I cannot trust either party to remain level-headed. With no emotional intelligence between them, there is no buffer to prevent the rapid escalation of conflict.

In March 2021, Alonniea Ford, an employee of a Houston fast-food restaurant, fired her handgun out of the drive-thru window at a car containing a family of three (including a six-year-old girl and a pregnant woman) in a dispute over curly fries.[3] Fortunately, nobody was injured. This case is extreme, but it is hardly an isolated incident in America. Just go on YouTube and search "Fast Food Fight." The platform is over-saturated with camera phone recordings of customers and employees acting out their extremes. Perhaps these types of incidents have always occurred in society, but their frequency has undeniably spiked in recent years.

Now that everyone carries a camera phone in their pocket, the consequences of having an extreme meltdown in public can be devastating. Not only will you likely lose your job (or be arrested), but you'll be turned into an internet meme and forever labeled a "Karen."

Recently, "Karen" has emerged as a modern archetype in American society, used to describe extreme behavior, entitlement, and anti-emotional intelligence. Karens are the opposite of role models. The videos of their meltdowns serve as cautionary tales. They warn us not to give into the destructive temptations of our extreme personality tendencies the next time the restaurant server gets our order wrong, an airline loses our bag, or a stranger steals our parking spot.

In 2020, YouTube was rife with a genre of content I refer to as "Karen freak-out videos," recordings of middle-aged women and men having epic infantile meltdowns and clashes with other people in public. In most instances, the encounters escalated to violence or arrest. Not once did any of the scenarios resolve amicably!

After copious research, I began to reach some fascinating conclusions about the Karen phenomenon and its genre conventions. First of all, it is my opinion that, in 2024, the term "Karen" has nothing to do with gender, race, or age (despite the label originally singling out middle-aged white women). These days, the term has been so overused that it generally

---

3. "Jack in the Box employee defends herself in shooting over curly fries," YouTube video, 3:07, posted by *ABC13 Houston*, September 23, 2023, accessed 2024, https://www.youtube.com/watch?v=GHk3ICTZdlI.

applies to any person acting out of their extremes in public, usually motivated by narcissistic entitlement (and occasional demonic possession). All jokes aside, you can find videos of "Karens" in all sizes, shapes, genders, colors, and socio-economic classes. The one thing they have in common is that they *all* behave out of their destructive extremes.

These extreme blow-ups can happen in different ways, depending on the person's personality tendencies. Using The Personality Color Matrix technology, we can begin to understand how and why people "Karen out." The motives vary and depend on a person's color blend when they are in their extreme. For example, some Karens are sticklers for the rules. Other Karens equate any enforcement of the rules whatsoever with oppression or discrimination. The scenarios vary.

Generally speaking, some personality color blends are more predisposed to confrontational Karen-like behavior, particularly those influenced by strong purple, red, and green coloring. The extremes of these colors can become authoritarian and militant; they combine to create a righteous person who not only demands that rules be unilaterally enforced but is willing to get in someone's face to make them comply. To elaborate further, I'd like to compare and contrast some of the most infamous Karen episodes on the internet to explain the specific extreme personality dynamics that can be at play.

Let's begin with the Central Park Karen incident that occurred in May 2020 in New York City.[4] It involved a woman named Amy Cooper calling the police on a man named Christian Cooper (no relation) who was birdwatching. Christian Cooper had asked Amy Cooper to leash her dog, as it was required in that area of Central Park. Amy refused, became agitated, and called 911, claiming that an African American man was threatening her. Christian recorded the incident on his camera phone, which went viral and drew significant backlash toward Amy for weaponizing emergency services as a tool of racial intimidation.

Although there was an undeniable racial subtext to the exchange, I would argue that the incident actually happened as a result of clashing extreme personality tendencies. In this case, Amy Cooper acted out of her yellow extreme. People with yellow personality tendencies are naturally averse to conflict. They like harmony and sunshine and walking their dog in the park undisturbed. They also want their dog to feel free and untethered. Out of courtesy, they'll unleash their furry best friends to play and

---

4. "The Central Park Karen Original Video," YouTube video, 1:09, posted by *Methodshop*, May 28, 2023, accessed 2024, https://www.youtube.com/watch?v=IFvM7-YtvbM.

explore, even if it's technically against the rules. In their mind, they aren't hurting anyone.

However, to a person with strong purple-blue (blurple) personality tendencies like Christian Cooper, rules serve a purpose and should be followed precisely. From his perspective, a dog running unleashed around the park, upsetting the birds he is trying to watch, is quite discourteous, especially when posted signs clearly show that dogs are to be leashed. This violation, combined with Amy's dismissive response to his initial request to leash her dog, sent Christian Cooper into his blurple extreme (whether he was aware of it or not).

In the age of the camera phone, one of the easiest ways to identify whether or not someone is in their extreme is if they are recording another person they are in conflict with. Although Christian never appears on camera, we can hear the frustration in his voice. The desire to record a dispute for the sake of collecting evidence implies that he is building a case against Amy to make her look bad. To a person who values strength, being held accountable may not seem like an act of aggression, but to someone who values warmth, it can feel like being singled out and harassed.

In her yellow extreme, Amy felt targeted the moment she realized Christian was recording her. Rather than leashing her dog, she seized her animal defensively by the collar and approached Christian, repeatedly demanding that he stop filming her. The bird watcher refused. In their extremes, people with purple personality tendencies often become overbearing and rigid in their enforcement of rules and policies. They tend to dismiss others' personal feelings as inconsequential if they fail to align with greater systems that necessitate compliance. For a person with strong purple personality tendencies, compliance is expected. In their extremes, obedience is mandated.

To discourage dissent and ensure the systems they oversee continue to function effectively, people with strong purple personality tendencies will not hesitate to threaten and enforce penalties on those who break the rules. They have little desire to entertain nuance or exceptions. In their eyes, rules are rules, and your excuses don't matter, no exceptions. Because they prioritize policy and efficiency over people and emotions, individuals with strong purple personality tendencies possess the ability to remain calm while they are in their extreme. People with strong blue personality tendencies can also appear calm in their extremes. However, this is because they consider overly emotional behavior to be irrational.

On the other hand, people possessed by yellow extremes find it impossible to restrain their emotions. This explains why Amy grows increasingly nervous and irrational the longer she is being recorded. In her mind, the stress of the confrontation is unbearable. When yellow extremes take over, people become inconsolable victims. In this fearful state of mind, their past traumas (and the personal stories surrounding them) consume and cripple them. They adopt whatever narrative framing portrays them as most sympathetic. They cry and act miserable and helpless to manipulate others to get their way or absolve them of guilt. In the process, they can become so absorbed in their victim narrative that they lose touch with reality. In the case of Amy, she became so panic-stricken on the telephone while informing 911 that someone was threatening her and her dog that she began to yank her poor pet by the collar, choking the animal and wrestling it to the ground until it yelped. Although Amy's narcissistic entitlement convinced her that she was the victim, she was the only one doing any harm to her animal.

After making a desperate plea to 911 to "send cops immediately!" Amy finally leashed her dog, at which point Christian Cooper said, "Thank you," and immediately cut the recording. The abrupt ending of the video reveals that for people with extreme purple tendencies, conflict is resolved at the moment of compliance. There is no need for lingering drama. For blurple extremes, it's time to get back to business and focus on the details. These birds aren't going to watch themselves.

As far as blurple extremes go, I have to commend Christian Cooper for remaining as calm as he did during the encounter. That's not always how it works with purple personalities in their extremes, especially if they are influenced by secondary colors like green, red, or blue. In that case, if you break the rules, purple-red-green extremes won't hesitate to call the police on your family barbecue at the park because you are using a charcoal grill in a restricted area.

Such was the case with Jennifer Schulte (a.k.a. BBQ Becky), who was inducted into the Karen Hall of Fame after she called the police on an African American family having a barbecue in an Oakland, California, park.[5] Jennifer informed the family (incorrectly) that the grill they were using was illegal. She sternly insisted, "There are laws about this park, and people should follow them." That is purple extreme talking if I have ever heard it!

The same goes for "Permit Patty," a Karen who became a social media

---

5. "Original BBQ Becky Meme Video - The First Viral 'Karen'," YouTube video, 24:52: posted by *Michelle Dione*, April 30, 2018, accessed 2024, https://www.youtube.com/watch?v=Fh9D_PUe7QI.

villain in 2018 after calling the police on an eight-year-old African American girl who was selling water in San Francisco outside her apartment without a permit.[6] While working from home, Alison Ettel, the woman dubbed "Permit Patty," found herself persistently distracted by her young neighbor, who kept shouting from the sidewalk to attract customers to buy her bottled water. Alison confronted the girl's mother and threatened to call the police after they failed to present a permit. She went viral when the girl's mother began filming her in retribution.

"You can hide all you want," the girl's mother said, following her neighbor with her camera phone as Alison ducked behind a wall to avoid being recorded (extreme yellow behavior). "The whole world is going to see you, boo." The mother's judgmental, condescending attitude in response to Permit Patty calling the police on her eight-year-old daughter is understandable. It is also how blue extremes sometimes appear in these heated camera-phone interactions. People with extreme blue personality tendencies will undermine, insult, belittle, and disregard anyone they consider uninformed or in the wrong.

One of the most notorious Karen videos on the internet involves a woman named Abigail Elphick, "The Victoria's Secret Karen," who was filmed having a crying fit in the lingerie store after she attempted to hit another African American customer named Ijeoma Ukenta.[7] Although we can clearly see Abigail is in her yellow extreme as she weeps in a puddle on the ground, it is less obvious that the woman filming her, Ijeoma, is also in her blue extreme.

"Oh, my God! Do you see this?" Ijeoma jeers behind the camera. "Karen had a breakdown. She tried to hit me." As Abigail curls into a fetal ball, squealing that she doesn't want to be recorded, Ijeoma continues to film, saying, "You should have thought about that before you did what you did." Ijeoma's words embody the merciless, sharp edge of blue extremes.

People in blue extremes can be haughty and demeaning. As I have mentioned, those with blue personality tendencies tend to be very rational. They remain this way in their extremes. Like people influenced by purple personality tendencies, they have a greater capacity to control their emotional volatility when they feel rage because they understand that

---

[6]. "Woman Dubbed 'Permit Patty' Calls Police On Young Girl Selling Water," YouTube video, 1:49, posted by *CBS Miami*, June 25, 2018, accessed 2024, https://www.youtube.com/watch?v=4Bftqi1FSOM.

[7]. "Karen Goes Crazy Part 1," YouTube video, 3:18, posted by *Mama Africa Muslimah*, July 10, 2021, accessed 2024, https://www.youtube.com/watch?v=u5g9K0xY0-g.

being overly emotional isn't logical or productive. Although they may appear somewhat calm, below the surface, they silently seethe and will say things to cut down people they deem to be unworthy of their respect.

Although Abigail begged, "Don't record my mental breakdown! Please. Please. Please," Ijeoma had no concern for her feelings. Why should she? Abigail was clearly in the wrong. Ijeoma's extreme blue felt righteous in mercilessly torturing her in retribution, refusing to take her camera off her as she wailed.

Even when asked by another customer if she would walk away, Ijeoma refused. "No! Why don't she walk away from me? No. I was here first. No. No. No. We're not doing this. Why don't I walk away from her? Why don't she get away from me? She can get away. Go wherever you want to go. This is crazy."

The video ends with Abigail, lost in her yellow extreme, collapsing onto the floor face down, pretending to fall unconscious. Honestly, you have to see it to believe it. The poor woman looks like an opossum playing dead. According to her police report, Abigail said that she knew "what she did was 'wrong' and that she experienced a panic attack after realizing Ukenta was recording her. She also said that she has an 'anxiety disorder' and was anxious about Ukenta recording her because she was 'afraid of losing her job and apartment.'"

In her blue extreme, Ijeoma was far less concerned with Abigail's mental health or the accusations of racism that would inevitably be raised against her. Instead, she was far more concerned with documenting the wrong that had been done to prove she was in the right. "I'm sorry," Ijeoma comments with a laugh at the end of the uncomfortable encounter. "I don't feel bad."

Following the incident, Ijeoma sued Abigail, the mall, and the security company because she believed they were negligent in their duty and failed to arrive fast enough to assist her after she was assaulted with prejudice. Through the discovery process of the lawsuit, it was revealed that at the time of the altercation, Abigail lived in "a complex reserved for residents with intellectual and developmental disabilities. Her behavior stemmed not from a 'race-based' problem, according to a complaint filed by her lawyers, but from the fear that being filmed would lead to the loss of her apartment and job."[8]

---

8. "Update: VIRAL Victoria's Secret Karen Story Gets More Complicated,"ouTube video, 16:11, posted by The Young Turks October 4, 2023, accessed 2024, https://www.youtube.-com/watch?v=867vhwWkhXY&feature=youtu.be.

THE PERSONALITY COLOR MATRIX

With that context in mind (which only emerged several years after the clip initially went viral), this particular Karen freak-out video requires more nuance and understanding than it was initially afforded. Outraged online commenters contacted the school district where Abigail formerly interned to demand that they fire their "racist employee." Court records show she received harassing calls and contacted the police to report threats of rape and death.

This unfortunate reality speaks to how internet commentators in our culture tend to demonize people and ruin their lives without understanding all the details of the situation that they are reacting to. The Personality Color Matrix technology allows us to examine misunderstandings and altercations between private citizens in far more shades than simply black and white. The more context we have, the more empathy we experience. The more empathy we experience, the less judgment we pass.

Besides acting superior and judgmental behind the camera, people with extreme blue personality tendencies are notorious for rebelling against rules, systems, and procedures they deem misinformed, pointless, or idiotic. During the COVID era, Karen freak-out videos commonly involved customers arguing with employees over temporary mask mandates. While a manager in their purple extreme would be prone to tell a customer, "Sir, this is a Wendy's. Put on a mask and follow the rules," a customer in their blue extreme would likely reply, "There is no scientific evidence that supports the efficacy of masks in preventing the spread of an airborne virus, you sheep. Do your own research and mind your own damn business. I know my rights." Unbeknownst to the customer in their blue extreme, by that point, it's more than likely that an offended employee with extreme orange, green, or red personality tendencies has spit into their Frosty.

People with strong blue personality tendencies love doing independent research. In their extremes, they love to inform others that they "know better." They will cite research studies and legal statutes to make their case. This type of Karen-esque behavior can be especially tedious for authority figures and service industry workers to deal with. Although someone in their blue extreme will usually present evidence to back up their outrage, their efforts to prove themselves correct are ultimately futile. Their righteous, rational appeals against "idiocracy" get them nowhere. Whether or not they are right, a purple employee or supervisor will insist on upholding store policy and call the police unless the extreme blue customer ceases their tirade. When blue extremes get mouthy with police officers and attempt to outsmart them or question their authority by citing the Constitution instead of cooperating politely, they usually end up making their inevitable arrest much harder on themselves.

Encounters with Karens in the wild don't always escalate to violence. However, when Karens become physically aggressive, we know we are dealing with extreme red personality tendencies. Red extremes are the reason we need the police. To get their way or deal with perceived disrespect, they will lash out physically, stealing people's camera phones, throwing fists, screaming, "Get out of my way!" and ramming people with their cars.

For example, when an unidentified Karen in Sacramento found herself unable to pull forward out of a fast-food drive-thru because the car in front of her was blocking her exit, she got out of her car and approached the vehicle in front of her.[9] Hammering on the window, she demanded that the driver move, insisting that she couldn't pull her car out and felt "unsafe." When the driver of the other car, who was still waiting for their meal, refused to move as she commanded, the unidentified Karen threatened to ram their vehicle. Returning to her car, the enraged woman threw her vehicle in reverse and slammed on the gas, plowing into the car behind her before speeding away from the drive-thru. Yes, you read that correctly. The Karen rammed the car behind her, not the car in front of her that belonged to the driver she was filmed threatening.

At their worst, people with extreme red personality tendencies can be dominating and destructive bullies. They have no regard for people's feelings, safety, or property. They will make a mess with no thought for those who have to clean it up. If you dare call them out for their disrespect, they will verbally assault you or physically attack you or your business.

One of the wildest Karen videos I have ever seen is of a woman in a convenience store doing her best to destroy everything in stock.[10] She removes item after item from the shelves, chucking them across the room, shattering glass. She breaks every bottle of wine and liquor she can get her hands on while going on a racist, anti-Semitic tirade. In her mind, the owners of the shop deserved to have their inventory obliterated for engaging in human sex trafficking and racking up prices. From the havoc she wreaks, it is evident that there is no convincing her otherwise.

When Karens become enraged with feelings of entitlement regarding

---

9. TapHaps, "Woman Claims McDonald's Drive-Thru Is Unsafe — See Why," accessed 2024, https://taphaps.com/unsafe-mcdonalds-drive-thru-24b/.
10. "Crazy Karen DESTROYS Convenience Store," YouTube video, 2:27, posted by *KAREN FREAKOUT VIDEOS by Endless Uploads*, February 1, 2023, accessed 2024, https://www.youtube.com/watch?v=lTd5jx994tA.

what is fair and what people "deserve," you can be sure that extreme green personality tendencies are at play. In their center, people with green personality tendencies are purpose-driven activists who see the big picture. They often join spiritual or ideological movements to find meaning and a sense of belonging. The identity provided by their beliefs makes them willing to sacrifice their money, energy, and time to create the change that they wish to see in the world.

Although people with strong green personality tendencies are non-confrontational by nature, once they feel unjustly wronged and enter their extremes, they become obsessed with retribution and vulnerable to radicalization. In their extremes, people with strong green tendencies can violate every belief they hold dear in their center. In Karens, green extremes show up in two forms: Karens who are easily (and perhaps overly) offended by free expression and go out of their way to silence or control dissenting opinions or behavior and Karens who are overly eager to be seen as martyrs to exemplify prejudice and systemic injustice.

In their extremes, people with strong green personality tendencies transition from activists to militants. Like people with purple personality tendencies, they seek to enforce rules, except the rules they are concerned about are political correctness and equity. They police other people's language and behavior, calling them out when they overhear or observe something that they deem to be morally unacceptable. In their eyes, nothing matters more than creating a sustainable and safe world for those they believe are oppressed. In that pursuit, conflict becomes justifiable.

Because people with strong green personality tendencies are so committed to their belief systems, when they go into their extremes, they perceive anyone who disagrees with their ideology as an enemy. While they may believe themselves to be righteous and accepting, they can practice exclusionary discrimination. This not only applies to "woke" social justice warriors but dogmatic religious fundamentalists. When green personality tendencies blend with purple personality tendencies, those who value inclusivity and fairness implement rules and policies to create safe spaces. Purple and green personality tendencies share a common chord of adherence and politeness. When green-purple personalities enter their extreme, they can become stringent conformists who show little tolerance for oppositional voices, classifying counter-narratives as misinformation and demanding censorship or penalizations for online "hate speech" in the name of public safety or national security.

The following is a transcript from one of my favorite Karen freak-out videos that perfectly captures the righteous and judgmental attitude of extreme green personality tendencies. Allow me to set the scene. On a flight from Baltimore to Seattle following Donald Trump's first inauguration, Scott Koteskey, a man wearing a MAGA shirt, sat down beside an elderly woman and her husband. Immediately, the woman became visibly upset by Koteskey's presence and passive support for the controversial president and signaled the flight attendants to request that the man be reseated because she was uncomfortable sitting next to him.[11]

Flight Attendant: "Is there going to be a problem?"

Karen: "There will be. I would like him to change seats with someone."

Flight Attendant: "Well, you don't have that right, so I will get somebody to come and talk to you."

(Flight Attendant leaves. Karen turns to man in MAGA shirt.)

Karen: "You pretend to have the moral high ground, but you put that man's finger on the nuclear button. That man doesn't believe in climate change. Do you believe in gravity? Did you know gravity is just a theory?"

(Flight Attendant Two approaches.)

Flight Attendant Two: "Excuse me, ma'am. Can you grab your belongings and come with me, please?"

Karen: "Where?"

Flight Attendant Two: "You have to be off this plane."

Karen: "I beg your pardon?"

Flight Attendant Two: "We have to take you off this plane right now. Can you grab your belongings and come with me, please? Please?"

Karen: "No. I paid for this seat, and I'm sitting in it. He is in my space."

Flight Attendant Two: "We can do this one of two ways."

That's some based purple behavior on display by Flight Attendant Two. It makes sense. As I've said, people with strong purple personality tendencies have no time for shenanigans. The airplane needs to take off on time, regardless of its passengers' petty political squabbles. Ultimately, the woman and her husband (who were reportedly on their way to a family funeral) were forced to disembark the aircraft as the surrounding passengers applauded. How tragic. I mean it. Being carried away by our extreme personality tendencies always leads to miserable dead ends.

"Fate, it seems, is not without a sense of irony."
– Morpheus
The Matrix

---

11. Facebook, "Video Post," accessed 2024, https://www.facebook.com/638719921/videos/10155758661609922/.

THE PERSONALITY COLOR MATRIX

The other way that extreme green personalities lead to entitled, Karen-esque behavior is when people who believe themselves to be victims of unfair or unequal treatment go out of their way to prove it and break the law in the process. Although they view themselves as martyrs, these Karens are only victims of their own sense of narcissistic entitlement and rigid limiting beliefs.

"This is my Rosa Parks moment. Don't play with me," said Karen Ivery, a 37-year-old African American woman, after police detained her in the manager's office of a Target in Blue Ash, Ohio.[12] In October 2022, Karen became furious with employs after they refused to give her $1,000 worth of merchandise for free. She explained that Target should cover her purchase as a part of the reparations that she was owed as a historically marginalized person of color. She told the employees that they lived a privileged life while she was disadvantaged and deserved to leave with the items in her cart, even though she didn't have enough money to pay for it all.

The checkout employees offered to put Karen in touch with someone from Target HR to see if a donation could be made, but they explained that nothing could be done that evening. Karen refused to accept that. She adamantly insisted on speaking to a supervisor until a loss-prevention manager arrived. When he also refused her unconventional proposal to give her everything that she wanted for free, she chased the manager into his back office. Here, we can see Karen's red extreme tendencies blending with her green to become a dominating force.

Acting in self-defense (and succumbing to his own red extreme), the senior manager punched Karen in the face when she entered his office, sending her sprawling to the floor. Immediately after the incident, the manager called 911. When police arrived, they questioned Karen, who considered herself the victim of the altercation and insisted that she had done nothing to warrant being assaulted. In her mind, she had "stood her ground," and her actions were not wrong because she stood in her truth.

"So what caused the issue here today?" asked the police.

"We were having a conversation about how to reconcile the fact that some people benefited off of a system that has been used against other people," Karen explained. "I asked nicely to have that conversation."

"What were you asking for?"

---

12. "'Don't Play with Me': Woman Punched in the Face by Target Manager After Charging at Him," YouTube video, 14:07, posted *Law&Crime Network*, April 19, 2023, accessed 2024, https://www.youtube.com/watch?v=aQm25YR-97U.

"To break the lies around money."

"What does that mean?"

"We all know that money has not been treating everybody equally," said Karen. "Money is not the only way for things to happen."

"Were you asking Target to make a donation?"

"I was coming up to the limit of where I had money. I was trying to ask if Target would compensate me the rest, and we would have a bigger conversation about why because I know the heart of this place. It's the right place for me to have this conversation."

"It's a good company," agreed the police officer.

"Exactly, and I was trying to have a hard conversation in a safe place. People hit me for that. I did it the right way. I went through the right steps. The reason that money doesn't work right is that it blocks me from my checkpoints, and I'm tired of money blocking good people out. You don't get paid what you deserve… not nearly as much because choosing to do the right thing in this world costs us monetarily. That's not fair. The system is rigged against people doing the right thing."

When Karen was informed that she was being charged with trespassing, the authorities told her that she could either leave of her own free will or be escorted out by police. She insisted on being handcuffed and arrested to protest the injustice. "When the laws are not right, you make a stand so things will change," she said, holding up an empowered fist. "If the laws are meant to hold people down, then you will fight for me and my community."

Her appeal did not persuade the police. "Just because your intentions were good, it doesn't mean that your actions were legal, unfortunately."

Karen Ivery was later convicted of disorderly conduct and sentenced to one day in jail and fined $110. In the end, she got exactly what she wished for. Coverage of her story went viral. Unfortunately, the public was unsympathetic to her plight.

The final Karen freak-out video I would like to highlight showcases the self-consumed and self-destructive nature of extreme orange personality tendencies. In July of 2023, an unidentified, unruly United Airlines passenger began arguing with flight attendants after being denied wine, repeatedly refusing to follow crew instructions to take her seat until the airplane was forced to divert. The intoxicated woman's insistence on causing a rebellious scene after being refused alcohol reflects the craving impatience, verbal hostility, and reckless shortsightedness associated with extreme orange tendencies.[13]

Another passenger on the flight by the name of Blake Perkins captured the incident on his cell phone, posting several clips to TikTok with the caption: "Another video of the Karen who couldn't get her wine. We had to land ... so she could get escorted off ... causing us even more delays than we already had. Over wine."[14] Upon landing in Phoenix, law enforcement removed the woman from the aircraft. She was consequently banned from future United Airlines flights. Hedonistic orange extremes can be impulsive, inconsiderate, and insulting, especially when prevented from indulging in their favored form of escapism. Their desire to be treated as the exception, along with their tendency to overindulge in vices and thoughtlessly seek instant gratification and attention, can derail their long-term personal well-being as well as inconvenience and endanger others around them.

As I said before, Karen freak-out videos are cautionary tales. They are also reflections of our entitled, emotionally stunted society. Being aware of our extremes does not mean we have to accept them. The choices we make under the influence of our extremes do not define who we are in our center. Nevertheless, extreme behaviors lead to confrontation and miserable outcomes for all involved and account for every cruel, bigoted, dehumanizing thing said in the history of our species.

Nobody is immune to entering their extremes. The impulse can be impossible to resist. Often, we do it daily. People with strong blue personality tendencies are the easiest to provoke. They don't even need other people to send them into their extremes. Just reading or watching the news is enough to trigger their discontent and outrage.

People with strong red personality tendencies are the second most likely to enter their extremes. The moment they encounter opposition, they will try to overcome it by any means necessary, including force.

Yellow personality tendencies are the third most likely to enter their extremes. Because they are so sensitive, people with strong yellow person-

---

13. David Propper, "Disruptive Passenger Temporarily Banned from United Airlines After Uproar Over Wine," *New York Post*, August 1, 2023, accessed 2024, https://nypost.com/2023/08/01/disruptive-passenger-temporarily-banned-from-united-airlines-after-uproar-over-wine/.
14. Monique Welch, "United Airlines Passenger Causes Scene over Sparkling Wine on Houston Flight," *Houston Chronicle*, August 2, 2023, accessed October 14, 2024, https://www.chron.com/news/houston-texas/transportation/article/houston-flight-wine-karen-18279371.php.

tendencies tend to take things personally and react passive-aggressively. Their natural aversion to conflict makes them feel anxious and disempowered whenever they sense that people are unhappy with them.

Green personality tendencies are the fourth most likely to enter their extremes. Like people with strong yellow personality influences, people with strong green personality tendencies are naturally averse to conflict. Their devotion and big-picture vision help them remain centered despite the hardship and personal conflict they endure in life. However, when they feel their beliefs are under attack or their identity subjects them to unfair treatment, they seek support from like-minded groups and organize extreme movements to enforce their ideological will.

Orange personality tendencies are the fifth most likely to enter their extremes. Because oranges are motivated by fun and good vibes, they tend to take life less seriously, using their natural charisma and humor to ease tension as well as manipulate people to get their way. They are happy to tell others whatever they want to hear and lie to their faces to avoid dealing with consequences. However, the moment a person with strong orange personality tendencies feels cornered or forced into a position where they cannot freely access their preferred means of escape (be it drugs or video games), they become enraged and use their way with words to deceive and denigrate anyone who refuses to enable their impulsive, reckless, and potentially destructive behavior.

Out of all the colors, purple personality tendencies remain the least likely to enter their extreme. People with strong purple personality tendencies value achievement and efficiency too much to see their productivity derailed by unruly emotions. If anything, in their extreme, they become taskmasters intent on planning to ensure order in the household or workplace. They are excellent at remaining level-headed during conflicts. Their problem is often working so much that they fail to invest enough time in their personal relationships and get accused of neglect by the people who love them.

Remember, no human being is ever defined by simply one color personality tendency. We also all say and do things in our extreme that we regret. However, in a culture that is armed and eager to capture one's emotional meltdown on camera and immortalize it as a meme, we need to be prepared to de-escalate conflict so that we are not defined by our extremes in perpetuity on the internet.

Each of us must take personal responsibility for the behavior we resort to in our extremes, as well as the consequences of those actions. To avoid suffering as a result of our unruly extreme behaviors, we must invest in

THE PERSONALITY COLOR MATRIX

learning how to center ourselves. The more wisdom and emotional maturity we cultivate, the more capable we are of recognizing when we enter our extremes. Once we are willing to admit that we are behaving out of our extremes, we allow ourselves a choice to return to center.

One of the prevailing narratives surrounding Karen freakouts is that they are racially motivated. I'm not denying that prejudice is a factor in many of these cases. However, I believe The Personality Color Matrix allows us to diagnose and treat the Karen epidemic by going beyond traditional frames of "racism" or "privilege." When we use loaded words to label people behaving out of their extremes, we don't afford them a way to navigate back to a place of harmony. The stigmas we assign to them are permanent and come with severe consequences. With no hope for redemption and reconciliation, our society grows more disconnected, isolated, and hateful.

The journey back to center is rarely easy. While pulling ourselves out of a wrathful extreme mindset can feel impossible, it is something we are all capable of, but not until we become aware of which colors we react out of in our extremes. This ability comes naturally when you work with The Personality Color Matrix and begin to recognize the centered and extreme tendencies associated with your unique color blend.

5

WHAT IS THE HELP PARADOX?

*"A hero is an ordinary individual who finds the strength
to persevere and endure in spite of
overwhelming obstacles."*
– Christopher Reeve

A paradox is a contradiction in terms, something that feels inconsistent or in conflict but, when investigated and understood, may prove to be founded on the truth. For example, confidence and humility may seem contradictory, but balancing or marrying these two traits makes a person more authentic, believable, charismatic, and effective. Paradox rules human beings. To obtain joy and success, two things must be fully represented. If you guessed that those two things are strength and warmth, I am proud of you for paying careful attention while reading this book.

Let's consider what it takes to be a great partner, parent, friend, or citizen. We must be willing to stand alone and take personal responsibility for our actions and our character. We are supported and held together by two magnificent truths that only appear paradoxical: our ability to be *self-responsible individuals* **defines** our character and integrity and strengthens our resilience (strength), while *our relationships with one another* **prove** it (warmth). Upon deeper reflection, we find that these paradoxical ideas are actually necessary and complementary sides of the same coin.

To review, you'll remember that strength is a person's capacity to make things happen with ability and force of will. When people project strength, they command our respect. Warmth is the sense that a person listens to or understands our feelings or point of view. When people project warmth, we like, trust, and support them. The goal is to learn the value of strength and warmth so that we respect them and can experience a greater balance between them in our lives and relationships.

An entitled, *extreme*-strength mentality corrupts our expectations. We begin to believe that we are entitled to *our way* in every aspect of our lives, whether that is relationships, our health, our work, or our service. An *extreme*-strength mentality infected by entitlement eliminates the ideal called sacrifice, or at least makes us believe that sacrifice is something someone else should be doing for *our* sake, not something we should be doing for the sake of another. When sacrifice is gone, what we are left with is a self-consumed, entitled, short-sighted version of human nature that is, without question, its lowest form.

Entitlement causes qualities like honor, service, and dedication to rot in cesspools of narcissism and replaces *centered* strength thoughts with corrupted ones like, "I am the one who matters" and "I deserve what I want, and I am willing to lie, cheat, and steal to get it." When strength turns extreme, it turns people into liars, predators, oppressors, and mongers poisoned by a self-consumed drive for more, always more.

Extreme warmth shows up differently than *extreme* strength. *Extreme* warmth dresses up as love. This *extreme*-warmth kind of "love" is often well-meaning, but it is still self-deceiving. It imagines itself to be a perfect example of true care and compassion. In reality, *extreme* warmth's overprotective lack of faith in the resilient capabilities of those they wish to help only serves to limit and damage the *centered* strength necessary for others to thrive.

An example of misguided *extreme* warmth is a person who wants to come to the aid of a butterfly that they perceive is struggling to exit its cocoon. It takes ten days of pupation inside the chrysalis before a healthy adult butterfly can emerge. A great deal of struggle transpires during these ten days. The timing of the butterfly's emergence from the chrysalis is key. If a well-meaning human interferes and tries to "help" the butterfly with its struggle, it will doom the insect because it will never develop the strength it needs to fly. When we are trapped in an *extreme*-warmth mentality, it is difficult for us to stand still as we watch another struggling.

Entitlement tells us that our children don't *deserve* to suffer or face difficult obstacles. In reality, it is adversity and opposition that build the resilience and fortitude that will hold them steady through the storms of life.

An *extreme*-warmth mentality does not "help." Instead, it hinders by enabling victimhood. When we begin to see ourselves as victims in an unpleasant, cruel, and unappreciative world, we limit ourselves. When we begin to see others as victims incapable of fighting their own battles and decide to fight for them, we limit them. A victimhood mentality deceives us with thoughts like "It's not right that my challenges seem more difficult than the challenges of others," "It's not right that the world isn't fair," or "I am simply incapable of _____ (you fill in the blank). I deserve someone to do it for me." When we face challenges, it is intoxicating to imagine someone rescuing us. But are those who "help" in these situations actually rescuing us? Or is that "help" only weakening our ability to develop our capacity and resilience?

Taking responsibility for another person's most difficult challenges doesn't help them because it never allows them the opportunity to realize how truly capable they are. What if the greatest help you can ever offer another is your belief in their capacity? *Extreme* warmth can cause us to resist the tenet that everyone is responsible for getting what they want and need in their life. For someone who has developed *extreme* warmth habits, it is difficult to restrain their intense desire to rescue. This creates what I have labeled the "Help Paradox."

I care deeply for those who are less fortunate and experience great need because I began life as one of them. I was born into the poverty, dysfunction, addiction, and lack of education that many of our most underprivileged experience. Most would say my life has been a success story, from rags to riches, ignorance to education, abuse to freedom. Because of my background, I feel that I have great insight into the needs, hardships, and hopes associated with people suffering from poverty. I also have great insight into how extremes of both strength and warmth steal and destroy hope and possibility, as well as how centered strength/warmth attitudes and behaviors encourage hope, self-responsibility, and hard work. Before I used statistics to make powerful, thought-provoking arguments, I was one. In great part, my early life and experiences defined my purpose.

My life began in a state of financial deprivation. My parents were uneducated. Both were raised during the Depression and had to quit school to help support their families. My father was one of eight children —until his baby brother, Johnny, was killed at three years of age. His family never fully recovered from the tragedy. My mother was the third child of five. Her father died when she was four years old from a hemorrhage in his stomach. Her mother didn't remarry until her five children were raised. There was not a day that my grandmother did not work. She was quite an extraordinary woman.

Early in my life, I didn't realize how poor we were. I often entertained my family with not-too-humorous stand-up comedy and helped my mother with the other children (sometimes without being threatened). I loved it when my father played the guitar and taught us to sing in harmony. I also felt special because we had a rather plush outside facility. My father had a gift for carpentry. When we moved into our house, it was a real mess. The old outhouse had completely collapsed and was lying on the ground, so my father designed a new one with two holes instead of one, allowing my sister and me to go to the bathroom together. His cleverness helped minimize our terror of going to the outhouse in the dark. Both my mother and father had a great deal of creativity. For outings, my mother would take us to the dump. It wasn't hard to recognize us; we were the ones carrying the couch into town tied to the top of our smoke-bellowing Ford Impala. My mother would strip the frame and reupholster the furniture from the dump for our home.

But there were struggles. My father was an alcoholic. It broke my heart when alcohol transformed him from a gentle, loving man to one consumed with rage. It was also a struggle to have no indoor plumbing, except for the cold-water pipe in the kitchen. We boiled water on the stove to take baths in the washtub.

When I entered first grade, how poor we were became glaring. I realized that other kids had different outfits for every day of the week. My sister, brother, and I got one pair of shoes (inexpensive tennis shoes) that were to last us throughout the school year. In the summer, we loved going barefoot. On the last day of first grade, all of my classmates were allowed to enter the new gym for the first time. Each child slipped off their shoes as we stepped into the new gym entrance. It was very exciting for me. The tile was beautiful. It was highly waxed and polished. It was so shiny that you could see your reflection. I stepped carefully, but with each step I took, the ammonia created from my worn-out shoes took up the wax on the shiny new tile. All the kids started pointing and laughing, saying that I was the girl with the rotten feet. I ran all the way home, crying. I was so embarrassed that I never wanted to have to see those children again. My mom had previously assured me that children were innately good and innocent and, if they died, they went straight to heaven. I wept into my pillow as I told God He could take me anytime before second grade began.

THE PERSONALITY COLOR MATRIX

When the time arrived to return to second grade, my mom had to threaten to spank me to get me to go. Have you ever wanted to be invisible? That is exactly what I wanted to be: invisible. I never wanted kids to laugh at me and make fun of me again. I entered the classroom where I immediately went to the back of the room and selected a seat where I could best hide. Putting my head down, I realized that on my desk, there was a flier about becoming a Brownie. I knew that Brownies got to wear uniforms because my older cousin got to be one. If I wore a uniform, no one would know I was poor and didn't have enough clothes. This was my answer. My heart began to pound with excitement as I folded the flier and stuck it in my blouse, anxious for the day to end, so that I could show it to my mother.

I rushed through our old screen door and handed the crinkled piece of paper to my mother. Needless to say, when she opened the flier, she took a step back, sat down, and began to cry. Through her tears she explained it would take a miracle for me to be a Brownie because we didn't have money for food, let alone a uniform or Brownie dues. Just at that time, my father walked in and asked, "Why is your mother crying?"

"I want to be a Brownie, Daddy. Brownies do good things, and if I can be a Brownie, nobody will know that we're poor." My father had been drinking and was already angry. He explained that life was hard for poor white trash like us and told me to stop living in a dream world. He insisted that I needed to grow up and understand three very simple rules about being poor.

One: Poor people don't get what they want.

Two: Good things happen to those who can afford them.

Three: Life is something one must simply endure until the constant disappointment is finally over.

I joined my mother in tears. I wondered why, if these three rules were true, they hadn't worked to spare *him* disappointment and heartbreak. At the time, I was too young to understand that entitlement was crippling and attempting to destroy my father's joy. My father had a great deal of extreme green personality tendencies that caused him to be furious at the unfairness of life, giving his extreme orange personality tendencies the perfect excuse to drink as an escape. His strong blue influence, when extreme, turned him cynical and ungrateful. He did not focus on the fact that he was an intelligent craftsman or a talented musician and singer or that he had survived the Korean War in one piece (at least physically). He did not focus on the good fortune that came with three healthy, gifted children. He did not focus on the fact that he had a loyal, caring wife who loved him.

My mother, who had strong yellow and green personality tendencies, which fed her hope and love for me, spent a nickel that she didn't have to buy me a book at a garage sale that was all about positive thinking, setting goals, making a difference, and living with purpose. It was called *Wisdom of the Mystic Masters* by Robert Collier. It spoke beautifully to my centered green personality tendencies. It told stories about people who started with nothing, yet became more. When my dad stepped outside for a cigarette, my mom grabbed me by one arm and said, "Dawn, darlin', hope is the poor man's bread. You eat your fill. Miracles do happen. If they can happen for other people, they can happen for you."

My mother backed up her claim of their existence with things like the movie *Miracle on 34th Street* and stories of the miracles that God had performed in the Bible. She needed hope as badly as she needed to teach me not to lose it. My mother insisted that my life was a gift, especially to her. I was much more drawn to my mom's story about life and possibility than I was to my dad's hard "facts" of life. As far as I was concerned, between God, my mother's unwavering faith in me, and Santa Claus, anything was possible.

The next day, at school, my second-grade teacher asked us to tell everyone about our favorite color and why it was our favorite. Some kids picked pink, yellow, blue, green, and red. Not me. I picked brown. Brown was the color of the dirt and the great things that grew from it. It was also the color of tree trunks, which held up the branches that produced the fruit. I explained that brown was the color of the uniform of the greatest organization in the world, Brownies, except I wasn't going to get to be one because we couldn't afford a uniform and dues.

Several days later, my teacher, Mrs. Jo Anne Stone, asked if I could stay after school for a few minutes. I said, "Sure." I liked staying after school. Sometimes, she let me clean the blackboards for her, and she made me feel very special. Besides, I only lived a few blocks from school.

When she invited me into her office, she was acting rather strangely, and I thought she might be angry with me. She noticed my concern, smiled, and told me that she had a surprise for me. She asked me to open the box sitting on her desk. I removed the lid to reveal a Brownie uniform. I couldn't believe my eyes! My teacher kept apologizing that the uniform wasn't new. She said that her sister had a little girl who was one year older than me, and this was her old Brownie uniform. She hoped it might fit.

The uniform was just my size. The material was soft from being worn.

THE PERSONALITY COLOR MATRIX

At the bottom of the box, I saw a beanie. When I placed the cap on my head, it felt like a crown. Wearing my new uniform, I knew I was meant to be more than poor white trash. I was meant to be something wonderful. I was meant to be a Brownie. I knew that my father was wrong—but not because he was bad. He simply never had a second-grade teacher like Mrs. Stone. Ms. Stone leaned in and whispered, "I am also paying your dues for the year, but I have one request. I want you to use this gift and opportunity to become the best you can be. I believe you have so much promise."

Becoming a Brownie was a great endowment. It wasn't an act of pity motivated by extreme warmth. Mrs. Stone did not look at me or treat me like I was a helpless victim. Although her kindness was unconditional, her expectations of my potential and capabilities were clear. Her generous act of centered affirmation provided me with a tool. After putting it into my hands, she stood back and said, "Take this. Learn to use it for you and the world's benefit."

> *"Nothing splendid has ever been achieved*
> *except by those who dared believe*
> *that something inside them was superior to circumstances."*
> – Bruce Barton

Several weeks later, the Brownies hosted a special father-daughter dinner. I had never had a date with my dad. My mother made him borrow a suit from a neighbor. I was so happy. I thought he was the most handsome man there. At one point, the daughters began to sing a song, "Let Me Call You Sweetheart." My dad lifted me up, stood me on a chair, and began to sing with me in harmony:

> *Let me call you sweetheart; I'm in love with you.*
> *Let me hear you whisper that you love me, too.*
> *Keep the love light glowing in your eyes so blue.*
> (He changed "blue" to "hazel" to match my eyes,
> even though it didn't rhyme.)
> *Let me call you sweetheart; I'm in love with you.*

There were tears in our eyes as we finished singing. He leaned over, kissed me on the cheek, and whispered in my ear, "When I see you in that uniform, it makes me want to believe in miracles." It was one of the most memorable, centered green statements that my father ever made. I will never forget that moment. I know he never forgot it, either. In that moment, miracles were as real as we were. The hope I gained from that experience has carried me forward ever since.

I often wonder: if the Brownie uniform had felt like an entitlement that I expected, instead of an endowment that I was blessed with, would it have made the same powerful impact on me? All I know for sure is that endowments, when recognized as the gifts they are, make more of us. Our greatest gifts are often wrapped in our greatest challenges. When we realize that truth, we can allow our challenges to make more of us instead of less.

Forty years later, I had the opportunity to publicly thank Mrs. Stone for her kindness. Mark Victor Hansen and Jack Canfield asked me to use the Brownie story in one of the *Chicken Soup for the Soul* books, and millions would read about her generosity. In front of approximately five hundred people, I shared the story that helped transform my belief in myself and, ultimately, my life. It was her last year of teaching. She was retiring and wondered if anything she had done had truly made a difference. She was stunned that an act that she perceived as a small gesture of kindness had made such a difference in my life.

We often never know if the kindness we show others transforms their lives, but we always know that each compassionate act has the potential if it is received as an endowment. Throughout our nation and around the world, there are many wonderful people like Mrs. Stone: generous, united souls who deeply care about the suffering and hardship of people, especially children. For all of you great teachers out there, your students may not return 40 years later to say thank you, but know this: with every kindness and belief in the potential of your students, you certainly transform the direction of their lives as well.

Multiplying centered strength and resilience requires personal dedication, hard work, and effort. Thinking someone owes us something or that we are incapable of building our capacity and need someone else to be responsible for us causes us to forget that life and its opportunities are gifts that only we can open. Once we accept our responsibility and develop our capacity, we can emerge from our cocoon with the strength we need to spread our wings and soar.

When I was in my late teens and early 20s, I trained to be a ballroom dancer. The first lesson we were taught was the critical importance of tension. By tension, I do not mean conflict or opposition. I mean just the opposite. Our instructors asked us to assume a position in which the woman placed the fingers of her right hand between the thumb and fingers of the man's left hand, allowing their palms to meet. The man would lift his right arm, bent at the elbow, and carefully place his right hand just under the woman's left shoulder blade. She was to rest her left arm on his. The man was instructed to keep his right elbow raised so that contact with the woman's left arm was constant.

Now, we were shown that if we maintained equal and consistent tension, the man pushing with the same pressure as the woman, like magic, we could glide around the dance floor with our bodies moving as one. The minute either partner did not do their part to provide the pressure to maintain this equal tension, their bodies could no longer move together. They would veer off course and no longer move in harmony. Our societal dance is the same. We must fight to balance and support citizens by building their *strength*, resilience, and personal fortitude while also encouraging and inspiring them to widen and expand their capacity for *warmth*, which means doing all they can to love and support themselves and their communities.

This is the true, powerful, positive paradox of help. Generosity alone is not enough to transform the realities of our disadvantaged families. Giving is only one side of the dance. Centered strength and centered warmth are needed in equal measure. Can a system be designed that attacks not just the symptoms of poverty but poverty at its core? Can a system be designed that, while helping, can also motivate people? As a harvester of hope, I believe the answer is yes.

However, for successful programs to make a real difference, they must encourage the people they desire to help to focus on how they can also serve themselves in the process. That means answering questions like "*Why* should *I* change?" "*What* should *I* do?" "*How* should *I* do it?" "*Where* should *I* go to learn what *I* need to know?" and "*When* should *I* have it done?" I advocate for both the government and citizens to join in being socially accountable. Our government is not *entitled* to squander and waste its citizen's money while showing no positive results and, in many cases, like homelessness, even making the situation worse.

> *"Persistence and resilience only come from having been given the chance to work through difficult problems."*
> – Gever Tulley

Mrs. Stone's generosity was the first step in the dance of opportunity and societal responsibility. My actions and commitment to make the very most of the gift were the second, followed by my continued commitment to feeling deep appreciation. I used the gift from Mrs. Stone and the many future endowments to transform my life. I then used what I created to benefit others.

I have dedicated my entire life to the positive transformation and welfare of families, especially children. Time and time again, the outcomes of centered warmth, dancing in unison with centered strength, have created a social environment where everyone can emerge from their struggles with wings strong enough to lift them to their dreams.

CORBIN'S THOUGHTS

Growing up, I struggled to fit into my clothes and in with my peers. In high school, my best friends affectionately dubbed me "Chubs." To this day, it's hard for me to imagine a worse nickname. Considering that I have strong blue, orange, and green personality tendencies and a deep desire to be liked, entertain, and occupy "the center of attention" as a creative force, being made fun of in school for being overweight and unattractive was particularly unfair and torturous. Although I excelled in the classroom and was highly confident in my academic abilities (thanks to my strong blue tendencies), I was deeply insecure about being called fat. More than anything, I wanted to shed the stigma of being overweight, which I blamed for my social exclusion.

Being confronted with my insecurities sent me to my extremes. When I was bullied, my extreme yellow tendencies would take over, and I would cry like an inconsolable victim. When I looked in the mirror, my extreme blue tendencies would judge me as inadequate. Whenever I felt worthless and lonely, my extreme orange personality tendencies would lead me to retreat to television and junk food for mindless comfort, and I would overindulge to escape.

Periodically during my life, I experienced success dieting, but the transformations were temporary. Throughout my teens and early 20s, my weight would rise and fall like a yo-yo. Since purple is the color that has the least influence on my color blend, I tend to lack the consistency and discipline required to maintain lasting results, leaving me stuck in a cycle of extreme blue self-loathing and extreme orange self-sabotage. While I can be more consistent and disciplined for weeks or even months at a time, those changes don't tend to last for years.

When I graduated from film school, I was the heaviest I had been in my life (up to that point). Although I had been very successful in college, after graduating, I was completely unsure how to make a name for myself in the film industry. At 21 years old, I felt as if I had been flown via helicopter out into the middle of the ocean and told that there was land in some direction before being promptly pushed out of the aircraft as the pilot yelled, "Swim!" I desperately wanted someone to help me. To my dismay, nobody came to my rescue. If I didn't want to drown, I had to develop the strength and resilience required to swim. Sure, I couldn't control a production company's decision to hire me, but I could control how I treated my body and what kinds of food I ate.

Around this same time, my father was diagnosed with type-two diabetes. The sight of him repeatedly pricking his finger to test his blood sugar levels throughout the day gave me a glimpse of the future I would inherit if I didn't alter my lifestyle. I had no desire to suffer numbness in my fingers and toes or inject insulin into my stomach to manage a preventable (and reversible) disease.

Determined to avoid my father's fate, I decided it was no longer logical to continue to neglect my health. I started running, reduced my caloric intake, shopped organic at the grocery store, and exercised regularly in my living room using Wii Fit. After two months, my habits shifted drastically. The more aware I became of how fast food was factory-farmed and processed, the less of it I consumed. I started reading labels and stopped purchasing foods that contained ingredients I couldn't pronounce. The blue part of my personality tendencies enjoyed studying nutrition and exercise as a science.

After several more months of mindful eating and working out, I was in the best shape of my life and had become an outspoken advocate for health and nutrition. Not only was I tremendously relieved to shed the stigma of being overweight, but I enjoyed an improved sense of confidence and self-esteem. Most importantly, I had hope for my future.

Hope is a powerful motivator. The feeling comes naturally to those with strong centered green personality tendencies, who look forward to the future and dream of how to make the world a better place for all. People with centered green personality tendencies are gardeners of hope. They plant and nurture changes that grow into movements that can transform the nature of the social landscape. In their hearts, they desire nothing more than to help people. They are very passionate about their message and the cause they support, whatever it may be.

In December 2009, my newfound passion for health and wellness culminated in a desire to produce an independent film that tackled the epidemic of childhood obesity in America. The idea delighted my strong green personality tendencies. I wanted to help others heal, grow, and experience the same health transformation that I had. I hoped the movie would motivate audiences (particularly parents and their children) to take personal responsibility for their health to curb rising trends of childhood obesity and the diseases associated with it. As the director of the film, my goal was to show that making a healthy change was possible for any child to achieve, regardless of their socioeconomic circumstances. Of course, overcoming the odds is never easy, but I wanted to prove it was possible.

Five years later, my vision was realized when the feature documentary *Bite Size* premiered on Netflix in 2014. The movie follows the day-to-day lives of four children (ages 11–13) as they struggle to reform their relationship with food and their bodies. The story then catches up with them one year down the road. It tracks the weight loss journeys of two boys and two girls, all diagnosed as clinically obese. Two are coastal kids, Emily in Florida and Moises in California, while two live in rural Mississippi, Davion and KeAnna.

I shared this story in this chapter because *Bite Size* could have just as easily been titled *The Help Paradox*. Although I intended the film to be a purely inspirational experience for the viewer, the final cut tells a far more nuanced story that perfectly illustrates how, no matter how hard we try (as parents, mentors, or peers) to help others transform their lives for the better, we cannot force other people to help themselves. Although we can serve as role models and positive influences, ultimately, the only lives that we have total power to control and improve are our own. To explain, I'll briefly summarize a few of the interwoven narratives that the documentary focuses on, along with my director's commentary.

The film opens in Cleveland, Mississippi, where we are introduced to a three-hundred-plus-pound 12-year-old boy named Davion, who dreams of playing football. Davion wants nothing more than to make the middle school football team and, one day, play the game he loves professionally, but his recent type-two diabetes diagnosis compromises his endurance and capacity to play.

Despite his disease, Davion refused to be stopped in the pursuit of his passion, displaying strong red personality tendencies. In our interactions, his personality seemed to be a blend of red, green, and yellow. His strong red tendencies made him tough and compelled him to put in the effort to train to make the football team and transform his health. His strong green personality tendencies inspired him to dream of being a part of something bigger than himself: a team. His strong yellow tendencies made him fiercely loyal, sensitive, and approval-seeking. All he wanted was for his mother and father to come to a game and watch him play. When they didn't show up or left the game before he took the field, he would often cry and take it personally.

In Davion's extreme, his red personality tendencies caused him to lash out physically, particularly when he was made fun of for his size. His extreme yellow personality tendencies made him partial to seeing himself as a victim of bullies and adults who didn't understand his struggle. When his extreme red personality tendencies took control, Davion would get into fights at school. These altercations threatened his ability to remain on the football team.

To resist the influence of his volatile and blameful red and yellow extremes, Davion leaned into his strong centered green desire to be a team member and live out his dream of playing professional football. Fortunately, he had a great coach, who, in addition to role-modeling strength and accountability, possessed strong centered green personality tendencies that helped center Davion and inspire him and his teammates to conduct themselves with respect on and off the field.

Over the course of a year, Davion learned how to better regulate his extreme emotions and developed a sense of belonging, a quality that people with strong green personality tendencies need to thrive. In front of the camera, he matured into a more responsible, confident, and capable young man. He also lost around 60 pounds, successfully reversing his type-two diabetes and eliminating his need for insulin. Despite his considerable disadvantages, he took responsibility for his self-improvement and displayed commendable resiliency.

The film also tells the story of Emily, a 13-year-old girl, as she returns home from a weight-loss boarding school called Mindstream Academy. For two semesters, Emily was sequestered on a ranch in what she described as a rehab center for kids. She characterized her food addiction as similar to drug addiction and jokingly referred to her experience away from her family as her own mini-version of *The Biggest Loser*, a popular reality TV show where contestants compete to lose weight. During her year away from home, her portions were carefully measured by chefs to keep her in a caloric deficit. At school, she abided by a strict daily schedule, which included multiple workouts, starting with a five-mile run at 6 a.m.

While in the idyllic, highly monitored Mindstream environment, Emily achieved great success, losing 80 pounds. Although she worked hard to achieve those results, when we met, she was apprehensive about returning home to the temptations of "the real world." She had never developed the inner strength to resist ritual snacking and overeating on her own and feared she might relapse.

As far as I observed, Emily's coloring was all warmth—a blend of orange, yellow, and green. I suspect it was her strong orange tendencies that made her inclined to be a part of the documentary. She enjoyed goofing off in front of the camera, laughing and having fun. That being said, her orange tendencies were restrained by the strict rules at Mindstream Academy. Every hour of the day was allocated to learning, therapy, or physical activity. There was little free time. When there was, Emily enjoyed watching TV, joking around with her friends, and video chatting with her mom and dad. Her strong yellow personality tendencies came through in her love for her family. She missed them terribly while she was away.

At Mindstream, Emily formed new friendships and affectionately referred to her classmates as the island of misfit toys. Before attending Mindstream, Emily had been mercilessly bullied; the kids at her former school had called her cruel names and even thrown rocks at her. Because of her strong yellow personality tendencies, these experiences emotionally wounded her. Now that she had transformed herself physically, she no longer saw herself as a victim. However, her self-confidence was still budding and needed to be nurtured.

Mindstream Academy was an ideal place for her to flourish. In addition to enforcing routine and structure, the school was also a very motivating, emotionally supportive environment. The atmosphere naturally resonated with Emily's green personality tendencies and inspired her to always do her best. While at Mindstream, she spent every day imagining a healthier future for herself and the world. She hoped that sharing her story of transformation would benefit others on their personal journey of recovery.

Once summer arrived and Emily was no longer restrained by the purple structure of Mindstream, her orange personality tendencies were free to spiral into their extremes. Returning to Florida, all she wanted to do was have fun, be free, and spend quality time with her family. Now that she was home, working out and running were the opposite of fun and felt more like chores, especially when her parents supervised. She resisted her parents' efforts to support her in staying active. She looked to her father and mother as resources for warmth. When they attempted to love her with strength by running exercise drills, throwing around a football, or helping her track her progress on the scale, Emily tended to shut down.

I felt for her parents, particularly her father, who was doing his best to be supportive in the same way the trainers at Mindstream had been. Like his daughter, Emily's father's personality color blend seemed to be composed of all warm colors, with orange being his primary color. Stepping into a strength-oriented style of parenting was a new role for him. Emily was not used to her father being a coach, channeling red, purple, and blue energies. She wanted him to hold her, laugh with her, and accept her no matter what.

However, Emily's parents had spent their retirement to finance their daughter's two semesters at Mindstream and knew it was important to establish and enforce structure to ensure their investment paid off and their daughter lived a happier, healthier life. As a teenager with strong orange personality tendencies, Emily naturally wanted to free herself from the pressure of expectations she was experiencing and assert her independence. In other words, she rebelled. Because of her orange coloring, she did it mostly with her mouth.

"You were so good at running," Emily's mother told her at dinner. "Why don't you like running anymore?"

With a defiant grin, born from her orange and green personality tendencies, Emily retorted, "Why don't you like running?" When her mother struggled to think of a response, the entire family burst into laughter to relieve the tension. According to Emily's green lenses, if her mother wasn't also exercising, it wasn't fair for her to pass judgment. In her green extreme, Emily positioned herself in opposition to her parents because she interpreted their good intentions as oppressive and unfair. It didn't help that her family's efforts to change their diets were largely ceremonial. Emily was expected not to eat junk food while everyone else in her family ate as they pleased. To Emily's green sensibilities, this was an obvious double standard.

As she had feared, Emily eventually began to repeat old patterns of behavior. When her strong orange tendencies turned extreme, she looked to food for a sense of escape. Now that there were no locks on the cabinets, she began to sneak food into her room and hide her snacking from her parents. As a fellow orange who has dealt with food addiction in my extreme, I empathized with her struggle. While one can always quit other drugs cold turkey, one can never stop eating altogether.

In interviews, Emily explained that she lacked impulse control and called herself "a never-ending trash can." She described her hunger as painful and feared there might be something medically wrong with her. When a visit to the doctor revealed everything was normal, Emily seemed more disheartened than relieved. She desperately wanted to find a solution to her dilemma, but instead of focusing internally and developing self-resolve, she searched for something outside herself to make life easier. Under stress, her warm coloring led her to prioritize comfort.

When our film crew returned a year later, Emily had regained a considerable amount of weight and confessed that she was mad at her old self. "I feel like a tornado just wrecked every good thing I thought about myself," she lamented, speaking from an extreme yellow state of mind. She seemed to feel powerless. The vibrant green part of her personality that had blossomed at Mindstream had faded into a resigned melancholy. Instead of being hopeful about her future, she felt guilty about her past, mentioning that her mother had said, "I hope we didn't waste our money."

Although Emily received a tremendous advantage, she was never forced to develop her own strength. The structure and discipline that initially helped her succeed came from outside of herself, not from within. Emily was like a tall flower that thrived because of a stake in the ground that held her upright and allowed her to grow. When the stake was removed, she lacked the strength to stand up on her own against the wind.

I like to compare Davion's and Emily's stories because I believe they reveal a great deal of insight into why some people succeed in their goals while others miss the mark. Although *Bite Size* is a very evenhanded film that leaves the viewer to interpret their own meaning from candid observation, I believe the film reveals the vital importance of individual responsibility and resilience to lasting success. Personal accountability and relentless self-belief combine to create the elusive X-factor. Both qualities come from within. They have less to do with our life circumstances and privileges and far more to do with our determination and perseverance. Even after we succeed, we must possess resilience to sustain those results.

Just as those who value strength can learn to be compassionate by interacting with those who value warmth, those who value warmth can learn to be resilient by interacting with those who value strength. By interacting, I don't mean simply tolerating one another in the same space. I mean actively listening and incorporating opposing perspectives instead of resisting them. The heartfelt compassion that those who value warmth naturally express can be healing and nourishing. At the same time, compassion can also be expressed through strength in the form of "tough love" that sets strict boundaries and enforces consequences to encourage positive self-development and teach discipline. This form of compassion is uniquely constructive and provides tremendous value.

Strength and warmth also express resilience differently. Those who value strength equate resilience with unbreakable will and individual determination. Because this type of understanding is self-sufficient and individualistic, it is more attractive to those with strong red personality tendencies. On the other side of the wheel, those who value warmth express resilience through unfaltering, unconditional love. Through the power of love and remembrance of unity, we can withstand any challenge and overcome all obstacles. This heartfelt commitment is fearless and faithful in its devotion. It is the assurance and motivation we need to face powers we can neither control nor explain and keep moving forward together rather than drift apart. This big-picture mindset is most appealing to those with strong green personality tendencies.

Resilience is not developed overnight. It requires time and struggle. The struggle ensures the transformation lasts. Most importantly, it necessitates that we never give up. This theme is recurrent throughout *Bite Size* and is further exemplified by the story of Lisa Ross, a compassionate school counselor who formed a weight-loss support group out of concern for the health and longevity of her overweight female students.

As a type-two diabetic, Ms. Ross felt compelled to intervene to save her female students from suffering the long-term health consequences of obesity-related diseases. "I'm sick and tired of sticking my fingers every single day," she said during one of our interviews as she checked her insulin levels. "I'm sick of us suffering from preventable diseases. I don't ever want them to suffer from diabetes. Who wants to suffer and lose their legs, their eyesight? No."

In her conviction to create a better future, Ms. Ross exhibited strong green personality tendencies. She was a deeply empathetic human being, which made her an excellent counselor. She was willing to take the time to help students work through their problems because, in her heart, she truly cared about making a difference in other people's lives. Ms. Ross was beloved by her students, especially the girls, who would loiter and dance outside her office before school until she shooed them off to class.

As a school administrator, she possessed a great deal of purple personality tendencies. Her job required her to enforce the rules when students got rowdy or violated the dress code. When students acted up, Ms. Ross was quick to throw them an evil eye, wag her finger, and exclaim, "Not today!" She was also one of the few members of the school faculty who danced with the kids. Her strong orange personality tendencies made her a riot to joke around with and a joy to film and interview.

After inviting 25 overweight girls to join her program, Ms. Ross asked the girls to come up with a name to describe their metamorphosis. The girls settled on *"Si Se Puede,"* a Spanish saying that translates to "we can do it" or "yes, we can." After securing a modest grant from a local foundation, Ms. Ross partnered with the middle school PE coach to create an after-school curriculum that would get the girls moving.

Over the course of a semester, she endeavored tirelessly to educate and empower the *Si Se Puede* girls to make better food choices, stay active, and learn to love themselves at any size. She chaperoned the girls on field trips to local parks and pools, as well as interactive learning centers. She held space for the girls to rehearse, exercise, and vent their feelings. She even took them camping and brought them together around a campfire to burn all the ugly names that bullies had called them and move past them. She did all of this for no additional pay but purely out of compassion to uplift her community.

People with green personality tendencies will sacrifice their time and energy to volunteer for causes they believe in. Because Ms. Ross possessed strong orange personality tendencies, it was important to her that *Si Se Puede* was not only educational but also fun. She wanted the girls to look forward to their meetups. Although the *Si Se Puede* girls tended to resist doing traditional aerobic exercises with their PE coach, they all loved to dance. To get the girls excited about moving, Ms. Ross enlisted a dance choreographer to help them come up with an original routine to practice three times per week and perform for their loved ones at the end of the semester. "I can't do it for them," she said, "but I can facilitate the change."

Although participating in *Si Se Puede* was undoubtedly beneficial to the mental health of all of its members, when it came time to weigh in and measure progress after nine weeks, Ms. Ross was disheartened to discover that few of the girls had actually lost weight. In fact, several had gained weight. Although Ms. Ross had done everything in her power to teach the girls how to make healthier lifestyle choices, she could not control whether or not the girls implemented those lessons at home.

For her program to be successful, she knew she needed to get the parents on board. Unfortunately, the few parents who accepted her invitation to speak after school had even less desire than their children to start incorporating fruits and vegetables into their diets. Even though many parents wished that they could cook or exercise with their children, they were often too busy or exhausted after work to do so. They would tell Ms. Ross to "be realistic." However, for an idealist with strong green personality tendencies like Ms. Ross, being realistic was no different than giving up.

"I don't think you ever give up on a child," Ms. Ross told me in an interview, "but there's some of them you won't be able to help because they don't want the help, but you still don't give up. You just hope, and you pray that one day, the light will come on."

At the end of the fall semester, she invited the *Si Se Puede* girls' relatives and supporters to a dance recital to celebrate the group's hard work. Above all, she wanted to change the story of how the girls felt about themselves by giving them a moment where they could feel proud of how they had grown more confident through the program. "If you don't feel good about yourself," she said, "I don't care how much weight you lose. It's coming back. The girls have to love themselves enough to want to change."

In the end, Ms. Ross concluded that the most she could do to help the girls was change her lifestyle to serve as a positive role model. "Trying to educate the girls as to healthy choices has left me with no choice but to try and set an example for them," she explained when our film crew returned one year later. While walking us through the lush organic garden growing outside her house, Ms. Ross shared how she had changed her diet and started taking daily walks. She had no doubt that the changes she had made had added years to her life. "What I learned from *Si Se Puede* was I want to live."

In addition to losing a noticeable amount of weight, she revealed that she had reversed her type-two diabetes symptoms and no longer needed medication. Although she had started the *Si Se Puede* after-school program to touch the lives of others, it was her life that was most transformed by the experience.

Sometimes, we see ourselves as helpless or hopelessly disadvantaged; however, directing *Bite Size* showed me that any individual, young or old, possesses the power to change their lives, regardless of their circumstances, by adopting personal responsibility. The secret to success lies in resilience. It all comes down to individual choice. Will we choose to help ourselves? To do so requires us to lean into strength.

> *"Sooner or later, you're going to realize just as I did that there's a difference between knowing the path and walking the path."*
> – Morpheus
> *The Matrix*

6

HUMANS BEING RIGHT

"Pride is concerned with who is right.
Humility is concerned with what is right."
– Ezra Taft Benson

The desire to be right—and to *right* things in our direction—is one of entitlement's slyest covert weapons. The insidious certainty that comes with being right invites entitlement to envelop our most sacred spaces. Entitlement can motivate us to value being right more than just about anything else. We will sacrifice love, connection, friendship, happiness—whatever it takes for the opportunity to be right. We rarely care if being right keeps us from feeling the unity, joy, and tranquility we long for in our relationships and homes or if our drive to be right keeps us from success at work. Remember, entitlement's purpose is to steal what is precious and leave us *right*eously bonded to our perceived injustices.

Therefore, one of our most destructive extremes is our desire to be right. People who feel strongly about the concept of "right" versus "wrong" can unknowingly base their self-worth on being right about everything and actually prevent themselves from learning from their mistakes, keeping an open mind, or listening to others they have deemed to be wrong.

Let's consider how people motivated by centered warmth and strength look at the idea of "being right" through different lenses. A person motivated by warmth might say something similar to this quote by Wayne Dyer: "Attachment to being right creates suffering. When you have the choice between being right and being kind, choose kind and watch your suffering disappear."

A person motivated by strength might say something like this quote from Barack Obama: "Fighting for what you think is right is always worth it." It is a "fight for your right" mentality. As you can see, the view of this important idea looks different depending on the perspective of one's values. A more balanced view is illustrated by a quote from Martin Luther King Jr.: "God has two outstretched arms. One is strong enough to surround us with justice, and one is gentle enough to embrace us with grace."

Both centered strength and warmth ideals have positive, inspiring, and necessary properties. As we have stated many times, strength and warmth ideals are meant to work in harmony, but when they morph into extreme versions of themselves, as we detailed in Chapter Four, entitlement would have us believe strength and warmth are deadly opponents and we must choose which of them we pay allegiance to.

As the quote at the beginning of this chapter says, "Pride is concerned with who is right. Humility is concerned with what is right." Our extreme color personality tendencies are always motivated by pride and arrogance, while our centered color personality tendencies are motivated by humility and a capacity for compassion.

Forty-five years ago, I attended a parenting seminar. I had just given birth to my first son, Tony, and the love that I felt for him was ineffable. I was furious with my parents for decisions that they had made while raising me, and my only goal was to learn to be a better parent than I perceived them to be. Although I went into the conference with an open mind, what I heard during the seminar shocked me. I thought we had gone there to learn how to be parents; instead, it appeared to be a room full of grown people complaining about their parents. I didn't mind. I was just waiting to build up the courage to stand and share my sad horror story of alcoholism, drugs, poverty, irresponsibility, and instability. People had great sympathy for many of the stories that were shared, and I certainly believed a little sympathy should be coming my way.

One woman stood and told everyone that she had been married four times and now finally understood why. She had gone to a therapist who had helped her trace her difficulty back to her childhood. Then, she told us a story about her mother. She was one of four children, and her mother had a big dinner at their home for her father's boss. She said that the children were thrilled because their mother announced that she had to have the day to cook and clean and asked them if they would rather spend the day at the movies or go to the local park and swim. They excitedly selected swimming. The mother then announced that they could each invite a friend since it was going to be a several-hour affair. She put the children in the van, picked up their four friends, and dropped them off at the pool. It was secure, and there were many lifeguards to watch over them.

The woman remembered the day vividly. She had a wonderful time, but when her mother arrived to collect the children, the littel girl realized she had forgotten her towel. Without telling her mother, she ran back to the edge of the pool to collect it. When she came back to where the van had been parked, it was gone. In all the confusion and hurry of the day, her mother had not taken a head count and did not realize that she had forgotten her daughter until they returned home. The mother panicked. Leaving her chicken to burn and her table unset, she rushed back to find her daughter, who was sobbing. Everyone was miserable. The dinner was ruined, and so was the little girl's life.

She determined that her mother had forgotten her because she didn't love her. She said she had come to realize that her four failed marriages were her mother's fault. Because her mother forgot her that day, she decided that no one would love her. Everyone would leave her sooner or later, and guess what? *She was right.* She wore her four failed marriages like badges of courage on her lapel, using them as conclusive evidence to prove that she had no value and could not succeed or ever be secure in a relationship. She was righteous, poised in her certainty, and unwavering in her story.

The instructor listened intently and then asked the woman how many times her mother had remembered her.

"What do you mean?" asked the woman.

"I mean, how many times did your mother remember you?"

"I don't understand the question," the woman stuttered. "I just told you *she forgot me.*"

"Yes, you did. Now I would like you to tell me how many times she remembered you."

"You mean every day when I was growing up?"

"Yes, you have shared one day; now, share with us some of the rest."

"Well, she didn't forget me any of the others," said the woman.

"Okay, so how many times did she remember you? Did she take you to school and pick you up?"

"Yes."
"Every day?"
"Yes."
"Did she take you to other places as well?"
"Yes."
"Every day?"
The woman frowned. "Well, almost every day."
"How many times would you say she remembered you?"
"Throughout my whole life?"
"Yes. Would it be one hundred?"
"No, many more than that."
"How many would you guess?"
"Thousands, probably."
"Thousands?"
"Yes."
"And she forgot you once?"
"But… it was her job to remember me. Parents are supposed to remember their children." The woman was now on the verge of tears.

"And I thought she did, in fact, thousands of times. Is that correct?" the instructor asked.

"I guess so," the woman answered hesitantly.

"So, although your mother remembered you thousands of times, you picked the one time she forgot you to base your life and value on? Do you know why?"

"I wanted to make her pay for forgetting me. I wanted her to see that forgetting a child can negatively affect their whole life. And *I was right*. It has."

"Maybe, but what if you have sacrificed love, committed relationships, friendships, a powerful relationship with your mom, and many other blessings so that you could be right? Has being right been worth it?"

"Yes… I mean, no… I don't know anymore." The woman began to cry.

"Very good," said the instructor. "You have taken your first step away from the limitations forced upon you by the certainty of being right."

"When we are not sure, we are alive."
– Graham Greene

There were many more stories—stories of abuse, neglect, perceived pain, and suffering. Each caused me to reflect on my own. My father was an abusive alcoholic. His entire personality would change with a drink. He would transform from a sweet and kind man into a nightmare of rage. He would hit, throw food off the table, knock holes in the walls, drive recklessly, and scare us to death. My mom was anxious and addicted to Valium. They would beat us until we bled and then cry about what they had done. We had no money, so when the bills were due, many times, we would just move.

In my junior year, I was selected for two college scholarships. No one in my family had ever gone to college, especially a girl. I had worked very hard, knowing that if I didn't earn my own way, it would not be possible. I was selected to be head cheerleader my senior year and kept my grades up so I could use both scholarships to attend college. I took a job that paid one dollar an hour as a carhop and walked three miles across the desert to work at the A&W Root Beer stand and home every day. For an entire summer, I only spent one nickel on a Coke, and I never let myself forget that nickel, as I had spent it carelessly.

By summer's end, I had saved just under $500. It was mostly quarters and one-dollar bills. I counted it every night. This cash would pay for all of my uniforms, my prom dress, and anything else I might need because I knew my parents did not have the money for those things. Everything was going according to plan until my father had a drunken breakdown near the end of summer, and I was told that we were moving to another state. I was in shock. How could they move me now? Everything that I had worked for up to this point in my life was within my grasp. If they moved me, I would lose it all.

I had no choice. They forced me to move. However, that wasn't the most painful thing. What hurt the most was that they couldn't afford to move without taking all the money I had saved. I have never felt so betrayed in my life. "It wasn't fair," I kept telling myself, consumed by my extreme green color personality tendencies. You see, when looking through green lenses, if something isn't fair, it just isn't right!

I swore to make my parents suffer. I chose to never read another book. Since I was a voracious reader, I would read until the last few pages and then ask someone to read the rest to me so that I could *be right* about not finishing a book. My parents told me the move was necessary to save our family and their marriage, but on graduation day, in a state far away from where I believed I belonged, when it was too late to be awarded a scholarship, my mother served my father divorce with papers. They had played this scenario out so many times before. Who knew if it would happen this time? All I knew was that they were no longer going to catch me in the middle of their dysfunction. The day after graduation, I ran away from home. Instead of going to college, I have worked every day since.

Sitting in the parenting seminar, I couldn't believe it had been seven years since I had run away. I was married and a mother to my own child, but I was still trying to be right about how my parents had wronged me. At least I wasn't alone. I was surrounded by a room full of people who were just as right as I was.

A man began to share with the group, interrupting my thoughts. He explained that all he had heard so far were stories about how parents had failed and abused their children, but his situation was different. You see, his parents were perfect. They attended church, went to his games, had sit-down meals at home, took family vacations, spent time together, and were extremely loving. "How can I compete with perfection?" the man asked with genuine distress. "Do you have any idea how much pressure I feel because of that? How do I ever live up to them? Their perfection has ruined my life."

At this point, I threw my head back and laughed, finally seeing the absurdity and futility of sharing these stories of perceived injustice. Being a parent can be a no-win situation. If you are too good, you lose. If you are lousy, you lose. What causes this? Entitlement.

The instructor asked the group to do an exercise with her. She told us to close our eyes and think of all the qualities that we loved and admired about ourselves. Then, she said, "Give your parents credit for the things you love and tell them thank you. Now, think of all the things that you dislike about yourself and your life. Picture them clearly in your mind. Take responsibility for them. They are yours, not your parents. You are the ones responsible for the kind of person you are today. Your gifts, your talents, your hopes, and your dreams belong only to you. Be responsible for them."

"I have to go," I said, turning to my husband. We had come in separate cars in case of an emergency; he was a surgeon and could be called out at any moment.

"Where?" he asked. "The meeting isn't over."

"I have to get to college before they close."

"College? What for?"

"To use the brain that God gave me. Who I am is up to me. I'm tired of making my parents pay. I am tired of being right about the fact that what they did to me was crappy. I want *my* life back. I'm taking responsibility for who I am and what I am." After kissing my husband, I left the room.

That day, I enrolled in my first college courses. I graduated magna cum laude, went on for my master's, and completed all but my dissertation toward my PhD. My mother was diagnosed with cancer, so I stopped before I was finished to care for her. Both school and caring for my mother during her illness taught me many things. The experiences changed my life forever. I changed my life forever.

> *"A day dawns, quite like other days;*
> *but in that day and in that hour the chance of a lifetime faces us."*
> – Maltbie Babcock

Love asks that we be certain only of our endowments, and we can only be certain of our endowments when we are standing peacefully and joyfully in our center. Peace and joy ask very little. They ask that we remember and appreciate how rich, rewarding, and fulfilling they make our lives. Our center is always what is best and most loving, intelligent, kind, and real about us. It is our truth. There, we remember that our endowments are real and precious. We remember what is truly worth our attention and focus.

When we feel and behave out of our personality extremes, attitudes of entitlement take us over, and we narrow our focus to scarcity, fear, disappointment, and the things we perceive we lack. Entitlement's extremes insist we concentrate wholly on where we perceive life has been unfair, unjust, and even unforgivable. Entitlement encourages us to hold on to our pain and use our agony and disappointment to validate all the perceived injustices and injuries in our lives. It suggests that even though we succumb to victimhood and may risk losing everything of any real value, at least we will validate the narratives of victimhood we cling to. Holding on to narratives born out of our extreme personality tendencies convinces us that the prejudice and injustices in our relationships, our communities, and the world are not only true but irreversible without a destructive revolution.

My parents taught me a great deal about endowment versus entitlement. They are, in part, a large piece of this book. They were perfect examples on both sides of the entitlement fence. Watching them taught me what living a life of entitlement can steal and destroy, as well as what living a life of centered endowment can restore.

After my mother's death, I struggled a great deal with entitlement around my father. I told myself, "I deserved far better." No little girl, or even grown woman, should have experienced such abuse and disappointment. I wanted to cling to "my truth" that my life had not been fair. I wanted to convince myself and those around me that my dad had made one horrible decision after another with little thought for me or his other children. He was wrong, which, of course, made me *right*.

Once again, I was offered the opportunity to evaluate the story that my entitled extremes had created. If I stepped away from viewing my life through the lenses of right and wrong and instead asked myself the hard question, "How are these victim narratives working for you?" I would have to admit that they were not working out very well at all.

It is not an easy journey to return to one's center when entitlement has you all worked up in a frenzy about perceived injustices. Although the steps are simple, they require great courage and determination to let go of righteous indignation.

Let me leave you with a very personal experience, one that showcases how entitlement and *being right* can strangle our hearts and leave us bitter and blind. It is a letter to my dad. It is the most personal gift I can offer, but entitlement and endowment affect those things that are most personal to us. As it reveals to you one of my personal battles with entitlement, review it, feel it, and use it as an endowment to your benefit. My hope is that it will inspire you to revisit your life, find the places dominated by entitlement, and set yourself free. My dream is that this personal gift will invite each of you to join me on the journey back to the fulfillment and peace that endowments bring to our lives.

Dear Daddy,

I didn't know whether to start this letter with "Dear Dad" or "Dear Daddy," I guess because those names represent the two men I have experienced in loving you. Daddy is the man with the golden voice, the one who taught me to sing in harmony, the one who could fix anything, the one who was so handsome and strong, gentle and vulnerable. The one who built a playground from nothing, the ingenious one who could transform trash into treasure, and whose arms protected me when I was frightened by the world outside; the one who looked at me with tears in his eyes as he spoke the words, "When I look at you, I can believe in miracles." Daddy was your beautiful center.

Dad was the man who showed up drunk, whose eyes burned with rage, whose arms stretched out to hit, whose fists knocked holes into walls, whose voice screamed with rage, whose words were cruel, whose love was as lost as he was. Dad was the one whose self-absorption left everyone in his wake empty and bleeding. Dad was the one whose cynicism choked the life out of every dream. Dad was the one who stole mother's pain medication when she was dying of cancer so that he could take it. Dad was the one who pulled the knife on hospice volunteers and threatened everyone's life for drugs and left me alone, as hospice refused to return to help me take care of my mom as she struggled to die with some sense of dignity. Dad was the one that attempted suicide as my mother was dying and none of us had the emotional resources to bear any more pain. Dad was the one whose heart and mind were flooded with angry and raging extremes.

I have longed to love you, but I must confess, Dad, it hasn't been easy. After Mom's death, I promised myself that you would never hurt me again. I separated myself from you. But I have discovered that until I create a new way to love you, your extremes and the addictions they fuel will not only control you but will limit my heart for the rest of my life.

I have resented your addiction and your choices. I have deeply resented that your need for drugs and alcohol was more important than me. But today, standing in my center, I am choosing to release my resentment. Your addiction is simply your addiction, not a monkey that I accept to carry on my back, poisoning my possibility of loving fully and being loved.

From this day forward, I choose your love, your center, as the truth of you—not your extremes, which want only to destroy the best of you. I refuse to let your extremes not only steal your life but steal the truth of your love for me. I know you in your center. You love me, Daddy, and I love you.

When you were centered and I felt your love, it was great—so great that I wanted more. You didn't fail me. In fact, guess what? I turned out pretty good. My first book has been wonderfully received and highly praised. I am proud of the way that I am sourcing my children in wonderful and remarkable ways, with great commitment and love. I touch the lives of thousands of at-risk children every year with my seminars and counseling. I help heal and unite people that entitlement fights to tear apart. Your grandsons are both great contributors to their communities and their worlds. One is blessed with special baby blood that saves the lives of hundreds of premature babies each year, and the other, your youngest grandchild, is the author of three books and was the youngest professional inspirational speaker in the history of the National Speakers Association at the age of 12. Because of his passion and love for the planet and our united commitment,

169,000 trees were planted in Oklahoma in 1998. We are making a difference with our lives. We are leaving a legacy of breath, love, and abundance for the future, and this marvelous adventure began as a gift from you and Mom.

I forgive you and release the narrative that you failed me. I am choosing to replace it with the centered truth that you gave me the gift of the wonderful life that I continue to create. You have succeeded because I have succeeded. Your extremes and the addictions they fueled could not steal your greatness. Your pain and confusion did not kill your legacy of love. Thank you for the moments of wonder, love, greatness, and, especially, harmony. They are the only moments that matter anyway. I will remember the harmony, for within it is where I will choose to live.

Dawn

This is not a letter I wrote once and put away. That is not how the hearts and minds of human beings work. We move into our extremes and out of our centers daily, sometimes hourly. Therefore, this is a letter that I am committed to reading every time entitlement wants to take me into my extremes and make me forget the truth about my father. You could say that both sides were true. His extremes were every bit as true as his centered behavior, but you would be wrong. Love is the only truth. Everything else is an illusion, a smoke screen to help confuse us and break our hearts.

Our extremes represent the worst of what we are capable of being. They do not represent the truth of who we were created to be. It is vitally important that we remember that a person's center is the truth. It is based on the beauty of the soul and the brightness of their potential. Just as light eliminates darkness, returning to the light and love of our center renders our destructive and vicious extremes powerless.

These words express my commitment to my center, truth, future, and life. They speak to my commitment to my children, my friends, and the amity I wish to foster. The words remind me that in the most fragile places within our hearts, where the edges are broken and sharp, it is my choice, and only mine, to remember and appreciate my centered endowments and allow them to ease the pain and dull the sharp edges of my extremes. These words are not simply words; they are a prayer, an action against, and a movement away from my entitled extremes. Each time I read them, they remind me of the path I have chosen, and they are a greater gift still.

With them in mind, I continue to set myself free from the tortuous prison of my extremes.

> *"Words can sometimes, in moments of grace,
> attain the quality of deeds."*
> – Elie Wiesel
> Nobel Peace Prize Laureate

CORBIN'S THOUGHTS

In our centers, we make observations about others and ourselves. However, the moment that we begin to make judgments, we move out of our centers and into combative and destructive extremes that insist on being "right." Trying to be "right" can devastate relationships. To this, I can attest. However, before I share the harrowing story of how my extreme personality tendencies sabotaged my marriage, allow me to provide some context about how my wife and I viewed the world differently when we were married and why we, and so many others, fell into the trap of trying to be "right" or focusing on what was "wrong" instead of simply being love.

Let me begin by saying that I have always adored my wife's centered blue personality tendencies, specifically her discerning intelligence and curiosity. In the context of our relationship, blue showed up as her tertiary color. In the context of work, blue was her secondary color. She is a critical thinker who does her own research. When it comes to parenting our son, I always trust her to make the most informed decisions for his well-being. When we were married, her independent study led her to have strong, unconventional opinions. When I occasionally objected to her ideas, she was quick to reference the experts she had learned from to prove she knew better.

As I've mentioned, blue is my primary color, and I also love to be "right." Too often, our stubborn blue extremes led us to argue. When things felt off in our marriage, we tended to become more critical of each other, pointing out problems between us. In our extremes, we transformed from lovers and best friends into bitter opponents, insisting that we were each right and the other one didn't listen or care. Most of the time, these disputes were easily resolved once my wife and I took the time to return to our centers to communicate consciously and pour love into one another.

Although we both possessed strong blue tendencies and loved to be right, the most effective way for us to connect was through our centered green personality tendencies—the part of us that was deeply spiritual, empathetic, and passionate about self-development and raising human consciousness. While people with strong blue personality tendencies are motivated by doing things the "right" way, those with strong centered green personality tendencies are motivated by doing what is "right" to create a better future. This forward-thinking headspace is naturally conducive to the prosperity of love and marriage.

When my wife and I met in our centered green personality tendencies, we focused less on pointing out the flaws in our relationship and more on the gratitude we felt for the gift of our love and the many blessings that had manifested from it: a healthy baby, a beautiful home, and two loving dogs. While succumbing to our scornful extreme blue tendencies would take our relationship to the depths of misery, cultivating our centered green tendencies would remind us that we had created paradise together.

However, I was not always mindful of how blessed we were. When a problem would inevitably arise in our house, such as a leaky roof or a broken garage door, I would stray into my blue-green extreme, feeling burdened by a way of life that I couldn't afford. The stress of managing a house, working on a marriage, raising a baby, writing a book with my mother, and living in a world full of needless division, violence, and suffering was too much to handle. As a result, I existed in a perpetual brooding blue extreme state of mind.

I did not wish to neglect my duty. On the contrary, the weight of my responsibilities provided meaning to my life. My desire to ensure my family's security and stability caused me to ruminate about my ability to provide financially for them. When I felt unsure about what was the "right" way to deal with all the problems I observed, I procrastinated. Rather than obsessing over dilemmas that overwhelmed me, I deferred to my secondary orange personality tendencies and sought to escape my problems through entertainment and (in my extreme) numbing distractions. Thanks to my YouTube algorithm, a majority of that entertainment consisted of talking heads with strong blue tendencies commenting on and debating the various controversies of the day. Unfortunately, watching other intellectuals deliver long diatribes or talk over one another to get their point across only plunged me deeper into an aggravated blue extreme as I yearned to talk some sense into these people!

Since green is my tertiary color, I am capable of eventually seeing the forest from the leaves. While being in a blue state of mind allows me to ingest a large quantity of information, it is only in a centered green state of mind that I can process the knowledge that keeps me up at night into wisdom that benefits my life. Although the blue portion of my personality color blend would like to think it comprehends the mysteries of life, it is only in a centered green space that I find peace with who I am and my purpose on this planet. Pursuing a centered green sense of meaning improves my mental health infinitely more than constantly worrying about how to win arguments (blue tendencies) or win over people (orange tendencies). These compulsions (which often pushed me to my extremes) came from a need to "be seen" and an entitled desire for validation.

My strong green personality tendencies are also the reason I care deeply about the big-picture future of humanity on Earth. If I didn't have as much green in my color blend, I wouldn't be nearly as invested in global harmony nor concerned with apocalyptic potentialities. Fortunately, my primary blue personality tendencies help me easily reign in my less-dominant, zealous green extremes with objectivity and reason. However, my tertiary green personality tendencies are less competent at wrangling my obsessive, irritable blue extremes. The choice to lean into my green center is usually a conscious one that requires meditation or a gentle reminder from my partner. In marriage, when I began to slip too far into my acrimonious blue and orange extremes, my wife was good at helping me remember to shift into a centered green headspace.

While blue was my wife's tertiary color, her primary and secondary colors were yellow and green. Although she was curious, at home, she was even more nurturing (centered yellow) and hopeful (centered green). In our relationship, she liked to say that she was the heart (warmth) and I was the head (strength). Because her color blend contained more green than blue, my wife found it easier to take a step back from the news and social media to see life's big picture. She preferred to focus her attention on those she cared about. Although she liked to stay informed on major current events, she was careful not to allow herself to be manipulated by agendas that promoted fear. She refused to allow bad things happening in the world to dictate her mood. Unfortunately, she still had to deal with me stressing about the news of the day in my extreme blue, ruminating about how the world was run by clowns and appeared to be on the verge of catastrophe.

On autopilot, my blue mind tends to get lost trying to discern the "truth." Because I am motivated by knowledge, I can be easily distracted by the pursuit of clandestine information. People with strong blue tendencies are naturally inquisitive. They can discern that the world is more complex than it appears on the surface and can't resist chasing white rabbits in search of answers to life's mysteries. Their desire to understand how the world works causes them to naturally gravitate toward science and fields of discovery. This is why blue geniuses created the microscope and telescope: to see the unseen and solve life's mysteries. However, in their extremes, people with strong blue personality tendencies can be driven mad by their genius. Although knowledge can inspire and protect us, it can also disturb and distract us.

If the official narrative put forward by the media establishment doesn't add up in my blue brain, I can't stop myself from scouring the internet for kernels of "truth" like a truffle pig with its nose in the dirt. Even though I like to believe that I am capable of confronting the ugly face of reality, sometimes, the possibilities that I am led to consider are unimaginably disturbing and strip me of the centered green hope that is crucial to my well-being.

The transition from centered blue curiosity to extreme blue rumination is subtle. When I am alone, the onset is almost imperceptible. It's not until I find myself around other people, watching them raise their eyebrows as I rant about the many ails that I perceive to be plaguing the world, that I realize how high-strung and seemingly unhinged I can appear. From my experience, the more knowledge I acquire, the crazier I sound to the uninformed. Although I understand how that statement might sound pejorative, my opinion is that those who can refrain from being engrossed in the news and needlessly fretting about the collapse of civilization are the smart ones.

A majority of the time that I attempt to discuss the events that are transpiring in the world that keep me up at night, most people have no idea what I'm talking about. Feeling informed while surrounded by perceived ignorance can be isolating and frustrating to people with extreme blue tendencies, who see themselves as one of the few sane people on the planet. Similarly, those with strong green personality tendencies feel isolated and frustrated by the prejudice and injustice they perceive around them. They feel morally superior even when their extreme green ideals compel them to commit hateful acts of violence. For people with judgmental extreme blue and green tendencies, it can be difficult to respect or tolerate other people when they believe their opinions are dead wrong.

Those who test high in purple, orange, yellow, and red are far less concerned with trying to make points or defend their beliefs on the internet. In general, they do not allow news and online commentary to consume their offline existence. Purples, motivated by achievement, don't have time to concern themselves with distractions that interfere with their productivity. Oranges, motivated by fun, couldn't care less about the news (unless they happen to be on it). Yellows, motivated by appreciation, purposefully avoid conflict and prefer to use technology and social media to stay connected as opposed to staying informed. Last but not least, reds, motivated by power, are so focused on their personal quest to get where they want to go in life that they're too busy to argue or even consider other people's opinions. To those with strong red personality tendencies, especially in their extreme, being right means nothing compared to being in control.

While the people who run the media likely possess extreme red tendencies that incline them to distort information to consolidate corporate or political power, they do not actively engage in the day-to-day online quibbles of the culture war. In the eyes of someone with strong red influences, actions speak far louder than written words. They oversee the implementation of their agenda from leadership positions, relying on purple administrative supervisors to exact their agendas and extreme green ideologues to battle like foot soldiers in the online trenches of social media to defend their cause.

My assessment is that a majority of the keyboard warriors who tirelessly engage in the internet culture war (including me) are people with strong blue and/or green personality color tendencies. While blues debate other blues over "facts," greens argue with other greens over "beliefs." When blues and greens face off, blues call greens "delusional," and greens label blues as "insensitive." While those with strong blue personality tendencies tend to be more rational and pragmatic, those with strong green personality tendencies tend to be more spiritual and empathetic. Although being "right" is important to both colors, it means something completely different to each of them. In the eyes of someone with strong green personality tendencies, what is "right" means what they feel is fair. In the eyes of someone with strong blue personality tendencies, what is "right" depends on what information can be certifiably proven.

While people with a lot of green in their color blend tend to make their voices heard online and in the streets, people with strong blue tendencies prefer to critique the world from behind a screen or debate via webcam. Those with strong blue personality tendencies tend to be more tech-savvy and spend time in front of a phone, tablet, television, or computer. Consequently, they are more prone to develop screen addictions. In the internet age, one might refer to this extreme blue behavior as being "terminally online." This phrase refers to people who spend excessive hours browsing the internet or social media to the point where they become seemingly mentally unwell. When combined with bullying extreme red tendencies or flagrant orange extreme tendencies, extreme blue-green keyboard warriors can transform into vile online trolls.

As disturbing as the comments that people post below videos can be, somehow the news is still worse. The more I learn about current events, the more unsettled and out of control I feel as I ask myself, "Why do whistleblowers and convicted criminals keep committing suicide before they are set to testify in court?" Diving headfirst into the rabbit hole, one rarely finds peace or resolution at the bottom. Once it becomes clear that the tunnel leads to a dead end and there is no breaking through to the other side, the blue mind has no choice but to muster the strength to climb out of the hole, touch grass, and move on with their life, having accomplished little other than wasting precious time and energy in an endless search for "truth." The process is more or less akin to a dog chasing its tail.

Because people with strong blue personality tendencies value accuracy above all, they only seek news from sources they deem credible. They are highly selective about where they get their information from and only listen to people they consider experts. They are innately skeptical and dismissive of news that they perceive to be manipulative or "fake." While people in their green extremes tend to argue based on righteous emotion and attack the character of those who question their ideology, people in their blue extremes cite research to back up their assertions, which makes them feel justified in insulting the intelligence or emotional appeals of their opponents.

To rationalize a belief or premise to support their bias, individuals with strong green and blue personality tendencies will concoct complex, illogical explanations. Such mental gymnastics allow them to avoid reckoning with uncomfortable, inconvenient, or unjustifiable truths. Although it can be difficult to change the mind of a person with strong blue tendencies (especially in their extreme), it is still possible to persuade them to reconsider their positions if one approaches them with irrefutable proof. However, to a person with extreme green tendencies, evidence is inconsequential compared to how they feel about a situation. Radical and fundamentalist mindsets are motivated by beliefs, which news organizations and online content creators are obliged to cater to for a paycheck.

Today, the blue-green color blend is evident in most cable news and online media personalities who engage in partisan reporting. Rather than impartially relating information, their beliefs and prejudice saturate the information that they share. In the era of cable news, this phenomenon became known as "spin." Prior to the rise of 24-hour news networks, the news media prided themselves on accuracy (in alignment with blue

THE PERSONALITY COLOR MATRIX

personality tendencies). The purpose of journalism was to objectively deliver facts to the public rather than opinions. However, when cable news networks began to intentionally design their programming to appeal to the ideological extreme green bias of their viewers to compete for ratings and keep their audience, the once objective news media transformed into the hostile, pandering, and sensationalized version of itself we know today.

In addition to problem-solving blue and green tendencies, people who appear on camera to report the news can also possess confident orange or red personality tendencies. Those with strong orange personality tendencies are naturally attracted to the spotlight, while people with strong red personality tendencies usually rise to prominence in whatever field they choose to pursue, motivated by their desire to be number one.

In the wake of the 2024 election, the news media landscape has fractured as if stricken by an earthquake. The common ground we once shared, divided as it may have been, has shattered further into islands of beliefs separated by chasms of opinion. Before the internet, one could only access news and information from a limited array of accredited sources. For a period, the mainstream media's unrivaled control over the steady leak of information facilitated a relatively cohesive picture of the world, i.e., "Truth."

However, over time, the news media industry's shift toward extreme green ideological, exclusionary, and divisive rhetoric has caused many to disengage from overtly biased cable news networks and print media in favor of independent online content creators and streaming commentators. Although many people still rely on traditional means to stay informed about the world, these models are also growing increasingly obsolete. Independent media channels have exploded in number and popularity across a multitude of platforms, most predominantly YouTube, which uses an algorithm that intentionally suggests content that caters to the interests of users, only delivering them information that passively affirms their pre-existing beliefs and biases.

The traditional left-wing and right-wing propaganda disseminated by establishment media channels must now compete with countless other online channels spreading information, misinformation, and disinformation online. The one thing all these voices have in common is that, in their opinion, they are "right" and others are "wrong." As satisfying as it can feel to be "right," immersing ourselves in self-constructed digital silos leaves us vulnerable to deception and manipulation. As a result, the type of news we receive (and thereby our beliefs about the world) has become highly dependent on our social identity and demographics. Differences in age, interests, political affiliations, sexuality, cultural beliefs, and personality tendencies can result in dramatically different information diets and, consequently, interpretations of reality.

For people to make informed decisions, they need access to reliable information that presents different perspectives fairly. When the news and information we consume online or through television becomes partisan and misinformative (poisoned by extreme green tendencies) or hardheaded and high and mighty (poisoned by extreme blue tendencies), it pushes the public into their extremes, leading to increased confrontation and polarization and a declining lack of public trust in the integrity of establishment media. The debut of extreme blue-green partisan news coverage coincided with the emergence of echo chambers, environments where people are only exposed to information, opinions, or beliefs that align with their own. The resulting lack of exposure to alternative viewpoints contributes to extreme green radicalization and extreme blue arrogance. Both of these extreme states can lead to demeaning and closeminded behavior, especially in an online context in which anonymity precludes any consequence for antagonistic or dehumanizing rhetoric.

In the social media age, the echo chamber phenomenon has been amplified by algorithms that, as I mentioned, cater content and information to the specific interests of users to keep them engaged on the platform. To many, this can be rather appealing. For people with strong blue tendencies, it makes us feel smart to hear others affirm our pre-existing conclusions. We like to feel correct. For people with strong green tendencies, it makes us feel virtuous when others reinforce our existing affiliations. We like to feel united and supported.

I have dedicated this chapter to thoroughly explaining the dismissive and denigrating extreme blue-green nature of our news media because, one, I am blue and can't help but overcomplicate things, and two, the hyper-sensationalized, fear-inducing, belligerent, and apocryphal nature of the current information ecosystem preyed on me personally. My habit of allowing the news to overwhelm, depress, and put me into a perpetual extreme state of frustration jeopardized the peace of my otherwise beautiful marriage.

My extreme blue personality tendencies made me feel hostage to the unpredictable chaos of the world. Streaming news updates from my phone caused me to grow increasingly fearful of looming threats like escalating war, economic collapse, catastrophic climate events, and the adverse outcomes of AI. Although I was aware that worrying about events I cannot control is a complete waste of time and energy, I couldn't seem to stop myself from focusing on all that I perceive to be wrong with the world and choosing to suffer on a daily basis. Taken to the extreme, my desire to "know" interfered with my ability to simply "be." Because my wife cared about my well-being, she encouraged me to deactivate my social media or reduce my screen time. However, my clever blue-orange personality tendencies couldn't resist the allure of forbidden knowledge, and I didn't want to miss out on the fun of social media drama.

Over time, my wife and I's attempts to be "right" bred resentment and a power struggle in our marriage. Despite our repeated attempts to repair the damage done to our relationship by our blue extremes, the tension and discontent between us escalated to the point where our differences became irreconcilable. She felt as if her feelings and perspectives were dismissed. I believed the same. We spent the majority of our time together in our silent extremes. I found myself miserable and hopeless on a daily basis. Everywhere I looked, I saw problems that I didn't know how to solve. I would stomp, slump, and huff and puff around my house like a petulant teenager.

Because my wife is deeply empathetic, seeing me depressed and angry every day made her anxious and resentful. She couldn't imagine being miserable with me, married to my extreme, for the rest of her life. Whenever either of us attempted to express our mutual fears or unhappiness, an argument would ensue that left both of us in our blue extremes, insisting that we were right. Instead of showing each other the affection and appreciation that was necessary to rekindle our romance, we would go to bed angry and frustrated. As a result, we grew emotionally distant, and our communication broke down.

One Easter morning, the conflict between my wife and I reached a boiling point. After getting into a heated argument that resulted in threats of separation, I found myself driving away from my house in my extreme, utterly lost. Even though I knew where I was, I didn't know where I was going. All I knew was that I felt like I needed to escape my relationship.

My orange personality tendencies led me to the parking lot of my local movie theater. Sitting in my car, watching it rain outside, I decided to wait 45 minutes until the next showing of *Godzilla x Kong: The New Empire*. I supposed that if I was willing to destroy my life, it was only fitting that I watch a bunch of monstrous titans wreak devastation on the planet. Although I tried to pass the time listening to YouTube, I found no relief or amusement in any of the content my algorithm had to offer. Every video in my feed cynically highlighted an imminent crisis threatening the stability of Western civilization. I could only bear to listen to a few minutes of a podcast before I decided that my overstuffed mind couldn't take any more negativity.

Frustrated by my inability to not only solve the world's problems but also the problems in my marriage, I knew my spirit desperately needed nourishment. Fortunately, it was Easter Sunday, and it was still early enough to catch the 11 a.m. service. Rather than attempting to numb my mind by watching oversized lizards fight giant apes, I decided to answer the call to return to church after many years and feed my centered green personality tendencies.

The sermon that awaited me that morning could not have been more poignant. The lecture was titled "Finding Love in Chaos." Judging by the name, I initially expected the preacher to explore how to reignite the spark of love in a troubled relationship. However, the message was actually about how to embody love in times of great uncertainty and chaos. Considering how distraught my daily news feed had made me, I was starved for hope and hungry to receive a centered green message that would help me navigate the paralyzing uncertainty of the world without growing sharp and antisocial and taking out my stress on the people closest to me.

By the grace of the divine, I received the answer I was searching for. As if he were speaking directly to me, the preacher summarized Christ's instruction for his followers as "I don't want you to be right. I want you to be like me." To me, that meant, "I don't want you to be extreme. I want you to be centered. I want you to be love." The profound simplicity of the concept moved me to tears.

In my quest for knowledge, one of the most painful truths that I have come to accept is that more "truth" will not heal the world. At this point, only love and a willingness to accept, forgive, and reconnect can bring us back together. The assurance of that grace is all the common ground we need to construct a more conscious future of centered coexistence. As our awareness grows, so does our resistance to misinformation and manipulation.

As someone who struggles with extreme blue and extreme green tendencies, I refuse to continue to allow myself to be manipulated by divisive partisan rhetoric. Ever since that Easter morning, the statement "I don't want you to be right. I want you to be like me" has served as a reminder to return to my green center and embody love. Whenever I find myself in a judgmental extreme blue or green state of mind, I recite the phrase internally.

I wish I could say that hearing these words and coming home to share them with my wife after church miraculously saved my marriage. By that point, a rift had formed in our relationship that we were unable to recover from. Although we spent considerable time and energy in counseling attempting to reconcile our differing perspectives, ultimately, my wife and I decided that it was best for both of us and our infant son to end our marriage and consciously co-parent rather than endlessly argue. Coming to that conclusion was incredibly difficult, but it is one that our rational, centered blue minds reached together. Fortunately, I can say that as co-parents, we never fail to unite in our centered green personality tendencies with the best interest of our child in mind. I will always love her and how much she loves our son.

Although the message that I received on Easter may not have prevented my divorce, it set me free from the grip of my extreme blue personality tendencies. As a recovering argue-holic, I remind myself daily to be "love" instead of trying to be "right." The words lead me forward as I carry on as a centered green messenger seeking to help people strengthen their connections. My goal is to empower others with insight to avoid my mistakes. Rather than dwelling on my past errors, I choose to let go of all my resentful thoughts and entitled opinions and remember to appreciate the love and meaning in my life that truly matters. At this point, that means setting my judgments aside and doing everything in my power to be uplifting, kind, and considerate of other people's feelings and perspectives.

> *"I believe that the Matrix can remain our cage*
> *or it can become our chrysalis…*
> *That to be free, you cannot change your cage.*
> *You have to change yourself."*
> – Lana Wachowski
> *The Matrix* screenplay

7

DO WE TEACH CAPABILITY OR VICTIMHOOD?

*"Suffering is universal. But victimhood is optional.
There is a difference between victimization and victimhood.
We are all likely to be victimized in some way in the course of our lives.
No one can make you a victim but you. We develop a victim's mind --
a way of thinking and being that is rigid, blaming, pessimistic, stuck in
the past, unforgiving, punitive, and without healthy limits or boundaries.
We become our own jailors when we choose the confines of the victim's mind."*
– Edith Eger
The Choice: Embrace the Possible

What is suffering? Synonyms are words like "adversity," "discomfort," "misfortune," "ordeal," "anguish," "hardship," "difficulty," "misery," and "torment." What do these words have in common? Entitlement is their root cause. As the quote above reminds us, we are all likely to be victimized in some way in the course of our lives, whether it be physical or emotional or from a family member or a complete stranger. No one's life is without suffering. However, victimhood does come from within. It is the narrative that we tell ourselves and others about our suffering that creates a victim mentality.

A *victim mentality* is a psychological term used to define a personality trait that allows an individual to play the victim anytime things get a little tough. Such individuals find it difficult, if not impossible, to accept responsibility.

> *"The victim mindset dilutes the human potential.*
> *By not accepting personal responsibility for our circumstances,*
> *we greatly reduce our power to change them."*
> – Steve Maraboli

People adopt a victim mentality out of fear and a subconscious, self-deceiving belief that life is beyond their control. A victim mentality is often a developed response to the perceived pain and trauma one believes they have experienced. The key word is "believes." In Proverbs 23:7, the Bible tells us, "As a man thinks in his heart, so is he." Whether or not you are religious, you can find sound social and human principles in religious teachings.

A victimhood mindset has never brought anything except feelings of entitlement and pain to those who are trapped by it. A victim mentality is about our beliefs, our mindset, our choices, and how we define ourselves and our circumstances. There is a huge difference between a victim mentality, or victim narrative, and an underdog narrative. Vivek Ramaswamy, an American entrepreneur who declared his candidacy for the Republican Party nomination in the 2024 United States presidential election, makes this clear distinction in his 2023 book, *Nation of Victims*:

Narratives about one's identity hold great power—not just the power to understand a life in hindsight, but the power to create it, the power to give it meaning and direction. At its core, the appeal of the underdog story comes from its promise that we can create something from nothing, imposing our will on an unforgiving universe. The narrative promises that we can choose our own destinies, no matter how humble our starting points. It offers the hope that if we work hard and attempt great things, we can succeed.

When I was growing up in severe poverty, a common belief I held was that working hard to overcome disadvantages would not only help me find the success I wanted and longed for but, much more importantly, would build my character.

Ramaswamy's distinction between an underdog and a victim resonated with me because it beautifully illustrates approaching the challenges of life from an endowed attitude versus an entitled one. Although underdog narratives and victimhood narratives can follow a similar broad outline, they are profoundly different. In Ramaswamy's words:

The most crucial distinction is that the underdog struggles and overcomes forces arrayed against them, but the victim's task is to convince others to overcome adversity for them. *The underdog makes a demand of themselves; the victim makes an* (entitled) *demand of those around them.*

The truth is, only you choose how you feel about your past or present experiences. You do this by choosing the expectations and interpretations of your challenges and circumstances. Ask yourself, *Am I an underdog with the tenacity, determination, and focus to meet my dreams head-on, or do I choose a narrative marinating in victimhood, seasoned with bitterness, frustration, lack of initiative, devoid of capacity, and waiting on someone to fix my difficulties for me?*

No matter what has happened to you or your ancestors, only you choose, and continue to choose over and over, how you will use those "shitty" challenging experiences to fertilize and help strengthen your resilience and your capacity for living into what is truly extraordinary about you. Ups and downs, joys and sorrows, tragedies, and triumphs are all part of life, *and* they are all endowments, gifts to be treasured, learned from, reflected upon, and used for growth. Your experiences will either make or break you simply because of the meaning you give to them. You get to choose which outcome will be the reality you live into.

If you feel like a victim or expect to be treated like one, guess what? That is what you will most likely experience. You are the only one who chooses your outlook and attitude. When my clients are trapped by their victim mentality, I recommend the steps below to empower their lives and futures with actions and thoughts that are truly endowed.

1. **Remember that you are the author of your life's story.** Look internally and ask yourself if a victim mindset actually serves your best interest. Does it bring you joy? Does it enhance your peace? Imagine how your narrative would be different if, instead, you saw yourself as an underdog who has yet to prove to the world your significance. It can be challenging to change your way of seeing and experiencing yourself, but consider the benefits of doing so.
2. **Focus on the next positive steps you could take.** A classic victim behavior is to think that unfavorable events happen for the sole purpose of causing them pain. Mentally limit the times you compare, complain, mistrust, are jealous, or feel entitled. Instead of asking, *Why is this happening to me? I don't deserve this!* ask yourself, *What can I do to use this experience to make me and the world around me better, fairer, more compassionate, more connected, and stronger? What actions can I take today that would not*

only inspire me to be and accomplish more but inspire those I care about as well?
3. **Count your blessings.** It is difficult to feel like a victim when you allow yourself to feel blessed. Appreciation is one of the most powerful and effective weapons against entitlement. Entitlement wants to blind us to the good we have in our lives. Try keeping a gratitude journal. Every day, write down a list of the things you are most grateful for. Consciously cultivate a healthier mindset of gratitude, unity, and joy. Why? Because it will make you feel better, it will improve your physical and mental health, and it will revive your potential.
4. **Do things that foster confidence and self-esteem.** Accept the fact that you are the author and creator of your reality. Set yourself on a hero's journey. Who are your heroes, and why do you admire them? Become the protagonist of your life's movie. Take the time to understand your strengths and then spend more time developing and realizing them. Treat yourself with dignity and respect. Act in ways that uplift and inspire not only you but those around you. You build your confidence and esteem. How you treat yourself is how others will treat you. Respect and compassion beget respect and compassion.
5. **Let grudges and past hurts go.** Don't feed your enmity. Hating people makes those feelings stronger. Hoping for retaliation rather than offering forgiveness traps you in anger's quicksand. Enmity always makes less of us. If faith matters to you, *let GO and let GOD.* Allow your faith in something good to direct your steps, not your fear and expectations of something bad.
6. **Avoid becoming dependent.** Keep your legs strong enough to hold you up. They are *your* legs and no matter how well someone else attempts to carry you somewhere, it will never be as wonderful and satisfying as when you get there on your own. When you can stand on your own, you not only feel stronger, but your actions prove it. When you think of yourself as being at the mercy of others, it can cause you to feel weak, confused, and even helpless. Your strength, resilience, and brilliance are your destiny to develop, strengthen, and share.

7. **Expand yourself and your possibilities by developing a wide variety of relationships.** Learn about others and give them the privilege of learning about you. Create relationships, nurture them, and build them as a loving fortress around you. Trade your enmity for amity. Amity and its harmonies, understanding, goodwill, warmth, and compassion, breathe life into relationships with others. You are not in this life alone. Even more importantly, you are not in this life with only one group identity. Don't be defined or limited by any category or group.

What you will discover is that each person has a story of pain and hardship. Each person has experiences that have challenged or victimized them. Every human being experiences the same negative emotions, just as they have the capacity to experience the same positive emotions. As Jane Elliot, an internationally renowned teacher, lecturer, diversity trainer, and recipient of the National Mental Health Association Award for Excellence in Education said, "We are ONE race. The human race." Rejoice and become a part of the fullness, diversity, and expanse of the positive possibilities of humanity.

A victim mentality is acquired. It is not innate. You learn to think this way; sometimes, you even teach it to others. With consistent effort and dedication, you can become whatever you dream or desire, but you have to understand the important distinction and choose to become an underdog on your way to greatness instead of a victim drowning in misery and lack.

Albert Einstein said, "There are two ways to live your life. One is as though nothing is a miracle. The other is as though everything is a miracle." What if, instead of taking on the limiting identity of someone who is or has been oppressed, you lived every day of your future truly believing that you are the miracle you choose to be? Imagine the difference that would make!

Reality is merely our brains' relative understanding of the world around us based on where and how we are observing it. So, how, exactly, is it that our relative perception of what is happening, or what we think will happen, can actually affect what does happen? One answer is that the brain is organized to act on what we predict will happen next, something psychologists call "expectancy theory." According to Sean Achor, a Harvard expert on positive psychology, in his book, *The Happiness Advantage*, "the expectation of an event causes the same complex set of neurons to fire as though the event were actually taking place, triggering a cascade of events in the nervous system that leads to a whole host of real physical consequences."[1]

How you act toward someone becomes the reality they live into. This phenomenon is known as the Pygmalion effect.

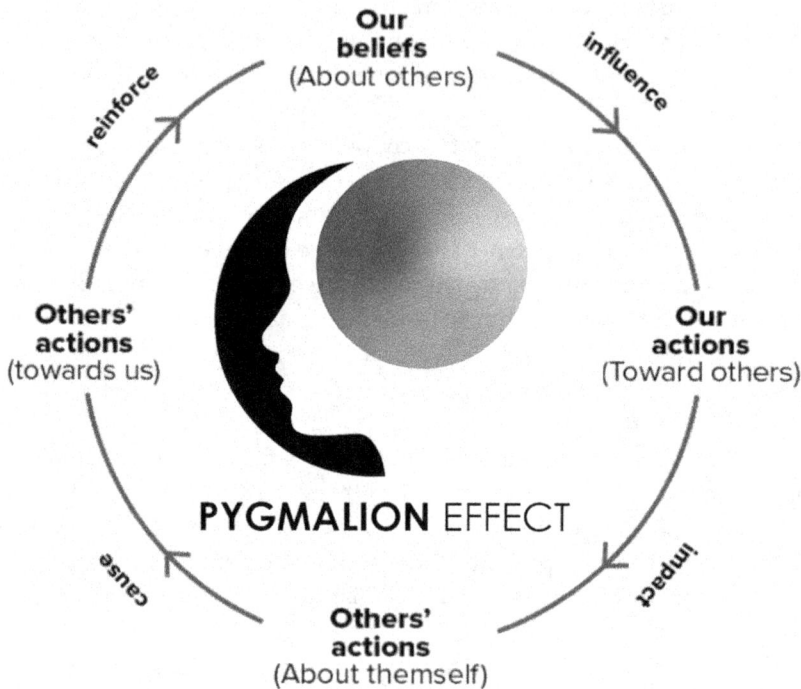

The work of Rosenthal and Jacobson (1968), among others, showed that teacher expectations influenced student performance. As the chart shows, positive beliefs and expectations about others influence performance and actions toward others positively, and negative expectations influence performance and our actions negatively. This continues as our actions influence others' thoughts about themselves and influence their actions toward us, which finally reinforces our beliefs about them. Rosenthal and Jacobson's original research focused on an experiment at an elementary school where students took intelligence pre-tests. By calculating the

---

1. Sean Achor, *The Happiness Advantage: How a Positive Brain Fuels Success in Work and Life* (New York: Crown Business, 2010).

results, Rosenthal and Jacobson identified the names of 20 percent of the students in the school who showed "unusual potential for intellectual growth" and informed the teachers that they would bloom academically within the year. Unknown to the teachers, these students were actually selected at random, with no relation to the initial test. When Rosenthal and Jacobson tested the students eight months later, they discovered that the randomly selected students whom the teachers expected to bloom scored significantly higher. Later, in a 1985 study, Rosenthal and Babad were quoted as saying: "When we expect certain behaviors of others, we are likely to act in ways that make the expected behavior more likely to occur."

We must train ourselves to see children, as well as ourselves, as passionate, capable, and resilient despite any adversity we may face. If we can help children believe in themselves and allow them to dream the biggest dreams in their hearts, their paths can be determined by their hopes and aspirations versus narratives of victimhood.

Happiness is not about lying to ourselves or turning a blind eye to any negative experience or event that may have happened. It is about adjusting our brains so that we can positively interpret what happens to us in a way that propels us forward, regardless of our circumstances.

CORBIN'S THOUGHTS

On January 19, 2019, police in Chicago responded to claims of a politically motivated, racist, and homophobic hate crime committed against Jussie Smollett, a television actor, singer, and outspoken social activist. When police arrived at Smollett's apartment, they found him bruised with a rope hanging around his neck and drops of bleach staining his sweater.

Smollett explained to the police that while he had been out walking to Subway at 2 a.m. for a late-night meal, he had been assaulted by two men wearing red hats and ski masks who recognized him from his role on the TV show *Empire*. According to Smollett, the men shouted racist and homophobic slurs at him, beat him, doused him with bleach, placed the noose around his neck, and shouted, "This is MAGA country," followed by racist expletives. There were no witnesses to the attack. However, Smollett was on the phone with his manager when it occurred. He claimed to have fought back during the assault, and he reported that his assailants had run away as suddenly as they had appeared.

News of the racist and homophobic attack against Smollett spread rapidly and was covered extensively by the mainstream media. The American people responded with horror and outrage. Many took to social media to express their support for Smollett and point out how the event encapsulated the fear and harassment faced by minority groups every day in modern America. Politicians, celebrities, and public institutions joined in expressing solidarity for Smollett and other victims of prejudice. In the wake of the attack, GLAAD issued a statement praising Smollett and condemning the attackers:

"Our hearts are with Jussie Smollett as he recovers from a hate-motivated and repugnant attack in Chicago. Jussie has always used his voice and talent to create a better world, and it is disgusting that anyone, especially someone who has done such good for so many, would be targeted by undeniable hatred."[2]

While many were quick to believe Smollett's story and rebuke the deplorable actions of alt-right factions in the United States, the Chicago police department remained skeptical of the victim's account. Although Smollett claimed he wanted to see his attackers brought to justice, he was largely uncooperative with police, submitting heavily redacted phone records, refusing to turn over his phone to evidence, and declining to submit a DNA sample. Naturally, the police were curious why the victim of an alleged hate crime would withhold evidence that could help solve the case. Smollett insisted that, as a black man, he didn't trust the police and wanted to protect his privacy and that of his contacts. However, as the investigation progressed, it became clear that Smollett was hiding the truth from law enforcement.

In a dramatic twist, police discovered Smollett had planned the attack on himself and paid two background actors who worked with him on the television show *Empire* to assault him on the street, promising to advance their acting careers in exchange for their help. Smollett's plan was to falsely portray himself as a victim of a hate crime to generate public sympathy, increase his notoriety, and command a higher salary. According to "Ola" and "Bola" Osundairo, Smollett's hired attackers, he "wanted to increase his star level… He wanted to be the poster boy for activism… He wanted to be the hero for gay people. The hero for black people."[3]

In this chapter, we will examine what compels someone to fake a hate crime against themselves for attention. Obviously, Smollett was acting out

---

2. *Good Morning America*, "'Empire' Star Brutally Attacked and Hospitalized in Possible Hate Crime," accessed 2024, https://www.goodmorningamerica.com/culture/story/empire-star-brutally-attacked-hospitalized-hate-crime-60701735.

3. "Brothers paid by Jussie Smollett share new details about the hate hoax," YouTube video, 7:52, posted by *Fox News*, May 17, 2023, accessed 2024, https://www.youtube.com/watch?v=Vawbuv9THt8.

THE PERSONALITY COLOR MATRIX

of his extreme personality tendencies when he plotted and carried out his conspiracy. Using The Personality Color Matrix insight tool, we can more thoroughly explain his behavior. Based on the evidence, we can surmise that Smollett's color blend consists of some combination of green, orange, and red. In their center, these colors combine to create a charismatic, driven, and compassionate activist/entertainer who uses their voice and talent to create a better world.

Is that not precisely how GLAAD described Jussie Smollett in their statement? That is very likely who Jussie Smollett is in his center and why he was beloved by many. However, in an extreme state fed by narcissistic entitlement, those same three colors combined to create a self-destructive, self-righteous, self-important extremist/con artist who used his voice and talent to manipulate others for personal gain. Do you see how, in our extremes, we become unrecognizable versions of our centered selves?

In his green extreme, Smollett yearned to be a political martyr for racial and LGBTQ+ justice so badly that he orchestrated his own oppression. His extreme orange tendencies thirsted for fame at any cost while failing to consider the long-term consequences that accompanied his lies. Extreme red tendencies drove him to take matters into his own hands and act out his victimization to advance his career ambition.

It's also worth noting that Smollett reportedly told the Osundairo brothers that he wanted to fight back during the assault. "That was very important for him," explained Bola Osundairo. "He said, 'Hey, don't just beat my ass. Make it look like I'm fighting back and whatnot. So we did that.'"[4] In an interview with Robin Roberts on ABC News, Smollett said, "I want a little gay boy who might see this to see that I fought the f@&% back… They ran off. I didn't."[5]

This insistence reveals the strong influence of red personality tendencies on Smollett's behavior. He did not wish to simply portray himself as a helpless victim, like someone with extreme yellow personality tendencies might have done. He wanted to present himself as someone ready and willing to fight back against intolerance and bigoted violence. As Jussie

---

4. "Brothers behind Smollett hoax share their story | Fox Nation Exclusive," YouTube video, 2:52, posted by *Fox Nation*, March 12, 2023, accessed 2024, https://www.youtube.com/watch?v=qXpIbM6p7DQ.
5. "Jussie Smollett FULL Interview on alleged attack | ABC News Exclusive," YouTube video, 16:35, posted by *ABC News*, February 19, 2019, accessed 2024, https://www.youtube.com/watch?v=pXLx5OY21Bk.

saw it, he was a champion of the people. In his first concert performance following the attack, he boasted that he was "the gay Tupac."[6]

Ultimately, the hoax orchestrated by Jussie Smollett wasted police and city resources, divided the nation, and did a great disservice to actual victims of hate crimes. It is a poignant example of how destructive entitlement and extreme behaviors can be. In addition, it reveals our culture's tendency to glorify and elevate perceived victims of injustice. Simply put, being a victim is in vogue.[7]

While Smollett's lies do not invalidate the struggles faced by minority groups in America, they do reveal our culture's predilection to celebrate and side with victims. Survivors of injustice are seen as underdog heroes and righteous martyrs. In a society that vilifies oppressors and sympathizes with the overlooked and oppressed, framing oneself as a victim brings tacit advantages. Essentially, "victim currency" affords one "victim privilege."

Victim privilege relates to a social currency that one can exchange for online support, media praise, credibility, notoriety, and lucrative financial opportunities. Those who value warmth are inclined to automatically perceive victims as innocent and/or morally in the right because they have been violated. Since their misfortune is out of their control, victims are not expected to take responsibility for their suffering. Instead, they prefer to assign blame and demand that others adjust their behavior to address their needs. Being a victim makes one sympathetic and powerful and gives the impression of unimpeachable moral character. This kind of social immunity can yield a tremendous advantage to someone with prideful green-red ambitions who desires to be the face of a political or cultural movement.

In Smollett's eyes, the obstacle in the way of social progress was racist, homophobic MAGA Republicans who harbored violent prejudice. To drive this point home, Smollett chose to include purposefully inflammatory details in his account. His story was devised to be as triggering as possible, touching on issues of political tribalism, racism, and homophobia. This reveals Smollett's extreme green tribalistic mindset, a state of being that is

---

6. "JUSSIE SMOLLETT 'S BACK & SAYS 'I AM THE GAY TUPAC'," YouTube video, :51, posted by *Miss Melody XOXO*, February 3, 2019, accessed 2024, https://www.youtube.com/watch?v=JWeQs6dkzpk.

7. Amanda Prestigiacomo, "Victimhood Is the New Currency for an Increasing Number of Teens," *The Daily Wire*, accessed October 14, 2024, https://www.dailywire.com/news/victimhood-currency-increasing-number-teens-amanda-prestigiacomo.

most susceptible to the influence of group identity—a person's sense of belonging to a particular community.

Partisanship, race, social class, religion, gender, and sexuality are all issues that deal with one's group identity. These aspects of the self are deeply meaningful, especially to people with strong green personality tendencies, who often develop group identities in accordance with their belief systems. At its center, group identity can provide a sense of purpose, pride, support, and solidarity among group members. At its extreme, group identity can motivate discrimination, segregation, and bloody conflict between different groups.

People with strong green personality tendencies desire equity and fairness. It is in their nature to look out for victims and marginalized groups and combat injustice wherever they perceive it. Collectively, they constitute the allies and activists that Jussie Smollett sought to be a role model for. In their center, people with strong green influences dedicate their lives to making a difference and creating a better world. They practice their beliefs in action. They march and volunteer for causes they believe in. They do this because they care. They are compassionate and trusting—some might say they are naïve.

Smollett intended to exploit the good faith of people with strong green personality tendencies, who shared his dream for racial, sexual, and gender equality, to exact personal gain and advance his political agenda. In other words, his extreme red tendencies baited the extreme green outrage of the public. To that end, he succeeded, becoming a household name, exactly as he dreamed. However, considering that the evidence proved that he fabricated the hate crime, he also became a felon and ruined his reputation and career in the process. His extreme manipulative scheme ultimately backfired.

In their extreme, people who value warmth can live in a perpetual state of insecurity and angst. For this reason, they often complain that they "don't feel safe" or claim harassment if they are subjected to speech they perceive to be harmful, even if there is no present threat of violence. As a result, what constitutes harmful conduct has slowly and steadily broadened to include unintentional verbal slights that cause emotional distress. Safety has always been a state of mind, but today, the term has become equatable with comfort.

I think it's fair to say that we live in relatively comfortable times, perhaps too comfortable. For our ancestors, survival was far more of a struggle. Whereas we once existed as perpetual victims of our environment, subjected to the oppressive force of nature, which constantly attempted to kill or eat us, the human species now presides as masters over a domesticated world. If anything, humans now oppress the planet with our reckless consumption. Humans have no natural predators. In fact, we don't have to hunt at all or even go outside to secure food anymore (unless you are planning to commit a hate crime against yourself on your way to Subway at 2 a.m.). Thanks to food-delivery apps, you can order steak after midnight in most major U.S. cities and have a driver leave it on your doorstep. At this point, the greatest threat to the survival of our species is our inability to provide for ourselves, given our reliance on convenience.

The ability to claim victimhood in the modern era of considerable civil privilege is in itself a luxury that only exists due to the success of the liberal ideals America was founded on. The goal of liberalism has always been the reduction of human suffering. At this point in our country's evolution, Americans suffer so little discrimination relative to our pre-civil rights past that activists resort to manufacturing persecution to affirm their extreme beliefs and advance their agendas.

A week before the staged assault, Smollett reportedly crafted a hateful letter to himself, which he mailed to Fox Studios in Chicago.[8] The hate mail arrived with an unknown powder inside the envelope (later revealed to be Tylenol) that resembled anthrax. The death threat resembled a movie ransom note, with individual letters cut out of magazines, and contained racist and homophobic slurs directed at the actor, as well as a drawing of a stick figure hanging from a noose while being shot in the head. The return address scribbled on the letter simply read: "MAGA." Based on the chicken-scratch handwriting on the envelope, the letter appears to be the work of either a highly deranged, mentally unstable person or a kindergarten art student. Considering how crude the letter appeared, the executives at Fox concluded that whoever sent it likely lacked the proficiency or mental capacity to pose a credible security concern. They paid little attention to the death threat, forcing Smollett to hire accomplices to actualize the implied threats.

---

8. "Brothers Say Jussie Smollett Helped Write Letter In Alleged Attack," YouTube video, 2:23, posted by *CBS Philadelphia*, February 20, 2019, accessed 2024, https://youtu.be/_pnBgHdVxLw.

THE PERSONALITY COLOR MATRIX

This letter illustrates the delusional victimhood caused by extremes. Those who live with a victim mentality are effectively in an abusive relationship with themselves. Just like people with extreme yellow tendencies in abusive relationships, victims will make excuses that enable and perpetuate their mistreatment. On a subconscious level, they can even convince themselves that they are unworthy and deserve to be punished. Living with the abuse actually becomes preferable to other, healthier alternatives because it is familiar. Rather than choose whatever is in our best interest, we regress to what is most comfortable.

Smollett's actions may seem like an extreme, isolated incident. However, I believe the case bears a striking similarity to the highly publicized Amber Heard vs. Johnny Depp defamation trial that dominated the cultural conversation in the summer of 2022. On December 18, 2018, one month before Smollett staged a hate crime against himself, actress and activist Amber Heard released an op-ed in the *Washington Post* titled "I Spoke up Against Sexual Violence—And Faced Our Culture's Wrath. That Has to Change." In the article, Heard portrayed herself as a victim of domestic violence at the implied hands of actor Johnny Depp. She also presented herself as a victim of death threats, sexist cultural outrage, and an industry that protects male abusers. In the same way that Smollett sought to be an icon for the gay community, Amber Heard positioned herself as a fierce advocate for women's rights in the face of oppressive patriarchal structures.

Two years ago, I became a public figure representing domestic abuse, and I felt the full force of our culture's wrath for women who speak out... I had the rare vantage point of seeing, in real time, how institutions protect men accused of abuse.[9]

Reading Amber Heard's words, one can discern a sense of victimhood stemming from her gender-based group identity. Although Amber Heard was initially celebrated by the #MeToo movement for her bravery in speaking out against the abuse that she had endured, after an exhausting, televised public trial with Johnny Depp, a jury found her guilty of defamation for the statements she wrote in her *Washington Post* op-ed.[10]

Caught in the extremes of their group identity, Amber Heard and Jussie Smollett portrayed themselves as victims to become the public faces of movements against group-motivated violence. In pursuit of this end, they fabricated alternate realities to support their entitled narratives. Their extreme narcissism turned their ideologies into "my-deologies." Considering the similarities between the disgraced entertainers' manipulative behavior, it should be no surprise that both exhibited color blends consisting of orange, red, and green personality tendencies. In the extreme, this triad is known as the Master Manipulator.

People with extreme red personality tendencies refuse to compromise or concede. They stubbornly insist that their personal beliefs about the world are *the* truth. Unlike people with extreme green personality tendencies, they couldn't care less about what others care about. The only narrative that matters is the one they choose to subscribe to. Not only do people with extreme red tendencies solely care about their truth, but they will not hesitate to forcefully impose their version of reality upon others by any means. They expect others to bend to their will. In pursuit of power and self-glorification, they do not consider the negative effects their bullying ambition has on others. When they feel wronged, they exact personal vengeance.

People with extreme orange tendencies will lie and manipulate others

---

9. *The Washington Post*, "I've Seen How Institutions Protect Men Accused of Abuse. Here's What We Can Do," December 18, 2018, accessed 2024, https://www.washingtonpost.com/opinions/ive-seen-how-institutions-protect-men-accused-of-abuse-heres-what-we-can-do/2018/12/18/71fd876a-02ed-11e9-b5df-5d3874f1ac36_story.html.
10. "Judge reads verdict in Johnny Depp-Amber Heard defamation trial | full video," YouTube video, 11:47, posted by *CBS News*, June 21, 2022, accessed 2024, https://www.youtube.com/watch?v=pGN2-MfKg9c.

to get what they want or avoid negative consequences. The problem is that they tell so many lies that they inevitably end up contradicting themselves and getting caught. Considering that people with strong orange personality tendencies are natural entertainers, many thrive as actors. However, for such people, the act never stops. They are deceitful and will adopt whatever persona is temporarily advantageous to manipulate whoever they are with to get what they want. Over time, their tendency to exaggerate or deceive strains their credibility, leaving others unable to trust them.

When they feel cornered, people with extreme orange tendencies will resort to malicious verbal attacks against their accusers. When extreme selfish red tendencies pair with extreme manipulative orange tendencies, an individual's personality can become highly vulnerable to self-deception. Eventually, these people convince themselves that the lies they tell are the truth. Jussie Smollett and Amber Heard certainly fit this description, especially considering both still insist on their innocence despite the evidence presented against them in court.

> *"Denial is the most predictable of all human responses."*
> – The Architect
> *The Matrix Reloaded*

Our minds long for confirmation of our beliefs and biases. In that pursuit, people in their extremes resort to constructing experiences of oppression to validate their narratives that the world is out to get them. We can only hope that figures like Jussie Smollett and Amber Heard serve as reverse role models. Their stories serve as warnings not to give in to the allure of victim mentality. Ultimately, it is a self-destructive state of mind that transforms you into the very thing you hate: a hateful person.

8

RIGHTS WITHOUT RESPONSIBILITY

*"Our privileges can be no greater
than our obligations.
The protection of our rights can endure
no longer than the performance of our responsibilities."*
– John F. Kennedy

The power in the above quote is in its expression of, and commitment to, personal responsibility. Self-discipline has fallen prisoner to the tyranny of our entitled self-consumption and self-deception. Personal responsibility is currently something we expect of others, not something we demand of ourselves. The original goal of creating the United States of America was to offer its citizens unparalleled freedoms and the safety and structure to enjoy the fruit of their labor. Our entitled extremes cause us to take extraordinary privileges for granted. What our forefathers originally intended as endowments have morphed instead into narcissistic entitlements. They are expected, demanded, and never enough.

Though imperfect human beings, our forefathers dedicated their wealth and lives to their intention of creating a free nation. There is no greater example of personal responsibility than committing all you have emotionally and financially to an intention. Now, hundreds of years later, the personal investments Americans are willing to make for the privilege of citizenship are minimal at best. It is my belief that every endowment (notice I did not use the word "right") implies a responsibility. Every privilege comes with an obligation as well. Endowments (great gifts lovingly provided for our benefit) come with the hope that those being endowed with such gifts remember it is their duty to honor and appreciate the value of those gifts by treating them responsibly and carefully.

According to Marianne Williamson, an American author, speaker, and political activist, who began her professional career as a spiritual leader, "A problem in America today is not that we have lost our rights, but that we seem to have lost our passionate connection to their historical significance."[1] We live in a time where the effort and personal investment that comes from sacrificing to win a privilege has been replaced by the simple act of being born. We forget that the gifts this earth provides us, like our relationships, our good genetics, and even our struggles, must be treasured. We take our freedoms for granted.

The cost of preserving our sacred endowments is no longer a willingness to risk our lives, our integrity and good names, or our fortunes. The cost is paid in the form of required taxes, taken from us, in most cases, before the money reaches our hands. Perhaps, if we paid our taxes after we received our paychecks instead of our employers serving as tax collectors up front, we would realize how much most of us are required to pay to live in this country. If we understood taxes and how many ways we are taxed, we would realize our tax bill is our largest bill, far larger than our house payment or the cost of raising our children.

Paying a bill of this magnitude each month might motivate us to be concerned that the money be used carefully, wisely, and responsibly. Instead, our present tax system is set up to take payment from most of us before we touch it, giving the government the privilege of using it without accountability. Anytime that we abdicate personal responsibility, we become dependent on someone else to pick up the slack.

Our government leads us to believe that any dependency it enables is done in our best interest, but are we being deceived? When we look carefully, we will discover that entitlement's real motivation is always power and control. Delegating important issues in our lives to third parties has become a culturally and politically endorsed habit. We depend upon attorneys, doctors, therapists, investment advisors, accountants, and news commentators to tell us how to think and what to do. This encouraged abdication compromises our ability to be self-responsible in critical areas

---

1. Marianne Williamson, *The Healing of America*, Simon & Schuster, New York, NY, 1997.

of our lives and creates an *excuse* mentality that serves only to perpetuate entitlement.

When we consider something an *entitlement*, receiving what we believe we have a "right" to requires nothing of us: no commitment, no challenge, no growth, and especially no self-awareness. It makes nothing of us. It requires no contribution or personal responsibility on our part because commitment, challenge, growth, and insight are all enemies of narcissistic entitlement. That which asks no effort or sacrifice of us is not the gift it pretends to be; it is a veiled thief who comes to steal our self-worth and leave us feeling inadequate, helpless, and dependent.

In stark contrast to feelings poisoned by entitlement, *feelings of endowment* bring with them gratitude and a personal responsibility to remember, celebrate, and develop the gifts and talents we are given. It requires that we work diligently to discover what is good and powerful within us and use those things for the good of humanity. We know that we have succeeded when what we have created with our gifts and talents benefits the whole as well as ourselves.

> *"To complain that life has no joys*
> *while there is a single creature who we can relieve by our bounty,*
> *assist by our counsels or enliven by our presence,*
> *is to lament the loss of that which we possess,*
> *and is just as rational as to die of thirst*
> *with a cup of water in our hands."*
> – William Melmoth

When we examine what our attitudes of entitlement have motivated us toward, we find a legacy of spoils, where greed and personal convenience guide too many of our decisions. We are obsessed with quick profit at the expense of long-term health and stability. Immediate gratification is the new norm, and instant is no longer fast enough. Our new, faster, improved society worships self-fulfillment no matter the cost. Reverence for life and the planet that sustains it are concepts that too many miss the joy of experiencing. We have become a drive-thru, throwaway, land-fill society. The garbage we produce is filling our streets, and what is worse, our lack of reverence negatively affects our hearts and minds.

President Kennedy said, "We enjoy the comfort of opinion without the discomfort of thought." It seems that everyone in America has opinions, but are we doing our best thinking? Think about the choices we are making. Are we truly so short-sighted, selfish, and entitled that we will allow our present irresponsible gratifications to endanger our futures? We are the models, the molders, and the mentors of the world. Our children will look at our actions and attitudes and build their lives around what they witness. What if we make a commitment to teach and model reverence and responsibility? Let us be eager students of great human beings like Albert Schweitzer, Jane Goodall, Martin Luther King Jr., Gandhi, William McDonough, Hemann Scheer, and countless others whose love had great purpose and passion to inspire and teach us. Let us always remember that life and the endowments we are granted are sacred, and it is our duty to cherish and respect them.

One of the areas in which personal responsibility has been strategically and systematically removed and replaced with an ever-present attitude of entitlement is our legal system. Lawyers have intimidated us into feeling impotent when we attempt to perform the most basic resolution skills on our own. The simple language of truth and resolution has given way to overly complicated legalese. Accepting personal responsibility in resolving our personal conflicts has been replaced by a system more concerned about monetary gain and competition than finding reasonable ways to resolve life's difficult and confusing issues. The question "What is best for both parties concerned?" has been replaced with a competitive obsession with winning. Facts are twisted, attention is refocused, and innocents become victims in the name of constitutional *rights*.

Our laws were written and established to create a vehicle that would ensure the protection of the original endowments of each citizen. However, in most cases, "justice for all" has been shrunk to "justice for those who can afford it." Notoriety can be gained through legal manipulation, as we have seen with such travesties of justice as the O.J. Simpson trial. On a less serious note, consider these two frivolous lawsuits.[2] In *Monkey vs. Photographer*, PETA, an organization well known for rational responses, sued a photographer on behalf of a macaque monkey. The monkey had taken a selfie using the photographer's camera, for which PETA believed it should enjoy copyright protection. The internet is already crowded with selfies. Perhaps it's best that we don't encourage the animal kingdom to join in. If that lawsuit isn't quite insane enough for you, consider this one: In 1996, a man named Paul Shimkonis visited a nude bar and later sued the establishment, claiming a dancer's breasts had given him whiplash. Shimkonis described the breasts as "cement blocks" which

---

2. Litera, "The World's 5 Most Frivolous Lawsuits," accessed 2024, https://www.litera.com/blog/the-worlds-5-most-frivolous-lawsuits.

had caused him physical and mental anguish. His request for $15,000 in damages was denied by the judge. Reading about the case, I found myself wondering what sort of gyrations could create that level of momentum. There is no shortage of ridiculous nuisance suits that are settled every day to avoid the circus of going to court. Unfortunately, the rule currently stands: whoever is the most difficult, annoying, and wealthy enough to hire a powerful attorney wins.

> "Our culture is so awash in self-seeking, self-fulfillment and simple selfishness that the merest suggestion of voluntary self-restraint is viewed as an interference with individual freedom... the freedom, that is, to hear no contrary moral argument."
> – Stephen L. Carter
> *God's Name in Vain*

Our ability to consider the whole truth has been overtaken by our ability to spin the truth. "Spin" is a rather mild term for twisting the truth out of something. It slithers through our culture like a python, choking common sense out of the very laws designed to protect us. Spin is used to reframe a given situation, to turn it, color it, and bend it until it looks like something else. To spin the truth really means, "I will exaggerate what is worst about my opposition, all the while comparing it to the very best of my position." According to Brent H. Baker, Vice President for Research and Publications at the Media Research Center (MRC) and author of *How to Identify, Expose & Correct Liberal Media Bias*, "Bias by spin occurs when the story has only one interpretation of an event or policy, to the exclusion of the other; spin involves tone—it is when a reporter's subjective comments about objective facts make one side's ideological perspective look better than another."

When examining how entitlement infects and corrupts our society through twisting and distorting laws, we can travel the spectrum from extremely serious legal issues to completely ridiculous examples. Take, for instance, the woman from Denmark, Anette Sorenson, who was arrested in lower Manhattan for leaving her infant in a baby carriage outside a restaurant while she dined inside.

The authorities accepted her argument that her behavior was normal in Copenhagen, so they dropped the charges. One would imagine that this decision was generous at its worst, but Anette sued New York for $20 million. She felt she had been humiliated and was *entitled* to compensation. She was not appreciative that the police officers could have saved her and her baby from great suffering had the baby been stolen or harmed. There was no gratitude, no humility, simply entitlement. *Entitlement* uses words to argue and justify its distortions. *Endowment* relies on respect and personal responsibility for protection. Acts of kindness, consideration, resolution, reverence, and respect cannot be spun by the twisted poetry of legalese.

To heal enmity's wrath, we must heal our entitled legal system. We must stop rewarding conflict and dissent and instead hold lawyers and plaintiffs personally responsible for annoyance suits. The epidemic of entitlement must be cured before it has a chance to destroy the true purpose of law. We must diagnose the sickness before entitlement turns our rights into nothing more than damaged, crippled versions of the sacred endowments they were meant to be.

> *"Do all the good you can, by all the means you can,*
> *in all the ways you can, in all the places you can,*
> *at all the times you can, to all the people you can,*
> *as long as ever you can."*
> *– John Wesley*

CORBIN'S THOUGHTS

In an era marked by growing nihilism and narcissistic entitlement, people increasingly indulge in self-serving interests under the pretense that it is their "right" to do so. As Americans, we use the term "rights" rather broadly and often. "Rights" can refer to the inalienable human rights with which we are all endowed at birth, or it can refer to the legal rights we are bestowed as citizens of a nation. In the United States, both human and legal rights are enshrined by the U.S. Constitution, particularly the Bill of Rights and the subsequent 16 amendments. However, our notion of rights is not limited to the terms outlined in this founding document.

Over the last several centuries, our rights have been steadily elucidated and expanded through legal precedent. For most of my life, Congress has leaned on the Supreme Court to preside over this process, legislating on issues ranging from voting rights to abortion rights to LGBTQ+ rights. That is to say, bills passed by elected representatives have not settled the debates surrounding these divisive topics. Rather, the decisions have been handed down largely by federal and state judges appointed to the bench. In this way, unelected officials have come to determine the modern rights of the people according to their politically biased interpretation of the Constitution.

My intention is not to condemn the system. I simply believe that acknowledging the court's modern role as bestower of rights helps clarify exactly what rights are, where they come from, and why they dominate the American political and cultural conversation. Although human rights are inborn, legal rights are something we receive from a group or nation-state. Because these rights are granted to us, the threat looms that they can be taken away by government regulation, particularly in the name of public safety and national security. Just think of policy aimed at restricting the Second Amendment and reproductive rights. Rights are thus expressed limitations applied to a wide group to protect the welfare of the individuals who make up that group. The inverse of knowing one's limits in society is understanding one's range of freedom. Freedoms are why rights ultimately matter and must be protected at all costs.

In a post-civil rights America, freedom pertains not only to one's self-expression but also to equal access and opportunity. Currently, it would be indefensible to deny any member of society access to a public or private institution based solely on the color of their skin. That's called segregation or an "apartheid system," and it is an extreme societal temptation that must be squelched. Fortunately, our country has largely overcome this form of embodied prejudice thanks to the civil rights movement. However, discrimination can take many forms to create a two-tier system of justice. Although business owners may no longer deny patrons service based on their race, they keep the prerogative to refuse service if the customer's expressed sexual orientation renders the service in conflict with the business owner's religious beliefs.

Naturally, those types of personal details don't come up when one goes to the butcher, but it's a different story at the bakery. In 2012, a same-sex couple, Charlie Craig and David Mullins, were referred by their wedding planner to Masterpiece Cakeshop in Lakewood, Colorado, to commission a cake for their upcoming wedding reception. The owner of the bakery, Jake Phillips, declined the couple's request.[3] In accordance with his faith, Phillips viewed marriage as a sacred covenant that only existed between a man and a woman. Therefore, he argued that crafting a wedding cake for a

---

3. Bill Hutchinson, "Sex, Wedding Cake, and Controversy That Made It to the Supreme Court," *ABC News*, June 4, 2018, accessed 2024, https://abcnews.go.com/US/sex-wedding-cake-controversy-made-supreme-court/story?id=55646970.

same-sex wedding, even if it included no overt symbolism or language in the design, would violate his religious convictions.

In response, Craig and Mullins filed a complaint with the Colorado Civil Rights Commission, claiming that Masterpiece Cakeshop had violated the state's anti-discrimination laws. Although the state of Colorado initially ruled against Phillips, the case was ultimately brought before the U.S. Supreme Court. In 2018, the Supreme Court issued a controversial decision in favor of Jack Phillips that determined that the Colorado Civil Rights Commission had shown hostility towards Phillips's religious beliefs, violating his right to free exercise of religion.

The case not only exemplifies the ongoing debate between religious freedom and LGBTQ+ rights, but it also demonstrates that our interpreted freedoms are often at odds with the perceived rights of others. Whose rights matter more: those exercising their right to free speech or those demanding the right to fair and equal service? Those who defend free speech insist there should be stronger protections for religious freedoms. They believe no one should be compelled to do anything that violates their beliefs. Those who defend fair and equal treatment under the law believe no business has the right to discriminate against someone based on their involuntary attributes. They believe no one should be excluded from the group.

Individual rights naturally clash. A journalist's right to a free press conflicts with a person's right to privacy. A squatter's right to occupy conflicts with a property owner's right to force them to vacate. A mother's right to choose conflicts with an infant's right to life. Disputes over rights take on a variety of forms and are more prevalent in an environment plagued by inequality between individuals in their extremes. Feelings of narcissistic entitlement and supremacy identity may lead some to believe their rights are more important than others, but this is never the case in reality. As citizens of this country, we all should enjoy equal opportunity.

As an American, I value the rights and privileges that facilitate the full expression of my sovereignty. Because of this, I look out for the rights of my fellow Americans. It doesn't matter if I disagree with what they say or find them to be unpleasant people. As a fellow citizen, I want the law to be universally upheld and equally serve the preservation of every American's sovereignty. Why? Because it serves my best interest in the long run to preserve the right to free expression for myself and my offspring. Simply put, protecting others' rights is my responsibility.

While America is a country composed of many sovereign individuals, together, we make up one nation. That is to say, although we are not all living in the same circumstances and hold wildly disparate values, we are united as one citizenry. But what does that mean? The concept of being a proper U.S. citizen means many things to many people. Of course, as I mentioned, this status comes with certain rights under the law. However, there is another essential component to citizenship: we pay taxes. Indeed, whenever I refer to the collective "we," I'm referring to U.S. taxpayers.

We pay taxes believing that the government will responsibly spend those funds. Unfortunately, a majority of the time, that is not the case. As the national deficit continues to rise and Congress continues to raise the debt ceiling to facilitate more government spending, it must be acknowledged that we, the taxpayers, also inherit this debt.

So, when I refer to the general "we," who suffer as a direct result of foreign and domestic policy failures, government cover-ups, corruption, and political polarization, I'm not appealing to a vague sense of patriotism or nationalist exceptionalism. I'm speaking quite literally of the collective U.S. citizenry who hand over a percentage of their hard-earned money to government agencies every year and are being slighted by poor policy.

When communication breaks down in government, taxpayers suffer because policy reform stalls. Legislative failures make it more likely for communication to break down in American households because families are, one, under undue financial stress, or two, divided by ideology. Thus, it is in the best interest of every taxpayer to not only hold government officials accountable for spending failures and corruption but also to take personal accountability for participating in this highly polarized climate. It is in our own interest to de-radicalize ourselves and return to center rather than linger on opposite sides of the courtroom in our extremes, waiting for the judge to rule in our favor.

Currently, our coexistence in this country is contentious and dysfunctional. The accumulation of power, as bestowed by the courts, is more desirable to both parties than achieving any sense of meaningful or respectful lasting compromise that considers the validity of all perspectives involved. The power yielded by rights equates to political leverage. Claiming a right is equivocal to winning a political argument. The competition to win rights further entrenches us in partisanship. The wedding cake becomes the metaphorical centerpiece in an ethical debate over fairness. However, what is fair depends entirely on what people believe is within their rights, which, if not explicitly specified by the courts, is based on their perspective.

We can see the influence of strong green personality tendencies driving the actions of both sides in the legal dispute over the wedding cake. Jack

Phillips's unyielding devotion to his religious beliefs is an example of the reverence and commitment demonstrated by people with centered green personality tendencies. At the same time, Phillips's choice to exercise his right to refuse service based on his faith indicates the intolerance and dogmatism displayed by people with green personality tendencies in their extreme.

As for Charlie Craig and David Mullins, it seems the couple inadvertently stumbled into the ordeal. The two were never activists in the gay rights movement. They weren't looking for notoriety. All they wanted was a beautiful wedding cake. It's understandable that the couple felt disrespected after being denied a service that they saw as a right. In their eyes, the situation was socially unjust and qualified as discrimination. As I have said, people with green personality tendencies value fairness above all. When they are wronged, their desire for justice (and broad retaliation in their extreme) consumes them.

Craig and Mullen spent the first six years of their marriage engrossed in the court case surrounding their wedding cake. As of 2018, both were forced to "put their career and personal ambitions on hold" due to the obligations of the case.[4] While Mullins "considered himself apolitical before the incident," both he and his husband now self-identify as "lifetime activists," willing to take on the burden of pressure and attention associated with the case to make a difference. For people with green personality tendencies who crave meaning that is bigger than themselves, standing up for their beliefs is worth the sacrifice. Nevertheless, my logical blue tendencies beg me to ask, why not just find a different baker?

Personally, I would tell any baker who refused to make me a cake because of my involuntary attributes to shove their buns in their oven, and then I would hire someone else for the job. As far as I'm concerned, the baker would be the one missing out on my business. However, I acknowledge that this is an individualistic, strength-minded perspective and, during my lifetime, Italians have never been considered a historically marginalized group. From the perspective of someone who values warmth and seeks acceptance, acts of discrimination leave deep emotional wounds. When warmth-minded individuals encounter discrimination in its various forms, whether it is directed at them personally or someone

---

4. Andrea Dukakis, "After the Masterpiece Ruling, David Mullins and Charlie Craig Hope to Move On," *Colorado Public Radio*, June 11, 2018, accessed 2024, https://www.cpr.org/2018/06/11/after-the-masterpiece-ruling-david-mullins-and-charlie-craig-hope-to-move-on/.

they care about, they tend to become lifelong advocates for social justice. The lingering sense of injustice they experience calls for reform on a societal level. In their center, this means sheltering and supporting the disenfranchised by championing an expansion of their rights and entitlements.

It is my supposition that those who value warmth tend to prioritize rights, while those who value strength tend to favor its flip side, responsibility. While rights are limits placed upon a group to protect individuals, responsibilities are the limits that individuals take upon themselves to sustain the group. As Jordan B. Peterson, best-selling author and former professor of psychology at the University of Toronto, points out in his lectures, responsibilities are the duties we know we should do.[5] They are accompanied by a sense of direction and purpose, which equates to a sense of meaning. In today's world, that is the most valuable asset we can possess if we seek to curate joy in our lives.

The same cannot be said for rights. Even if we are granted rights, we are not provided any instruction as to how to meaningfully exercise them. Just because we know what we are allowed to do, it doesn't mean we know what we should do. Although our rights are extremely precious, without responsibility, they are aimless and serve no interests other than the procurement of more power.

Today, responsibility is an afterthought in the cultural or political conversation, dominated by sub-groups competing for rights. Rights are noisy and combative. Responsibility is silent and dutiful. Rights intrinsically revolve around group identity categories, such as race, ethnicity, nationality, gender, and sexual orientation. These qualities have to deal with aspects of the self that are intrinsic. Because we do not choose these characteristics, we can assume no responsibility for or take pride in possessing them.

In contrast, our responsibilities directly result from our choices and define our actions. Whereas rights are received from a group, responsibilities are self-determined and arise naturally as one develops a sustainable relationship with our surroundings. For a long time, that simply meant surviving nature. Now that human beings from different backgrounds with different beliefs all live together in highly condensed populations and engage in anonymous conversation at all times through the internet, we have to survive one another. This means developing our capacity to show respect for other people's perspectives and beliefs.

---

5. "Jordan Peterson: Rights VS Responsibility," YouTube video, 3:54, posted by *Western Civilization*, December 12, 2017, accessed 2024, https://www.youtube.com/watch?v=2md-fEK-ies.

The necessity of responsibilities long predates the introduction of rights and relates to the ancestral traditions and practices of indigenous cultures. In a short film, "Rights Versus Responsibilities: An Indigenous Perspective," posted by Films For Action, Toghestiy, one of the hereditary chiefs of the Wet'suwet'en nation, explains, "In our language, we don't have a word for rights. We have words for responsibilities."[6] This is not to say that rights are not essential in modern society. However, it is crucial that they are accompanied by responsibility.

Before nation-states and courts existed to extend and revoke legal rights, one learned responsibility by practicing stewardship of the planet and sharing harmoniously in its abundance, never taking more than necessary. The land and its fruits and the rivers and its fish were not seen as resources or commodities. In this respect, responsibility not only embodies the value of centered strength but also the conscientious heart of centered green tendencies. We do not act for ourselves; we act for those seven generations from now.

To bear the burden of responsibility is hard work. It is akin to carrying a load on behalf of others. This act of service necessitates strength and fair compensation. If one receives no credit for bearing responsibility, why bother showing up or doing your best? Compensation doesn't always have to be financial. Sometimes, respect, recognition, and appreciation are enough to make one's duty fulfilling. Regardless, the fruit of responsibility (a sense of purpose) is its own reward.

In a community, one's capacity to take on responsibility makes one admirable and desirable to be around. Responsible people are role models. In their center, those who value strength create stability and order in the lives of those who depend on them. They take pride in waking up on time every day and reporting to work. These are the essential workers upon which societal infrastructure functionally depends. They are practical, resilient, level-headed, and law-abiding. They don't worry about what could be or what may happen generations down the line. They are concerned with how to effectively and safely deal with reality and solve problems so they can put food on the table. They can't afford the time or expense of spending six years arguing over a cake out of principle.

The rise in popularity and notoriety of Jordan B. Peterson personifies responsibility's appeal to strength-minded individuals. Peterson rose to

---

6. "Rights Versus Responsibilities: An Indigenous Perspective," YouTube video, 3:15, posted by *Films For Action,* January 28, 2019, accessed 2024, https://www.youtube.com/watch?v=z40kI4qRGNM.

prominence with the publishing of his book *12 Rules for Life: An Antidote to Chaos*. Although some consider him to be a controversial figure due to his occasionally provocative rhetoric, over the last decade, he has emerged as the single most outspoken advocate for responsibility in the cultural arena. While many critique Peterson for attracting a predominantly conservative male audience, I would assert that the audience that Peterson's lessons have resonated with the most are people (specifically young men) who value strength. Based on their values, these people yearn for strategies to help them improve their effectiveness in life. Though they feel disempowered by circumstance, they are hungry to develop a sense of responsibility to ascertain meaning in a nihilistic world. I consider myself a part of this audience.

One of Peterson's 12 rules for life that particularly resonated with me was the call to pursue what is meaningful as opposed to what is expedient, swift, or easy.[7] Things that are easily accessible often hold little value. In his lectures, Peterson cites the story of Pinocchio, in which the puppet visits Pleasure Island and is slowly transformed into a donkey while enjoying the attractions and amenities. The moral of this part of the story is that having the freedom to overindulge in extreme narcissistic entitlement leads to one's corruption. The parable is still analogous today, as teenagers and adults alike make asses of themselves on the internet in the pursuit of "clout."

However, I believe the concept of expedience extends beyond hedonistic impulses. Expedience is the path of *least* responsibility. Responsibility carries a negative stigma because it is associated with consequences. When consequences become severe, they can be perceived as infringements on personal rights. In the court of law, responsibility implies legal fault. Although the prosecution and defendant maintain conflicting rights, only the losing party bears responsibility.

Responsibility is a burden. It makes life harder for ourselves but easier for others. It can be inconvenient and disruptive, but the time we invest is rewarding. More often than not, responsibility compels us to compromise our personal desires for the betterment of the collective, whether it be our family or our nation. In the famous words of John F. Kennedy in his first inaugural address: "Ask not what your country can do for you. Ask what

---

[7]. "Pinocchio and the Abandonment of Responsibility," YouTube video, 38:42, posted by *Jordan B. Peterson Clips*, October 13, 2022, accessed 2024, https://www.youtube.com/watch?v=OSiLUddcE6k.

you can do for your country."⁸ This statement speaks to the importance of assuming individual responsibility, in addition to claiming our rights, to contribute to society. The right to drive comes with the responsibility to obey traffic laws. The right to drink comes with the responsibility of not getting behind the wheel of a car. The right to vote comes with the responsibility of educating oneself on history and the issues at hand. The right to citizenship comes with the responsibility of respecting the sovereignty of other citizens and their beliefs.

It seems to me that the root of the imbalance between rights and responsibilities stems from the increased division and subsequent lack of communication between those who value strength and those who value warmth. This is an eternal struggle that supersedes our country. As populations grow and technology evolves, human rights will continue to evolve and clash in myriad forms. However, what must remain consistent is our responsibility to engage in civil dialogue over these issues and resist the temptation of entitlement and enmity to infringe upon the rights of our perceived opponents. If those who value strength and those who value warmth cannot learn from each other, the imbalance will persist. The pendulum will swing from one side to the other in a perpetual fight for power.

The only way to stop the momentum of this back-and-forth swing is to not allow ourselves to get swept up in the inertia of oscillating extremes. It requires a rare sense of restraint to remain centered despite the push and pull of politics and the culture war. This self-control equates to responsibility. We should ask ourselves, to what degree are we willing to detach from our partisan identity for the sake of collective unity and progress? Instead of categorizing people according to the immutable aspects of their group identity, we should seek to relate to them by understanding their contextual color blends. In this way, we deal more with the substance of who people actually are as individuals rather than group members.

To honor ourselves and future generations, we must forgo trifling debates over rights and focus on the crisis of meaning facing our world due to our collective irresponsibility. Rights, as valuable as they are in a free nation, do not yield any sense of meaning. Responsibility does. That is to say that developing a sense of responsibility is the antidote to a crisis of meaning.

---

8. "President John F. Kennedy Inaugural Address 'Ask Not What Your Country Can Do For You'," YouTube video, 4:31, posted by *Educational Video Group*, October 14, 2019, accessed 2024, https://www.youtube.com/watch?v=P1PbQlVMp98.

THE PERSONALITY COLOR MATRIX

The first way one can assume responsibility is by choosing to return to the center instead of regularly engaging in extreme altercations (verbal, anonymous, or otherwise) for the sake of divisiveness. When we are willing and ready to exit our extreme, defect from polarization, and unite in mutual love and acceptance, we can collaborate in our center toward mutual promise. Our first responsibility is to appreciate the gift of life and citizenship that we have been given. These are treasures on this planet that are worth preserving for ourselves and others.

Tolerance is not a right. However, it is our responsibility to embody it and choose not to unnecessarily initiate or escalate conflict for political leverage. In our interactions, we must ask ourselves, is our goal to be restorative or retributive? If the answer is the latter, those desires have likely been infected by entitlement or enmity and may be counterproductive to tolerable coexistence.

Recently, Colorado cake baker Jack Phillips once again found himself embroiled in a multi-year legal dispute that, as of the writing of this book, has yet to be resolved.[9] This time around, he is accused of discriminating against Autumn Scardina, a transgender activist attorney, who, it seems, crafted her case against Phillips prior to placing her order. Although Masterpiece Cakeshop initially agreed to honor Ms. Scardina's request to craft a pink cake with blue frosting, Jack Phillips refused after Ms. Scardina explained that the cake was going to be used to celebrate her transition from male to female. Scardina's lawyer, John McHugh, insists that Phillips and his cake shop "object to the idea of Ms. Scardina wanting a birthday cake that reflects her status as a transgender woman because they object to the existence of transgender people."

Although Phillips was victorious in his Supreme Court trial in 2018, he has lost several appeals in this new case, and it is likely the matter will once again be brought before the Supreme Court to determine. Regardless of the outcome of the case, Jack Phillips will have spent the past 12 years fighting legal battles over cakes instead of baking and decorating them. I'm sure that because of the influence of his righteous extreme green and stubborn extreme blue personality tendencies, he would insist that standing up for his beliefs has been worth the sacrifice. Nevertheless, my rational, centered blue tendencies beg me to ask, why not refrain from designing custom cakes and sell pies instead?

---

9. EWTN, "Christian Baker Loses Appeal Over Transgender Birthday Cake Case," accessed 2024, https://ewtn.co.uk/article-christian-baker-loses-appeal-over-transgender-birthday-cake-case/.

9

WHO HAS THE REAL POWER?

*"Nearly all men can stand adversity,
but if you want to test a man's character, give him power."*
– Abraham Lincoln

Entitlement craves advantage, influence, power, and control while shunning responsibility. Entitlement hates being limited or restricted in any way, but it restricts and limits everything, especially our tolerance and ability to experience peace, joy, connection, or anything positive. Let's begin this chapter by considering those who are most vulnerable to corrupted power—children.

We'll start by examining the power abuses perpetrated by Big Tech. A September 2021 article posted on commonsense.org, titled "Why We Can't Trust Facebook to Keep Kids Safe, states:

> Our research has long shown us that social media can negatively impact kids' mental health—especially for kids with depression or other mental health issues. And we've been sounding the call for years, asking social media platforms to take action to protect kids. It turns out that Facebook and Instagram have long known that Instagram is harming adolescent and teen users, and they have lied about the impacts instead of making substantive changes.

Internal research documents released by a whistleblower reveal just how much Facebook knew. Some of the findings:

- *"We make body image issues worse for one in three teen girls."*
- *"One in five teens say that Instagram makes them feel worse about themselves."*
- *Teens "often feel 'addicted' and know that what they're seeing is bad for their mental health but feel unable to stop themselves."*
- *32% of teens feel they "don't have enough friends" due to Instagram, and 22% feel "alone or lonely."*

Because Big Tech's business model depends on commanding as much consumer attention as possible, companies push content to kids they know to be psychologically addicting. An article titled "Why Section 230 Hurts Kids, and What to Do About It" addresses the issue, stating:

All the tricks of manipulative design that make Big Tech dangerous for society—autoplay, badges, and the like—put young people at the greatest risk. In the early days of the web, a New Yorker cartoon showed an image of a dog sitting in front of a desktop, and underneath was the caption, "On the Internet, nobody knows you're a dog." On today's internet, nobody cares if you're a kid.[1]

The article goes on to say:

What might kids find on YouTube? YouTube videos aimed at kids have shown all manner of violence and perversion, from Peppa Pig armed with guns and knives to sex acts with Disney characters like Elsa. The Maryland couple behind FamilyOFive, a once-popular, now-terminated YouTube channel that attracted over 175 million views, posted viral prank videos of child abuse perpetrated against their own children. Perhaps most troubling: YouTube's behavioral algorithms appear to steer children into harm's way.

---

1. Bruce Reed and James P. Steyer, "Why Section 230 Hurts Kids, and What to Do About It," *Build Back Better Act: Hearing Before the Subcommittee on Health*, 117th Cong., 1st sess., December 1, 2021, https://www.congress.gov/117/meeting/house/114268/documents/HHRG-117-IF16-20211201-SD019.pdf.

THE PERSONALITY COLOR MATRIX

An exhaustive research study funded by the European Union found hundreds of disturbing videos, with hundreds of thousands of views, aimed at children between the ages of 1 and 5. The report concludes, "Young children are not only able, but likely to encounter disturbing videos when they randomly browse the platform starting from benign videos." Kids are growing up in the darkest age of children's entertainment in American history. As technology writer James Bridle warned in 2017, "Someone ... is using YouTube to systematically frighten, traumatize, and abuse children, automatically and at scale, and it forces me to question my own beliefs about the internet, at every level."[2]

It is important to note that children are like sponges: they soak up what is around them and then release it when squeezed. If you question this fact, simply reflect on the dramatic increase in violence and sex in our middle schools and high schools in the past two decades. If kids are to develop their ability to center themselves to make the best decisions and choices in their lives, adults must take responsibility for the many ways they are affecting our children negatively.

According to an article in Allina Health, Post-Screen-Time anger and Frustration in Kids, Aditi Garg, MBBS, explains, "In multiple studies, excessive screen time has been linked to school problems, anger, aggression, frustration, depression, and other emotional problems. Over-stimulation causes kids to have poor focus and depletes their mental energy, which often leads to explosive behavior."

According to the Council of Communications and Media,

The major setting for violence in America is the home. Television programs, video and computer games, Internet content, and movies frequently show graphic acts of violence. When children view this content, it can affect them just as much as if it were a "real life" experience.

By the time children reach middle school, they may have watched as many as 8,000 murders and 100,000 other acts of virtual violence through the media.[3]

---

2. Reed and Steyer, "Why Section 230 Hurts Kids."
3. Craig A. Anderson et al., "The Influence of Media Violence on Youth," *Psychological Science in the Public Interest* 4, no. 3 (2003): 81-110, accessed October 14, 2024, https://pubmed.ncbi.nlm.nih.gov/26151870/.

In 2024, your child can immediately access images and videos of brutal bullying, beat-downs, and even murder online. These are not "movie" murders but real-life people being killed.

In September 2023, mainstream media news aired a video that showed a young man filming while his friend drove his car into a bike lane, sped up, and ran over a 64-year-old. The victim was Andreas "Andy" Probst, a retired chief of police for the city of Bell. You could hear the boys laughing while it was happening. They left his crumpled body in the road. "The worst part about it in the video is you hear that everything was intentional," Las Vegas Metropolitan Police Department Detective Lt. Jason Johansen said.

The driver can be heard asking his giggling friend, "Ready?" as he speeds up directly behind the retired cop.

"Yeah, hit his ass," the passenger tells the driver before the car plows into the retiree.

The 17-year-olds from Las Vegas were arrested and are facing murder charges. However, recent clips of them in a courtroom show their total lack of remorse and defiant disrespect for the legal system.

The same pair allegedly struck a 72-year-old man around 5:30 that same morning, leaving him with non-life-threatening injuries. Police said the teens stole at least four cars to carry out the violent spree.

Too many people will shake their heads and ask, "Why would they do such a thing?" I am here to help you understand that the root of all cruelty and evil is narcissistic entitlement. These young men felt entitled to be criminals and destroy the lives of strangers they did not even know.

Commercial television for children is rated 50 to 60 times more violent than prime-time programs for adults, and some cartoons average over 80 violent acts per hour. That is double the number of violent scenes that they will see on television or in feature films.

But what do researchers say about all of this violent influence? According to an article from the National Library of Medicine, "Desensitization to Media Violence: Links With Habitual Media Violence Exposure, Aggressive Cognitions, and Aggressive Behavior," portrayals of violence in media increase the likelihood of aggressive behavior. Studies of the effects of television violence on children and teenagers found that children become immune to horror or violence, gradually accept violence as a way to solve problems, imitate the violence they see on television, movies, and music videos, and identify with certain characters, victims, and/or victimizers. Two surveys of young males convicted of violent crimes found that 22– 34 percent had imitated crime techniques they watched on television.

Now we have the internet to train kids on how to be criminals. Research examining violence toward women found that a viewer could be emotionally desensitized toward violence perpetrated on women after viewing as few as two films with sexually degrading and violent themes.

Now let me turn your attention to *Skibidi Toilet*, a computer animated series of YouTube videos and shorts created by Alexey Gerasimov, a content creator from the country of Georgia. Produced using Source Filmmaker, the machinima series follows a fictional war between human-headed toilets and humanoid characters with electronic devices for heads.

"Skibidi" is a wacky word that references or makes fun of the absurdity of slang. Depending on the context, it can mean "cool," "dumb," or "bad." It can also just be used as a filler word. For example, one might say, "You've got that skibidi rizz," meaning "you've got crazy charisma." The word is associated with meme culture, brain rot, and absurdist humor.

Skidbidi Toilet has become so popular with young children that it is now associated with a developmental syndrome similar to severe iPad addiction.[4] Recently, parents have documented their children displaying concerning behavior after watching the show. Kids appear to become "obsessed" with Skibidi Toilet, singing and crouching in containers to imitate the meme. While that may sound cute, children with Skibidi Toilet syndrome also tend to scream and lash out in rage when they are banned or restricted from watching the videos.

The series' chief appeal to young minds, children from the ages of three to six, seems to be its blend of potty humor and absurdity that caters to their playful sensibilities. The same kind of kooky content was popular with Gen Z and millennials, too. Think of the outrageous and irreverent children's programming like *South Park* on Comedy Central in the late '90s and early 2000s and the silliness of early viral videos like Salad Fingers, Charlie The Unicorn, & Annoying Orange that shaped Gen Z's absurdist and ironic sense of humor.[5]

Are these ridiculous videos evil or good? Regardless of the answer, they appear to have effectively captivated the world's youngest minds.

---

4. Elle Hunt, "'Skibidi Toilet': How a Surreal YouTube Series about Sinister Toilets Became a Viral Hit," *The Guardian*, January 22, 2024, accessed 2024, https://www.theguardian.com/culture/2024/jan/22/skibidi-toilet-youtube-series-viral.

5. David Firth, *Salad Fingers*, YouTube video, 5:45, posted July 1, 2004, https://www.youtube.com/watch?v=M3iOROuTuMA; Jason Steele, *Charlie the Unicorn*, YouTube video, 3:46, posted November 26, 2005, https://www.youtube.com/watch?v=CsGYh8AacgY; *Annoying Orange*, "The Annoying Orange," YouTube video, 2:37, posted October 9, 2009, https://www.youtube.com/watch?v=ZN5PoW7_kdA.

Skibidi Toilet resonates particularly with Gen Alpha (those born after 2012). Members of Gen Z humorously lament that this is the first internet joke they are too old to get.

Experts believe that *Skibidi Toilet* is so addicting because the videos are short and have a mysterious narrative that draws young minds in. They provide an immersive experience, especially if you are watching them on your phone. Sometimes, they even feel like a VR game (but with more toilets). Personally, I find the crude faces coming up from the toilets to be grotesque, even disgusting, but I'm 71 and have long lost my fascination with poop, fierce violence, and explosions. However, I'm not sure if the same can be said for *Armageddon* and *Transformers* director Michael Bay. He is set to collaborate with Alexey Gerasimov on a new Skibidi Toilet cinematic universe. Are you kidding me?

TikTok and YouTube shorts are feeding Gen Z and Gen Alpha children with millions of hours of content every day. These media platforms are shortening attention spans with their 15- to 60-second videos. What's even more unique about these videos is their niche approach, taking advantage of the applications' algorithms to direct viewers to them.

More recently, a new phenomenon has emerged, significantly impacting the academic landscape for Gen Z students. Dubbed "brain rot," this trend describes an obsessive engagement with digital media. As predicted, "brain rot" often negatively affects educational pursuits and intellectual growth. The term brain rot is frequently used in the context of Gen Alpha's digital habits, with critics arguing that this generation is excessively immersed in online culture.[6] According to a Newport Institute article: *Brain Rot: The Impact on Young Adult Mental Health*:

> *Brain rot, sometimes written as one word, "brainrot," is a state of mental fogginess and cognitive decline that results from excessive screen engagement. Is brainrot real? It's not a medically recognized condition, but it is a real phenomenon.*
>
> *When we spend hours surfing and scrolling, we consume huge quantities of meaningless data, negative news, and perfectly retouched photos of friends and celebrities that make us feel inadequate. Trying to absorb and cope with massive amounts of content creates mental fatigue. And that can*

---

6. "Brain Rot," *Wikipedia*, last modified August 3, 2023, https://en.wikipedia.org/wiki/Brain_rot.

THE PERSONALITY COLOR MATRIX

lead to a drop in motivation, focus, productivity, and energy over time, especially in young people.[7]

For me, brain rot language is complete gibberish. Honestly, I believe anyone over the age of 18 who was forced to listen to it would be confused. However, Corbin insists this is "cap."

To define brain rot in more psychological terms, it's essentially a state of cognitive overload and distraction. Children are constantly bombarded with short, highly engaging content that provides immediate gratification, like dopamine hits, but lacks intellectual depth. This can lead to a reduced attention span, as well as an upward spike in disinterest when it comes to engaging in or completing academic tasks. In short, this suggests that brain rot leads to a deterioration in attention spans, memory, critical thinking, and problem-solving skills. Just what every child needs, right? Holy night, of course not.

So, what should we do? First, do all you can to ensure that this Skibidi Toilet franchise gets flushed. If we, as parents, grandparents, and citizens, are unhappy with messages or values supported by particular products, we don't need to argue. We don't need to rage. We need to come together quietly and forcefully and simply put our money where our values are. We must have the courage to stand up to, with, and for our children. We need to carefully explain why we refuse to support messages that are devoid of decency, heart, or benefit.

Corbin is now 36, but when he was just ten years old, his father purchased him a *South Park* video game without consulting me. His dad had no idea of what the game was all about. He just knew that Corbin wanted it badly. I happened to be with my son when he opened it and played it for the first time. His face was flushed, and he was obviously uncomfortable and embarrassed at the thought that I was hearing the language and seeing the images that he knew would offend my sensibilities and values. I told him that we had to talk about the game.

"You can't take away a Christmas present from Dad!" he exclaimed.

"I will not take your game without your permission," I replied, "but we must have a serious conversation before you can play it again."

"Okay," he said, turning off the television.

"When you were born, it was one of the happiest days of my life," I

---

[7]. Newport Institute, "Brain Rot: The Impact on Young Adult Mental Health," Newport Institute, accessed October 14, 2024, https://www.newportinstitute.com/resources/co-occurring-disorders/brain-rot/.

said. "I promised myself that I would love you and always, no matter how difficult it was, put your best interest in front of everything else. I am proud to say that I have done that. I have loved you more each day, and I am proud and appreciative of the fact that I was given the privilege of being your mother. So, now I must ask you something."

"What?" He braced for the question.

"If you had a ten-year-old son that you loved with all of your heart, would you let him play this game with this language and this content?"

His hands clasped tightly around the game. "You can't take away my game."

"I gave you my word," I reminded him. "But I must ask again. If you had a ten-year-old son that you loved with all of your heart, would you let him play this game?"

His eyes started to tear. He lowered his head. "Honestly..." He tilted his head down as if to muffle the words into his collar, "No."

"If you can love an unborn son that much, how can you possibly expect me to love a son that I have cared for every day for ten years any less?"

"That's not fair."

"No, I don't think it is fair that companies can market games to ten-year-old boys that are inappropriate for their hearts and minds. You are right. It's not fair."

"That's not what I mean, and you know it."

"You decide," I said. "I promised that I wouldn't take your game unless you gave it to me."

He pouted as he threw the game to me. "If I give up this game, can I get a different one that you approve of?"

"Absolutely. I want you to own and enjoy wonderful games. But because I love you, I must do what I know in my heart is right for you in the long run."

We ended up trading in the *South Park* game for a wonderful racing game that he greatly enjoyed.

You may not agree with the stance I took in this story. I completely understand and respect that. But the point of this example is not to sway you to my way of thinking. The point is that whatever you care about and value, you need to continue to fight for your children. Make sure your children are introduced to your values and not simply programmed by the media and programming that surrounds them.

It is hard to teach our children to refuse the garbage that is out there. It's everywhere! Parenting is not for the faint of heart. It is natural for our children to be curious and to want to do what others think is cool, or skibidi (remember, this stupid word can mean cool, bad, and dumb). But with consistent love, expressed through honest, open dialogues about values, we can lead our children in directions that are healthier for their hearts and minds.

Of course, I am biased and believe that the more we understand our personality color tendencies, especially those of our children, the better we can nurture and support one another. Battles for control seldom, if ever, work because they are not centered. Uncentered communication always comes from an entitled bias. Learn about personality color tendencies, both yours and your children's. Then arm your children with the information they need to better understand themselves and others.

When my youngest son, Corbin, turned seven, the only thing that he wanted for his birthday was a dog. We looked everywhere—shelters, pet stores, and in the newspaper. We must have looked at 30 dogs before he chose a little white ball of fur that he named Ozzie. He loved his puppy.

We had only owned Ozzie for a couple of months when, one day, I stepped into the garage to find Corbin holding the puppy over his head. The next thing I knew, he dropped the puppy onto the cement floor. This was completely out of character for my son. He had always been a sweet and gentle person, so I was stunned by what I witnessed. I rushed to the puppy to make sure that it was okay. Once I knew that the puppy was fine, I knelt in front of my son, grabbed him by the shoulders, looked into his eyes, and, with anger and frustration, asked, "What in the world were you thinking?"

His eyes glazed over and began to tear up. "I… I… I wasn't thinking," he stammered. "I… I just finished watching B… Bart Simpson. He was throwing a cat off the roof and out of the car window. He said that cats always land on their feet, and I just wanted to see if dogs always land on their feet, too. I'm sorry. I'm sorry." With that, he began to sob.

I told him that I was sorry, too. He had made a terrible choice that day, but I had failed in my job of teaching and loving him. "From now on, we will watch television together," I promised, "and when you have questions, you can ask me." I made a vow that day to not allow Bart Simpson to educate my son. We began watching television that would educate and inform Corbin in ways that I believed would benefit his life.

One night, we were watching a man named Les Brown. (You can buy his tapes from Nightingale Conant, and I would highly recommend them for you and your children). He was speaking in a powerful, booming voice as he looked at his audience and said, "Do you know what I see when I look into your eyes? I see greatness!"

My son looked at me and asked, "Mommy, what do you see when you look into my eyes?"

I said, "Oh, honey, I see greatness." That became our mantra. Every morning, when he came down for breakfast, I would say, "Hey, Corbin, do you know what I see when I look into your eyes?"

He would smile and say, "Yeah, Mom, greatness."

"Yes," I would say, "and what great thing are you going to do today?" It is not enough to tell children that they are great. We must expect their actions to prove their greatness.

A couple of months later, Ozzie escaped his protective gates and, on his way down the hall, kidnapped a shoulder pad that was in a pile of laundry. Corbin took after the puppy, and I took after Corbin. After the garage incident, I had been watching Corbin's interactions with the dog more closely. Corbin, unaware that I had followed him, chased the puppy into a large closet.

"No, no, Ozzie. You can't eat my mom's shoulder pad," he said as he wrestled the shoulder pad out of the puppy's mouth.

After putting the shoulder pad out of harm's way, he knelt and put his hands on each side of the puppy's face. Looking deep into the puppy's dark brown eyes, he said, "Ozzie, do you know what I see when I look into your eyes? I see greatness, and I expect you to behave as a great dog would." With that, Corbin picked up the puppy, kissed him on the forehead, and carried him gently back to his protective gated area.

> *"Our character is basically a composite of our habits. Because they are consistent, often unconscious patterns, they constantly, daily, express our character."*
> – Stephen Covey

Our children, like each of us, can only give back the values and the learning that they are given. Whatever we focus on the longest becomes the strongest. What input is determining your life and the lives of those you love? How do we teach ourselves and those we love to make choices that are centered, compassionate, and fulfilling? I believe we can use what I call "the four-wins philosophy." Most people have heard of Stephen Covey's "win-win" philosophy from his book *The 7 Habits of Highly Effective People*. Covey believed that the fourth habit of highly effective people was making choices from a win-win perspective. "Win-win requires that we be both high in courage and high in consideration, that we approach others with generosity and a sense of partnership. When we do that—

when we demonstrate our investment in their interests and successfully advocate for our own needs—we build stronger, more trusting relationships." I also believe that, but I like to take the win-win concept a bit further. I believe that adding a couple of wins can strengthen the integrity, courage, and consideration of any choice. Most of us have witnessed choices made by two people that are wins for them, their company, their greed, but if we pull out and look at some of these choices, we can find that others suffer, the planet suffers, or there can ultimately be negative outcomes. But if we add two wins, we can ensure you win, I win, friends, family, strangers benefit. But finally I make all decisions with the fourth win in mind. If I make this choice considering the questions, "Will God find it edifying? Will it be in alignment with love, integrity, and compassion?" that fourth win is always a centered win for everyone.

> "Imagine what you could accomplish if you could get yourself
> to follow through on your best intentions no matter what."
> – Rory Vaden
> *Take the Stairs*

What must be done is simple, but it certainly is not easy. The real power is within each of us. We cannot legislate values. We must choose to speak them, model them, and, with honor and dedication, live them. It will take *centered*, disciplined effort and conviction from each of us. You must take better care of what the media, social media, and even teachers are feeding children's minds. Are our children's centers being fed loving, forgiving, kind, empathetic, and understanding principles that will fortify them as partners and parents in the future? If not, you must take a stand to devotedly teach them centered principles that can help protect them.

> "We are divinely created spiritual beings placed on earth for the
> purpose of creating the good, the true, and the beautiful.
> This goal, when embraced by the human heart,
> is a compelling force that motivates us to higher heights
> than any contest or economic stimulus
> could ever come close to matching.
> There are within each of us God-given talents
> that do not respond to market pressure yet spring
> to life in the presence of honor and respect."
> – Marianne Williamson
> *The Healing of America*

CORBIN'S THOUGHTS

When we ask ourselves, *Who has the real power?* we must also ask, *Who and what are we giving our power away to?* and *How aware are we that this energetic transaction is even happening?* More often than not, in our society, the answer to these questions is fear. Fear takes on many forms, but its essence remains the grand architect of deception that fuels our individual and collective suffering.

Fear is a natural human condition that can be necessary for our survival. Fear tells us to get out of the way of oncoming traffic or avoid someone with a weapon. In the short term, fear is an instinctive reaction to conflict that can actually be constructive and even life-saving. However, when sustained over a longer period, fear becomes a programmed mindset that perpetuates conflict, entitlement, and enmity, all of which are destructive forces.

In this way, fear stands in direct opposition to love on the spectrum of human choice. Just as darkness is the absence of light, fear is the absence of love. At all times, we can choose to proceed towards love or withdraw from it. In this binary, love is the constant, and fear is the variable. When it comes to sculpting our world in a more heavenly manner, the transformation we desire can only be brought about by love. Fear serves no role and has no place.

The media we consume tells us that there is reason to fear, but is there? By all appearances, our material world is dualistic. Our planet is literally divided by day and night, life and death, cold and hot, land and sea, predator and prey. These are just a few examples of the natural binaries we observe.

Over millennia, humans have constructed our civilization to reflect the duality we witness in nature. We tell stories of good and evil, light and dark, death and rebirth. In the political and cultural realm, we pick sides by declaring allegiance to one of two parties and wage war against the opposition. In the modern era, the polarization is exacerbated by government theater, media partisanship, and predatory technology. Rather than attempt to understand and learn from our rivals, we are all too eager to condemn them as "bad" in an effort to establish ourselves as righteous defenders of "good." These labels may carry weight and legitimacy in our minds and among our social circles, but they are hardly universal truths. They are perspectives.

Our fears stem from our perceptions and the social narratives that arise from them. In moments of immediate threat, fear can be a useful ally, but if the danger we feel is not physical or implicit, our fears are not always rational or concrete. More often than not, they are extreme reactions that should not be trusted. Fears play on our biases and our predispositions to suspect the worst.

When I was in the sixth grade, my brother came home from college to visit my family. While I was still at school, he happened to be in my room, searching my drawers for a video game that I had borrowed. As he was digging through my desk, he stumbled upon a conspicuous can of whipped cream. My brother immediately confiscated what he suspected to be contraband. Based on his experience, he feared I was using whippets, inhaling the nitrous oxide in the whipped cream canister to get high. When I returned home from school, he confronted me in my room.

"What was this doing in your desk drawer?" he asked, throwing the whipped cream canister at my chest.

I frowned and set down the can to cover my face in shame. "I know. I've been bad. I have a problem."

My brother shook his head. "This is serious, Corb. I'm only saying something because I care about you."

"I know," I groaned. "I just can't resist. I'm weak."

"You're not weak, but you're definitely too young to be messing around with drugs."

"Drugs?" I shouted in indignation, leaping back from the canister of whipped cream as if it were a stick of dynamite. "I didn't do any drugs!" As a recent graduate of the D.A.R.E. program, I was offended by the accusation.

"Then how do you explain this?"

"Whipped cream is a low-carb snack," I explained, fixing my hands on my hips. "I've been keeping it in my drawer to cheat on my diet."

"Oh..." My brother froze. "I was afraid something else might be going on."

"What did you think was happening?" I asked, raising my eyebrow in suspicion.

"Nothing," my brother answered awkwardly, backing away. "Forget it." He quickly turned to leave the room.

"I don't understand!" I shouted after him. "Can you get high from whipped cream?"

This humorous misunderstanding is an example of the way we sometimes allow our fears to get the better of us, especially when it comes to protecting our loved ones. That is not to say that we do not also intervene to shelter those we care about in the name of love. Looking back, that is how I view my mother's choice to confiscate my *South Park* game. Although she feared that the game's profane language and crude obscenities would be a negative influence on my vocabulary and behavior, she ultimately replaced the game out of love and a desire to preserve my innocence.

In that instance, I must agree with her parenting decision. Had I been exposed to the game, it's likely that I would have started cursing and responding with attitude and disrespect like a kid from *South Park*. Considering I was already a smart-ass, it would be an easy character for me to imitate.

I believe now, as I admitted then, that the material in the game was not age-appropriate. To be honest, it wasn't the substance of the game but the forbidden nature of it that made it so desirable to my pre-adolescent mind. However, compared to *Deadpool & Wolverine* and modern *Mortal Kombat* fatalities, the objectionable content in the game seems rather tame, which only goes to show how far the envelope has been pushed by shock entertainment. That being said, the covenants my mother and I entered into regarding my video game usage did not end at *South Park*.

Following the 1999 Columbine shootings, many news outlets reported a correlation between the rise in school shootings and the introduction of violent video games to the market. Because it was revealed that the Columbine shooters enjoyed playing first-person shooter games like *Doom* and *Quake*, researchers investigated if engaging in simulated gun violence inspired young men to commit mass murder in real life. When my mother learned about the looming threat of first-person shooter games, she approached me after school and asked me if I owned any.

"Only one," I replied with a gulp.

"What is it?" she asked.

"Come on, Mom. They can't all be racing games."

"What is the shooting game called?"

"*Goldeneye*," I stuttered, overcome by a flood of apprehension. I knew my mother was going to ask me to give up the game. If you are a child of the '90s, you understand the prize that was at stake.

"Do you kill people in this game?"

"I mean… yeah," I admitted, rubbing my neck, "but only bad guys. It's a James Bond game. We saw the movie."

"What kind of weapons do you use?"

"All kinds," I answered, trying desperately to form a response that didn't include the word "gun." "You can lay remote mines. There's spy gadgets, lasers, and rocket launchers—"

THE PERSONALITY COLOR MATRIX

"So, guns?"

"Mom, please don't take away *Goldeneye*!" I pleaded on my knees, on the verge of a meltdown. "You don't understand. It's all my friends and I play. It's the best game on the Nintendo 64."

"It doesn't matter how popular *Goldeneye* is. I don't think you should be playing any games with guns where you shoot people. If you had a son who was your age, would you let him play *Goldeneye*?"

"Absolutely," I said without hesitation. (I wasn't about to fumble on this play a second time). "This isn't a bad influence like the *South Park* game. There's no cursing. You don't pee on snowballs and throw them at people."

"No, instead, you shoot them with guns. That isn't any better, Corbin."

"But *Moooom*," I groaned, dragging out her name just like Eric Cartman. "I understand how playing a *South Park* game could make me rude and act out, but it's not like playing a James Bond game is going to make me kill people. That's crazy! *Goldeneye* was the game of the year last year. It's a piece of history! I'll do anything you say. Just please, please, please let me keep it."

My mother paused in silent deliberation. I could see that she was conflicted. Although the yellow part of her personality desired strongly to shelter and protect me from bad influences, the green part of her personality could understand that it would be unfair to simply take the game away from me. "Can you play this game without using guns?"

My face lit up with hope. "Yes. Why, yes! You can."

My mother nodded toward the game room. "Show me."

After blowing into my Nintendo 64 cartridge as if making a wish over a birthday cake, I inserted the game into the console and turned it on. I pressed the start button hastily to skip the intro animation, where James Bond shoots the camera, and a curtain of blood descends over the lens. I knew my mother wouldn't react well to the sight.

When the first level started, my character raised a polygonal pistol by default, at which point, my mother threw me a sideways glance. "Wait!" I pressed a button to un-equip the gun. Once I was disarmed, every time I pushed the trigger button, my character swiped the air in a flailing karate chop. Running up to a lone guard patrolling the dam, I struck the enemy repeatedly in the neck to knock him down. "See!" I waved to the screen as if there was nothing to worry about. "No guns."

"If you give me your word that you won't use any guns, and that goes for lasers and rocket launchers, then you can keep the game."

"Great!" I exclaimed, relieved to strike a compromise. My sense of satisfaction was short-lived. The agreement I had entered rendered the game essentially unplayable beyond the first stage. Unsurprisingly, only being able to charge and judo-chop my enemies made me a very ineffective secret agent. Although I could manage to down a guard or two at the beginning of a harder level, I could never complete one. Nevertheless, I honored the pact that I had made with my mother (even though it was absurd) until the game was no longer relevant.

The next time that my friends came over to my house to play *Goldeneye*, everyone seemed perplexed when I came running at them, senselessly karate chopping the air. Every time I rushed them, they dispatched me with ease.

"Corbin, what is going on, dude? You're just running into my bullets."

"My mom said I can't use any guns when I play *Goldeneye*. Technically, I think I'm allowed to use a knife, though."

"Wait," said one of my friends with a laugh. "So, you can only kill people with your hands or with a knife? Somehow, that seems even more brutal."

My mother's concern regarding my *Goldeneye* game was not too dissimilar from my brother's outrage when he found the whipped cream can in my desk. Of course, my mother's fear that violent video games might be linked to aggressive behavior wasn't totally ungrounded, but the abundance of studies conducted since 1999 have found no evidence that violent video games and other media inspire individuals to replicate gun violence in real life. That's not to say there isn't any evidence, but it hasn't been conclusive. Nevertheless, video games are still blamed for mass violence.

That being said, video games can be harmful to development if played in excess, just as most good things become destructive when done to the extreme. For one thing, video games are distracting and consuming, like any other vice to which we surrender our time, money, energy, and power. Studies have shown a link between playing violent video games and increased levels of aggression, but this should come as no surprise to anyone who has seen a gamer scream in frustration after losing.

When I was seven, my mother had to take away my Sega Game Gear after I began convulsing in a crying fit because I couldn't beat the final level of my *Lion King* game. What we witness during such freakouts are not expressions of hate but perfectionistic blue, ultra-competitive red, and volatile orange personality tendencies in their raging extremes. While these types of behaviors should hardly be encouraged, broken controllers and keyboards usually bear the brunt of this form of aggression, not innocent people.

While consuming violent content doesn't necessarily make us act out violence, it can make us more callous to the cruelty we encounter in the real world. This is of particular concern to me as I believe we have all grown too complacent to the scenes of violence that are fed to us through our screens. Murder, war, and genocide are unacceptable crimes against humanity. They should not be something we simply swipe past on our quest for dopamine. When will we reckon with the poly-crisis facing our civilization and choose to curb concerning societal trends instead of retreating to our vices?

In my opinion, desensitization is the true threat posed by any type of violent media, whether it be news or entertainment. A diet that is dense with violence feeds a narrative that our world is more threatening and divided than it actually is.[8] In the 1970s, Dr. George Gerbner coined the term "mean world syndrome" to describe this phenomenon as he researched the effect of violent media on the worldview of human beings. Because scenes of abuse in popular entertainment constantly bombard us, we are conditioned to accept war and oppression as regrettable but unpreventable "norms" of human behavior. In response to the cruelty and injustice we ingest on a daily basis, we develop a cognitive bias that makes us more suspicious, paranoid, and pessimistic about our world and society. In this way, the material we fill our minds with is literally toxic because fear is poison.

The constant depictions of crises that circulate through films, social media, and news are so overblown, and the systems that distribute them are so corrupt and consolidated that we feel that it's impossible to change course. We are embedded in a system. In addition, the more we are exposed to negative stimuli, the more we come to expect it. In our anticipation of more bad news, we become vulnerable to spreading misinformation and falling victim to predatory algorithms and sensational outrages that play off of our cognitive bias.

Manipulation is rampant in the political arena. Both sides are guilty. As misinformation spreads, the search for "truth" becomes an obfuscated and futile venture. With the advent of AI image-manipulation software and

---

8. "How Society Is Making Us More Scared Than Ever," YouTube video, 10:41, posted by *Aperture*, January 6, 2023, accessed 14, 2024, https://www.youtube.com/watch?v=9lz3DfOXQ4c.

deep-fake technology, it is becoming increasingly difficult for internet spectators to distinguish between fact and fiction, truth and deception.

Interestingly, the veracity of our fears matters little when it comes to how much they affect us. Dr. Gerber's research concluded that it doesn't matter whether we know the content we are consuming is factual, like a news report, or fictional, like a movie; the effect is the same.[9] Regardless of whether there is any validity to news reports that first-person shooter games inspire gun violence, the president colluded with Russia, and America is on the verge of a second civil war, the fear of these notions lingers. We remain suspicious of others as a divide slowly widens between ourselves and the world. The more desensitized we become, the more disconnected we feel from our fellow citizens, the story of our country, and meaning in general. The resulting isolation fuels depression and extremism.

I believe that the violent and offensive media we engage with is less the root of our social distress and more a part of the subconscious conditioning that gradually wears down our resistance to cruel injustice until we accept violence as an invariable condition of a dualistic human existence. Perhaps conflict is inevitable, but it is within love's power to resolve the disputes that arise from judgments and fear. The question is, how do we embody love instead of fear? The answer is simple: we choose.

In 1999, my mother and I bought two tickets to see *The Matrix* the weekend that it opened. At the time, neither of us had read reviews of the film or knew anything about the plot. We were simply in the mood for a Sunday movie and big fans of Keanu Reeves. My mother and I have always shared a common love and enthusiasm for cinema (and popcorn). However, looking back, I am convinced that if she had seen the trailer or knew anything about the gun violence in the film, she would have never taken me to see it. Although she was strict about what media I consumed, occasionally, she would allow me to tag along with her to an R-rated movie.

That being said, my mother was notorious for walking out of films that she found distasteful, disturbing, or unsuitable for my eyes. For example, in 1996, when *Black Mask* was released, starring Jet Li in his first leading role after his captivating debut in *Lethal Weapon 4*, my mother took me to the theater on a whim to see the film. To her horror, the fighting was far more gruesome than the average Jackie Chan films our family was used to. After a tank rolled over a soldier's legs, she promptly pulled me out of the

---

9. "How Society Is Making Us More Scared Than Ever."

theater ten minutes into the movie. Rather than go home, we settled in a neighboring theater to watch *Notting Hill*. Although I have nothing against Julia Roberts's romantic comedies, I had my hopes set on watching spectacular fight choreography. To my disappointment, Hugh Grant did not seem to know karate.

I say all of this to explain why, as I watched *The Matrix* with my mom, I half-expected her to get up at any second and pull me out of the movie. To my surprise, she was as captivated and impacted by the story as I was. We both share strong green color tendencies and are intrigued and interested in the interrelatedness and meaning of things. The philosophical questions posed by *The Matrix* resonated with us so deeply that we remained in our seats after the credits rolled, realizing we had both just witnessed something very special. We didn't get up to leave until the lights turned on and the movie theater attendants began to collect trash and sweep popcorn off the floor.

Exiting the theater, we found ourselves inspired and profoundly impacted by the themes and visual storytelling. My eleven-year-old mind had never witnessed such spectacular special effects and elaborate fight choreography. I also had never imagined that reality as I understood and experienced it could be a simulation, like a waking dream constructed of intricate code. To this day, I contend that despite having lackluster sequels, the original movie is a cinematic landmark and is my favorite film.

My mother and I spent the whole car ride home discussing our respective interpretations of the film. "What do you think was the key to Neo unlocking his full potential?" she asked.

"Belief," I answered in the passenger seat. "Like Morpheus said, he had to believe that he was the One in order to be the One."

"You're right, but it's also deeper than that. What did Neo believe in? What was it that gave him the strength to control the Matrix and bend it to his will?"

I shrugged. "By the end, he could see everything was code. He had a deeper understanding of reality."

"What gave Neo that ability?"

"Trinity told him that she loved him."

"That's it!" My mother patted the steering wheel. "Love was what changed everything. Love resurrected Neo. It empowered him. When the agents shot at him, he stopped the bullets with love. He simply refused to be hurt by the assault and took away all of its power with his mind. He didn't even send the bullets back at the bad guys. He just let them all drop at his feet. That is how you deal with negativity. You simply say, 'No,' and protect yourself. There doesn't need to be retaliation when you are operating on that level."

"Well, he did destroy Agent Smith," I reminded her.

"Yes, but how did he do it? Did he shoot the bad guy like the bad guy shot him?"

"No, Neo charged Agent Smith and jumped inside of him. They became one briefly until Neo burst out of Agent Smith."

"And what did that look like?"

"Like what I imagine God looks like," I said. "An explosion of bright, heavenly light."

My mother nodded. "Darkness cannot drive out darkness. Only light can do that. Hate cannot drive out hate. Only love can do that," she said, quoting her hero, Martin Luther King Jr. "Thanks to Trinity, Neo chose love. That choice made him unstoppable in overcoming the fear in his path. With love, he could see he was one with the world. With love, he could effortlessly disarm his opponents. He could anticipate and dodge their attacks with one arm behind his back. At a certain point, he didn't even have to fight anymore. He simply was the light. At that point, the moment he integrated with the darkness, the darkness ceased to be, and the other bad guys retreated like shadows from the light. The enemy is powerless against love. When we choose love, there is no limit to the possibilities we can create. That is the ultimate power, and it's accessible to everyone. Anyone can be *the* One."

That conversation planted a seed in my subconscious that eventually grew into my personal interpretation of reality. Just as the Matrix is constructed from binary code, our dualistic reality consists of two opposing alternatives: love and fear. Fear creates conflict. Love creates unity. Love ends conflict because it bridges the divide and embraces differences instead of allowing them to separate and divide us. To respond with fear is to fail to see yourself as interwoven in the code or fabric of reality. The fact that you are not separate from your surroundings means that you have nothing to fear. All is one.

As our consciousness rises, We come to see our outside world as an extension of our inner body. In *The Book: On the Taboo Against Knowing Who You Are*, the popular Eastern philosopher Alan Watts writes, "The skin is always considered as a wall, barrier, or boundary which definitively separates oneself from the world– despite the fact that it is covered with pores breathing air and with nerve-ends relaying information. The skin informs us just as much as it outforms; it is as much a bridge as a barrier. Nevertheless, it is our firm conviction that beyond this "wall of flesh" lies an alien world only slightly concerned with us, so that much energy is required to command or attract its attention, or to change its behavior. It was there before we were born, and it will continue after we die."[10] In essence, the separation is purely mental and a construct of the individual experience. However, we tend to imagine ourselves like birds nesting in the tree of life, able to fly free from the branches at will, rather than fruit growing from a common tree. If we could collectively see that we share a single trunk, a common origin, perhaps we could remember who we are and reconsider the power we give to fear.

Is there any good reason to fear ourselves? Although duality would lead us to believe there are opposing sides to the coin, we must remember that from a three-dimensional perspective, both faces belong to one coin. It simply depends on which dimension you observe the object from. This speaks to the underlying unity that binds strength and warmth (even in their extreme) despite their contrasting ideological values. To put it simply, we are not the same, but we are one.

The kind of vision that can see the big picture and recognize the whole, despite the illusion of opposing sides, is associated with strong, centered green personality tendencies. As I mentioned, this is a quality that my mother and I share, and it is why *The Matrix* spoke to us both with such profound meaning upon our first viewing. In a centered green headspace, we focused on the inspirational themes of free will, personal awakening, and the transformative power of love.

It was a highly romanticized interpretation, considering the movie would soon come under tremendous fire when tragedy befell Columbine High School less than a month after its release. At the time, political and social commentators attributed the massacre to the effect that consuming violent media had on the minds of young people. The school shooters had worn black trench coats reminiscent of characters from *The Matrix*, causing concerned parents to wonder if the intense gun violence portrayed in the film had inspired the children to bring guns to school to terrorize and execute their peers.

As you can imagine, my mother was mortified by the news of the Columbine massacre. In a green extreme, she sought emotional support from her sister, who mentioned that *The Matrix* may have inspired the attacks. The idea confused my mother, considering she and I had both loved the film and found it so uplifting. After hearing that my mother had

---

10. Alan Watts, *The Book: On the Taboo Against Knowing Who You Are* (New York: Pantheon, 1966), 59.

taken me to see the film, my aunt was outraged. She could not comprehend how my mother would refuse to let her children play with toy guns yet take them to see an R-rated movie filled with gun violence. My aunt insisted that *The Matrix* was poison. It was the exact type of desensitizing, graphic, corruptive media that my mother so vehemently opposed.

My mother insisted that she and my aunt had seen two different movies. My aunt invited my mother to go with her to the dollar movie theater to see the film again, intent on proving how harmful it was. Her mission was successful. The second time my mother watched *The Matrix* through the extreme red-purple lens of my aunt, a perspective centered around censorship, she could not see past the excessive gun violence. Rather than being swept away by the story, she couldn't wait to get out of the theater. She regretted ever allowing her 11-year-old child to be influenced by such graphic material.

She expressed her regret to me after I got home from school the following day. "I am so sorry for taking you to see *The Matrix*. Oh, what a terrible mistake!"

"What are you talking about?" I blurted out. "It was incredible! We loved it!"

"It was way too violent!" my mother insisted. "I don't ever want you watching it again."

"Woah, woah, woah," I said as if trying to calm a spooked horse. "It's a movie, Mom. There's nothing to be afraid of. Where is this coming from? What changed?"

"What changed is that I went to see the movie again with your aunt yesterday, and I was appalled by all the guns and the killing. I'm shocked I didn't see it the first time."

"What about the love?" I asked.

She paused. "What do you mean?

"The first time we saw the movie, you kept talking about how Neo was revived by the power of love. Did you see any love this time?"

She shook her head. "None."

"Were you looking for it?"

"No," she confessed. "I was looking for the violence."

"No wonder that's what you saw." I held my mom's hand. "Don't let other people's words and projections subtract from the beautiful experience we shared. We saw good. We saw light. We saw God. That is how I will always choose to see it."

My mother's eyes misted. At that moment, she returned to her center and realized there was nothing to fear. Knowing I had chosen to focus on the positive, she chose to do the same. Twenty-five years later, *The Matrix* remains a film we both cherish.

Awakening to The Personality Color Matrix is not easy. It requires unplugging from fear and choosing understanding and love instead. I would like to stress that loving one another does not mean agreeing on every issue or even getting along. It means cooperating in earnest toward the interest of equanimity and human progress. Love means caring enough to invest the time and energy to communicate with the goal of mutual understanding rather than block or censor dissent. It means taking a step toward the person we are arguing with, despite our differences, embracing them, and joining as one, dispelling fear in the process. To withdraw from love is to proceed toward fear in the search for some ulterior "truth" to replace that which we already are: love.

Fear is born from our extremes, so it is naturally divisive. It stifles communication, cooperation, and friendship. However, it is natural and, to an extent, involuntary. The objective is not to eliminate fear. The goal is to not allow ourselves to be manipulated or distracted by it. In this way, we reclaim our power. That means more than putting away our phones at the dinner table or turning off the news during a conversation in the living room. It means not exploiting anonymity and a lack of consequences to spread hate in petty internet squabbles. It means refraining from leaving scathing comments on our loved ones' social media accounts, stopping the metaphorical bullets mid-air, letting them fall harmlessly to the floor, and making the choice to proceed toward love even in the face of oppressive forces. It is time to take back our agency. It is time to choose love and become the One our relationships need.

> *"I can't tell you how to get there,*
> *but I know if you can free your mind,*
> *You'll find a way."*
> – Lana Wachowski,
> *The Matrix* screenplay

10

IN CONCLUSION: YOU CHOOSE

*All of the data, statistics, and behavior patterns
of our past or present may be shared as knowledge.
Wisdom, on the other hand, is how we live our knowledge."*
– Gregg Braden

When I was young, my father used to say, "Remember Dawn, it is *what* you know that matters most." Although he was forced to quit school in the seventh grade and go to work, he was strongly influenced by the blue personality tendencies of his color blend and greatly valued learning. He had great respect for the human brain and believed we should use it.

In my teens and early 20s, I began to believe it was *who* I knew that mattered most, influenced by my highly sociable orange personality tendencies. After all, I believed that knowing the right people could be fun and definitely have its advantages. My next flash of inspiration was realizing the importance of gaining insight into myself and others, inspired by my matured green personality tendencies, which continue to play a critical role in my legacy of work. As I continued to grow in wisdom, I began to understand that it is not just what we know (blue personality influence), who we know (orange personality influence), or even if we know ourselves (green personality influence) and feel we understand others (yellow personality influence) that form this thing called wisdom. I was missing two vital strength components of red and purple influence. I needed to add the *plan* and *do* the pieces necessary to implement wisdom. I realized that it is the plan or roadmap we create for our lives, as well as what we choose to courageously *do* with that knowledge and understanding, that truly matters. Unless we combine the strength and warmth, the mind and the heart, how can we use what we know and understand to bring more peace and joy to ourselves and others?

Although I believe that the opportunities before us are unlimited, I also believe that our destiny is shaped by two major mind/heart choices.

1) **Reactionary extreme choices.** When you put your energies and attention toward things you fear and despise, you fuel and strengthen them. Like Agent Smith, the rouge destructive virus in *The Matrix* sequels, your extremes multiply your challenges, anger, and hostility. They move you toward bitterness and misery and multiply more of what you do *not* want. Creating from your extremes, whether consciously or unconsciously, will lead to outcomes that devastate and disappoint you.

2) **Conscious centered choices.** Your centered choices and the actions they inspire nurture love and understanding. By turning your focus toward centered respect, compassion, kindness, appreciation, helpfulness, and excellence, you multiply more of what the world needs to thrive. Conscious, centered choices based on awareness require dedication, discipline, and focus, while behaving out of our extremes requires nothing but reacting on impulse.

> *"Each moment is a choice.*
> *No matter how frustrating or boring or constraining*
> *or painful or oppressive our experience,*
> *we can always choose how we respond."*
> – Marc Brackett

Carefully choosing your thoughts is not easy. The better you know and understand yourself, the better equipped you are to choose your thoughts, your words, and even your prayers wisely. The danger is in allowing your extremes to become habits that become an automatic, entitled default setting.

When you take personal responsibility for what your thoughts create, you choose to stop creating that which you do not want. Your power is choice and focus. You must focus on your deepest desires for healing, abundance, joy, and peace in everything. This beckons you to take your life seriously and realize you are not a victim of your past, your culture, or even societal influences. You are the creator of your joy. You create your future by choosing the ways in which you respond today. But as powerful as your thoughts are, they are emboldened, enriched, and encouraged by your feelings.

> *"Our oldest and most cherished traditions remind us that there is a divine language, One that has no words and doesn't involve the usual outward signs of communication that we make with our hands or bodies.*
> *It comes in a form so simple that we already know how to "speak" it fluently. In fact, we use it every day of our lives-*
> *it is the language of human emotion."*
> – Gregg Braden
> *The Divine Matrix*

Ancient traditions and modern sciences suggest that prayer is a sophisticated technology that allows us to recognize the possibilities of future outcomes and choose which outcome we experience. As we become the very conditions that we choose to experience in our world, we attract the outcomes that mirror our choices. When combined, thought and emotion produce feeling. Feeling produces the vibratory patterns that affect our world. As we change the frequency of our feelings, we change the pattern of vibration, thus shifting patterns in our outer world, leaving ripples in our wake.

What does this spiritual (and scientific) mumbo-jumbo have to do with us needing to learn to manage and reframe thoughts poisoned by extremes and narcissistic entitlement? The answer is everything. The Essenes believed that among emotion, thought, and feeling, although closely related, thought and emotion must first be considered independently and then merged into a union that, once named and claimed, becomes feeling, the silent language of creation.

We begin with emotion. The words "emotions" and "feelings" are often used interchangeably, but emotion requires no thought. It is automatic and begins in the primal cortex. It is built-in, basic, and active. Human beings are capable of two primary emotions: love and fear. Once an emotion moves from the primal cortex to the frontal cortex, we can name it, and then it becomes a feeling. Emotion is considered the source that drives us toward our goals in life. Feeling is the union of emotion and thought. Thought may be considered the guidance system that directs our emotions. The image created by our thoughts determines where our emotions and attention are directed. In the absence of emotion, there is no power to make our thoughts real.

To have a feeling, by definition, we must first have both an underlying thought and an emotion. When we examine, name, or claim a feeling, we have united the power of emotion and thought. When we allow our emotions to be based on fear, our thoughts will be entitled and become the seeds of misery in our lives. If our emotion begins as a part of the fear family (anxiety, fear, hatred, sorrow, frustration, etc.), we must consciously choose to move that emotion into a positive category (hope, forgiveness, happiness, and possibility). When we are in our centers, we create an endowed garden for those thoughts to grow into reality.

I have spoken at length about the power of the quality of your thoughts and the words you use. I know people can be numb to the importance of positive thinking or thought management, but let me share some important and impressive research that adds an exclamation point to my insistence.

Below are a couple of experiments referred to and edited from Gregg Braden's 2007 book, *Divine Matrix*.[1] These experiments prove that DNA, emotion, thoughts, and feelings work together in wonderful and mysterious ways.

EXPERIMENT 1)

A 1993 study in *Advances* journal reported that the Army performed experiments to determine precisely whether the emotion-DNA connection continues following a separation and, if so, at what distances. The researchers collected a swab of tissue from a volunteer's mouth. The DNA was isolated and taken to another room in the building, where researchers investigated a phenomenon that science says shouldn't exist.

In a specially designed chamber, the DNA was measured electrically to see if it responded to the emotions of the person it came from. The subject was shown a series of video images designed to induce states of emotion in their body. Although the donor was hundreds of feet from the DNA sample, the DNA acted as if it were physically connected to the body!

Dr. Cleve Backster designed this experiment for the Army. When the

---

1. P.P. Gariaev et al., "Investigation of the Fluctuation Dynamics of DNA Solutions by Laser Correlation Spectroscopy," *Bulletin of the Lebedev Physics Institute*, no. 11-12 (1992): 23-30, cited by Vladimir Poponin, "The DNA Phantom Effect: Direct Measurement of a New Field in the Vacuum Substructure," *Update on DNA Phantom Effect*, March 19, 2022, accessed October 14, 2024 (Dead Link).

subject was moved further and further away from the DNA, the results stayed the same. Their DNA and the subject were still connected. Even measuring responses with an atomic clock proved that there was no time lapse in the DNA's response to the emotion.

EXPERIMENT 2)

In 1991, the HeartMath Institute was formed to explore the power that human feelings have over the body and the role those feelings play in our world. One of the most significant findings is the documentation of the doughnut-shaped field of energy that surrounds the heart and extends beyond the body.

Researchers began by isolating human DNA in a beaker and then exposing it to a powerful form of feeling known as coherent emotion. They analyzed the DNA both chemically and visually. The results were undeniable, and the implications unmistakable. Human emotion changed the shape of the DNA without physically touching it!

We've been conditioned to believe that our DNA doesn't change in response to anything that we do in our lives. However, these two experiments show us that nothing could be further from the truth!

Many studies on the brain have proven just how powerful our words are. In the book *Words Can Change Your Brain,* authors Andrew Newberg, M.D., and Mark Robert Waldman write:

> *By holding a positive and optimistic [word] in your mind, you stimulate frontal lobe activity. This area includes specific language centers that connect directly to the motor cortex responsible for moving you into action. And as our research has shown, the longer you concentrate on positive words, the more you begin to affect other areas of the brain. Functions in the parietal lobe start to change, which changes your perception of yourself and the people you interact with. A positive view of yourself will bias you toward seeing the good in others, whereas a negative self-image will incline you toward suspicion and doubt. Over time the structure of your thalamus will also change in response to your conscious words, thoughts, and feelings, and we believe that the thalamic changes affect the way in which you perceive reality.*

Words are energy in the form of vibrations. It is believed that these vibrations create our reality. The Bible tells us that God said, "Let there be light," and spoke it into existence; sound became form. Thoughts become words, and words become reality. Similar stories of thoughts, words, and vibrating sound creating the world are told in Hinduism and by Native American tribes. According to Rory Vaden, MBA, CSP, CPAE, and *New York Times* bestselling author of *Take the Stairs*:

> *"When we can actually envision something in our minds, see it clearly, feel it, love it, get excited about the possibility, we can bring that vision to life. A vision is an inspiring mental picture that propels you to take action. The more clearly you see your vision, the more you can focus on it, and the more you focus on it, the more it draws you to action. A great vision is like a powerful magnet pulling you into a future of becoming a better you."*

We believe that better you is, of course, the centered you. A centered, powerful perspective allows you to move positively forward in your life, trusting that through your prayers, you can plant seeds of new possibilities. In this knowledge, your prayers become expressions of thanks, giving life to your choices as they blossom in the world.

> *"Prayer is to us as water is to the seed of a plant."*
> – Greg Braden

What if the feeling is the prayer? What if it is not just the words we choose to speak but the feeling we allow to influence and empower the words we speak that initiates creation? When we begin to understand this spiritual fact, we begin to grasp the enormous importance of each thought and feeling we allow in our lives.

Researchers of the brain tell us that you can only hold one feeling at a time in your mind. Which thoughts, words, and actions will you choose to create with? You manage your extremes by noticing when they fill your mind. Once you recognize them, you can choose to replace them with feelings that are more joyful, interesting, welcoming, and empowering.

Once you understand the centered and extreme tendencies of each of the six colors that make up The Personality Color Matrix Wheel, you can begin to discern the color blends of the people you meet and interact with. For example, in most contexts, my primary color is green. I, too, believe in a bigger vision of equality, respect, fairness, and the power of dreams. I am a gardener of hope and desire harmony over opposition. I very much desire for people to realize that they are creators of their reality. In a personal or relationship context, my secondary color is orange. I love to laugh and enjoy my family and friends. My tertiary color is yellow. My friends and family are very important to me.

A professional context alters my color blend. My dominant or primary color remains green. (I love words; the more descriptive and inspiring, the better. As you have probably noticed, most of the quotes that I have chosen were also written by people who have a great deal of green influence in their color blends.) At work, my secondary color is red. I love excelling. I love carving out new paths to explore. I love being my own boss. I am a serial entrepreneur. Building a reputation that is respected is as important to me as making a difference in the world (an example of my red and green personality influences working together). My tertiary color in a professional context is purple. I need purple influence to organize and manage my thoughts and have the discipline to write every day to be a successful author. I do not believe people's personalities are stagnant snapshots of who they are. Just as we can develop and strengthen our emotional intelligence, we can develop personality skills and talents that do not come "naturally" to us.

When you begin to recognize a person's color tendencies, you can better understand how to speak to their preferred listening. To explain, I am going to ask a question and change the wording to appeal to different color personality tendencies. The first is an example of how I might speak into the listening of what we consider the warmer colors on The Personality Color Matrix Wheel.

If each one of us is an artist expressing our deepest passions, fears, dreams, and desires through the living essence of a mysterious quantum canvas, will we wield our brushes like machetes in extreme, wild strokes, cutting into the hearts and minds of those around us, or choose to create from our center—beautifully, kindly, thoughtfully, and wisely?

Now, I will rephrase the question for the listening of more strength-related colors: blue, red, and purple. They are more direct, get-to-the-point people. For example:

If you understood that extremes are ineffective, harmful, and control your most important relational outcomes and that YOU have the power to manage them, would you use your strength to do so?

Of course, many people's personality color blends are a combination of strength and warmth colors. Every color of our color blend influences how we perceive and interact with the people around us. The difference in how the above questions are phrased is a small example of how important our choice of words can be. When you understand how people with different personality color tendencies approach situations differently, you are better equipped to communicate effectively. The power of words not only impacts our communication; we also use words to imagine and create our realities.

To some, the implications of being surrounded by a malleable world that we actively help create can be a bit terrifying. It can feel daunting to realize what powerful creators we are. Because of the strong green influence in my color blends, I love hope, change, possibility, and growth. What frightens me is when people do not understand or accept that each of us has a critical role to play in the quality and health of our relationships and the health of the heart of the world.

> *"We are dangerous when we are not conscious of our responsibility for how we behave, think and feel."*
> – Marshall B. Rosenberg

My clients will often confess how they hate their extreme thoughts and behaviors. Some have said they want to eliminate them, get rid of them, or destroy them. Do you hear the intensity of the feelings in those statements? Even though the outcomes of extremes are destructive and miserable, we can never kill or eliminate feelings of hatred, bitterness, anger, or confusion by continuing to give our extremes our passionate, creative power. Emotions are energy that cannot be distinguished. However, they can be transformed into centered feelings that have the power to create positive things in our lives.

Daryl Davis, an accomplished black musician who plays R&B and the blues, is a fantastic example of this kind of conscious manifesting. Davis played with musical icons like B.B. King and Chuck Berry. He even played with Bill Clinton. He is known for befriending Ku Klux Klan members.

According to a conversation Yoonji Han had with Daryl Davis for a 2023 *Insider* article, Davis learned about racism in 1968 when he was ten years old. He was in the fourth grade in a newly integrated school in Massachusetts. All of his friends were white, and they invited him to join the Cub Scouts. He remembers they had a parade for Patriots Day. He was the only Black scout. The sidewalks were lined with white people waving and cheering—until a few of the people started throwing bottles and soda pop cans.

THE PERSONALITY COLOR MATRIX

I didn't understand what was going on. I thought these people just didn't like the Scouts. It wasn't until my Scout leaders came running over and covering me with their own bodies that I realized no other Scouts were getting hit.

That night, my mother and father sat me down, and explained to me what racism was. You may find this a little hard to believe, especially in this day and age, but I had never heard the word "racism" because it had not existed in my world, growing up surrounded by people from all over the world. We all got along, even if we didn't speak the same language.

This early incident created an insatiable desire to understand the roots of racism so that he could help end it. Davis continued:

My first encounter with a member of the Ku Klux Klan was in 1983. I was out playing at the Silver Dollar Lounge, which has a reputation for being an all-white lounge, in Frederick, Maryland. I had just finished playing the first song when someone put an arm around my shoulder. It was a white guy with a big smile on his face.

He said, "I sure like your all's music," and said I was the first Black guy he'd seen playing like Jerry Lee Lewis.

I was not offended by the statement, but I was surprised that he didn't know the Black origin of Jerry Lee Lewis' piano style. So I proceeded to tell him that Jerry Lee and myself, we learned from the same place: from Black blues and boogie-woogie piano players.

He tried to debate me, but I said, "Look, man, Jerry Lee Lewis was a very good friend of mine. He told me himself."

The man was fascinated, and offered to buy me a drink. He said it was his first time sitting with a Black guy, and I asked why. His friend next to him elbowed him and told him to tell me why.

The man looked at me and said, "I'm a member of the Ku Klux Klan."

I started laughing—I thought he was joking. But he pulled out his wallet and handed me his KKK membership card. I stopped laughing then. It wasn't funny anymore.

We still talked, and the man gave me his phone number and told me to call him whenever I returned to the Silver Dollar Lounge, because he wanted his friends to see the Black guy who plays like Jerry Lee.
It only dawned on me a couple years later that I blew my chance to ask them the question that had been plaguing me since I was 10 years old: How can you hate me when you don't know me? Who better to ask that of than someone who went out of their way to join an organization that has, for over 100 years, practiced hating people who don't look like them?
I spent the next several years traveling across the country, interviewing the man from that night, Klan leaders, and Klan members, and eventually writing a book about it.

I used diplomacy in my conversations, likely a result of my upbringing living in a diplomat's family. I've learned that every human being wants to be loved, respected, heard, treated fairly and truthfully, and wants the same things for their family. If we can learn to apply those five core values, we can navigate even adversarial situations much more smoothly and positively. Yes, I have been the impetus for that conversion, but I don't go to them with the intent of influencing them. I go to them to find out why they believe what they believe. The more we conversed, the more people would change. When I say respect, I don't mean I necessarily respected what they said, but rather their right to say it. One time, someone said we should put Black people down. But I sat there calmly, and asked if they'd be curious about why I didn't fight back. Now their ears are open. Now we can nourish those seeds, water them, and, in most cases, they bloom.

Of course, some people go to their graves with hatred in their hearts. But what gives me hope, despite the current state of this country, is the fact that I've seen it work. I've seen people change.

Davis says he did not convert anybody. However, when they realized their hate might be misguided, over two hundred Klan members converted and gave him their robes. Davis collected the robes and keeps them in his home as a reminder of the dent he made in racism by simply sitting down and having dinner with people. The words we choose and the conversations we have shape our social reality. We make sense of things through conversation, and what emerges as knowledge is a broad social agreement created among people through the words they exchange.

THE PERSONALITY COLOR MATRIX

"In the end, a person is only known by the impact he or she has on others."
– Jim Stovall

Daryl Davis's thoughts and words were his prayers that came to fruition. Prayer is not something we save for church or sadness. Prayer is not begging for help. God, Heavenly Father, the Divine Mother, the Universe, the Higher Power, or even the Prince of Darkness, it doesn't matter what you call the designer of creation. It matters most that you realize that you are, at all times, consciously choosing to co-create in your divine creator's image. Daryl went about his life doing, saying, and being a *centered* human being who chose to be curious about and interested in other human beings. We are hungry for more people like Daryl Davis in the world. We are starving for the center, yet gorging on extremes. No wonder much of the nation feels like throwing up. When we focus on extremes (the places where human beings have failed, fallen short, are blind, confused, self-deceived, and have behaved in hideous ways), we encourage more of the same. This is the complete opposite of what most of us want.

Centered, inspiring words can change a person's life for the better, while extreme, toxic words can cause irreparable harm. Do you really want to change the world? Do you really want the tolerance, equality, equity, justice, and compassion you seek? Give your extremes less power in your life. If you want to experience examples of extreme, toxic, and destructive words being wielded like sharpened swords by dysfunctional adolescents, simply turn on your television or scroll any social media platform. It is difficult for me to understand how adults on both sides of the political aisle have become so toxic and vile. Although we have mentioned the damaging influence of political entitlement, I want to believe that we are capable of so much more than the enmity and rage that our political leaders currently model.

So what can we do? We need to relentlessly seek that which is inspiring, uplifting, encouraging, hopeful, helpful, compassionate, and understanding. Let us emulate Daryl instead of the lost, entitled, and harmful criminals that surround us. What do you imagine might happen if each of us were to consciously choose our words from our centers? What if we fought to focus our attention on creating new possibilities for respect, understanding, connection, and amity? What if we could imagine the world and our relationships healing, growing, and being filled and enhanced by all that is necessary for them to thrive? Would it alter the care with which you chose to use your words if you knew that choosing your words carefully from your center could invite those around you to believe in the world differently? I want you to understand that you *are* that powerful and intelligent. Your superpowers are built into your DNA. A person's greatest challenge is learning how to manage, direct, and consciously create with their words. You are a great creator in your center. You create chaos and destruction in your extremes. Whether you create consciously or unconsciously, whether you create peace, possibility, joy or misery, depression, frustration, or rage, you are creating with every emotion and thought that becomes your feelings.

Can we, as human beings, accept the power of creation we have been endowed with and let go of our death grip on misery and pain? Can we recognize the difference between the centered thoughts and actions that create growth, happiness, peace, and connection? Can we, with careful discipline, avoid giving power to thoughts born out of our extremes that will always bring destruction and devastation to the world?

Consciously choose your center. Your center is your protagonist. It is your advocate and champion of your greatest hopes and dreams. Your extremes are your antagonist: a sociopathic, hostile adversary with only your destruction in mind, an enemy who pretends to be your greatest friend. With each lie, entitlement's extremes steal, damage, and destroy. When you choose your center, you choose what is best about you.

> *"Creation follows a simple and powerful pattern:*
> *You think it, you speak it, you act it, it happens."*
> – Rory Vaden

If you take with you only one truth from these pages, let it be that ***only you can choose the thoughts, words, and attitudes that determine the quality of your life***. Wake up and start creating. Every day, your extremes will scream that you are *entitled* while your center will whisper the truth: you are beautifully and wonderfully endowed by your creator to be a creator in your life, expanding peace and liberty and modeling joy and appreciation. The greatest prayers are words of centered gratitude. We ardently thank anyone who joins us on this journey. We need you. We love you. We welcome you.

CORBIN'S THOUGHTS

Although we have arrived at the final chapter, our journey to understanding is far from over. My mother and I have so much more to share to help you learn how to strengthen your centered personality tendencies and navigate out of your extremes. We are nearing the completion of a follow-up book that will identify specific, actionable steps that you can take (based on your unique coloring) to return to the center and regain control over your life.

By raising our awareness, we can develop the capacity to resist fear's manipulations and reclaim our centered and purposeful power. To do so, we must not be afraid. We must be love. In our centers, we embody love. Love is the single most powerful transformative force on the planet. Let us not forget that love was the key to both Neo and Trinity's transcendence of the limitations imposed by the Matrix. Love lets us take flight and inspires others to soar beside us. With love, we possess the power to reshape and reunite our divided culture. When we restrain our judgments and release the extreme feelings of entitlement that isolate and blind us, we increase our capacity to appreciate our blessings and connect with others. Each of us has an essential role to play in the process of reconciliation. To this end, we each must identify the rituals, invocations, or exercises that help center us whenever we inevitably stray into our extremes.

The only thing that will prevent us from building a more compassionate and conscious world is fear. When we are afraid, we relinquish our power. Fear's goal is to immobilize us. When we feel overwhelmed and out of control, we can become apathetic and anxious. When we are afraid, our focus narrows, causing our challenges and threats to loom larger. Rather than put out the emerging fires, we become obsessed with the size of the shadows they cast on the walls.

According to a Swedish proverb, "Worry often gives a small thing a big shadow." Depending on how far we distance ourselves from the light, fear's shadows grow larger and larger. When we attempt to defend ourselves against them, we are merely battling projections.

Fear cannot be overcome by trying not to fear. The fear must be replaced with another emotion that we choose to feel instead. The energy we spend attempting not to think of something tends to only empower it. We must actively give our power to something else, preferably uplifting thoughts. As I described in Chapter One, the only way to dispel darkness is with light. When we fill our minds with grateful, kind, loving, hopeful thoughts, we leave no space for fear to fester. Rather, we change the inner Matrix where our thoughts develop.

Just as turning on a light drives away the shadows from a room, thinking positive thoughts pushes our negative thoughts to the corners of our minds. Although this action begins with conscious choice, with practice, our brains grow even more adept at producing affirming thoughts that return us to our light-filled centers.

Epictetus said, "Man is not worried by real problems so much as by his imagined anxieties about real problems." Much of the fear we allow to control us exists only in our imaginations. However, that doesn't make our premonitions of doom feel any less real. Even if the potential danger seems absurd or defies logic, it does not diminish fear's power to steal our joy and terrorize us.

In 2021, my wife and I invited a medicine man named Mark, who previously lived in Sedona, Arizona, to stay with us. At the time, he spoke very highly of a psychic healer named Joey, whom he was studying with, and invited us to meet him via video chat. Although I was curious to meet this new character, I was also highly skeptical of his powers of prescience. After listening to him pontificate about his abilities for 15 minutes without providing any evidence to back up his bold claims that he used to perform remote viewing work for the government, I decided that participating in the conversation was no longer worth my time. Waving goodbye as politely as I could, I got up and went on with my day.

The following morning, Mark approached me in earnest. "Joey mentioned that he was really impressed by you. He told me that you have a very powerful aura."

"Oh, yeah?" I said, feeling flattered. Perhaps this psychic knew what he was talking about after all.

"He'd like to help you. He told me that he can show you the blocks that are holding back your career so that you can remove them."

"Why not?" I shrugged. "I suppose it couldn't hurt."

Once again, we sat down for a videoconference with the psychic. After asking me for a few personal details, Joey appeared to plunge into the astral realm. He raised his hand and wiggled his fingers as if sifting through invisible files in a cabinet. Then he made whooshing and clicking noises with his mouth as he traversed the astral halls of the Akashic records. The search took a surprisingly long time, and he grimaced in frustration. When I glanced sideways at Mark, he nodded reassuringly as if to tell me to trust the process.

Joey squinted and squirmed in his seat as if trying to approach a destination from multiple directions, only to find that every path was obstructed. "I see..." he murmured in a vague and ominous tone.

"What do you see?" I asked, holding my breath.

Joey's eyes remained closed as he answered, "Looking down your life path, I can see what's keeping you from achieving the success you desire."

"What is it?"

"Your path ends," he said gravely. "There's no way I can move forward to observe it."

"Okay…" I stammered. "Are you saying what I think you're saying?"

"I'm afraid so." Joey opened his eyes. He wore an expression of condolence. "I see that you have about seven months."

"Before I die?" I asked. "Just to make sure we're clear."

Joey nodded. "From what I can tell, it happens because of something you ingest."

My jaw dropped. Surely, I was being pranked. I glanced at Mark to confirm that this was really happening. To my dismay, he appeared as shocked and disturbed as I was.

"I wish I could help you," Joey said with a shrug. "I can't say much more for sure."

The months that followed the premonition of my untimely demise were filled with an astonishing degree of undue anxiety. Internally, I battled against the daunting shadows cast by the prediction of my death. Even though the fatalistic premise was utterly absurd, I became very careful about everything I "ingested," especially in the final month before my supposed expiration date. Every time I swallowed, I was reminded of the prediction. I have never chewed so thoroughly in all my life.

The good news is that I am still alive. The psychic was obviously mistaken. The unfortunate part is that, for seven months, I allowed a stranger, whom I initially got up and walked away from, to control my life. The psychic planted a seed of worry in my mind that led me to suffer unnecessarily for more than half a year. That idea may seem ludicrous to you as you read it… because it is. However, the experience taught me that when we don't take responsibility for our thoughts, we can unconsciously surrender our power to others, allowing them to manipulate and rule us with fear. Even though the entire scenario was preposterous, it led me to seriously contemplate matters of death, judgment, and the afterlife.

Being a musical artist, I focused my creative angst on a musical and literary project that I called *Inferno: Descent*. The album and accompanying audiobook were a modern reimagining of Dante's classic. The story details my descent into the underworld, with each layer presided over by a particular vice, including lust, gluttony, greed, violence, and fraud (all extremes). One chapter of the story described my attempts to break free from the manipulations of media corporations and reconcile with my mother, an experience that my words consciously manifested.

In the end, the *Inferno* project didn't end with my descent. In the midst of creating it, I realized that just focusing on the extremes and fear left out the most beautiful, centered parts of life. To create balance and inspire hope, I composed and released a second adjoining album called *Inferno: Ascent*, which included songs aimed not just at pointing out problems but embodying solutions and embracing love over fear. If you are so inclined, you can enjoy these albums and accompanying audiobook by visiting YouTube and searching "Floowood Inferno." Please enjoy the art and music as my gift; it would thrill me if it brought you insight and inspiration on your path.

This world desperately needs centered role models who can embody love, tolerance, and compassion. Let us embody a love that is so undeniable that it positively transforms everyone we come into contact with. When we consciously live from our centered color personality tendencies, in the spirit of love and appreciation, our thoughts and behaviors become capable of manifesting wondrous things. We now have the opportunity to manifest a new era of understanding and forgiveness. Although forgiveness is a display of warmth, it is also an exercise of strength. When we forgive, we allow ourselves to move forward. When we reconcile, we allow ourselves to move forward together.

> *"When I used to look out at this world, all I could see was its edges, its boundaries, its rules and controls, its leaders and laws. But now, I see another world. A different world where all things are possible. A world of hope. Of peace."*
> – Lana Wachowski
> *The Matrix* screenplay

After putting down this book, I encourage you to step into wonder. Commit yourself to finding meaning and gratitude in the smallest breakthroughs. You are endowed with everything you need to realize your most extraordinary purpose. Don't allow yourself to be deceived by entitlement's lie that the world in which you live is grotesque and cruel. Yes, there will always be examples of hideous, hateful behaviors because some people will continue to choose their extremes, but with the knowledge we have shared, you have the tools necessary to make yourself a powerful and positive force of understanding. You, too, can choose to see the beauty in *The Matrix* despite the violence. We see what we seek. You can see yourself in prison or paradise.

I'm reminded of the climactic finale of *The Matrix Revolutions* as Agent Smith stands triumphantly over Neo and asks, "Why Mr. Anderson?

THE PERSONALITY COLOR MATRIX

Why? Why do you persist?" As Neo rises from the ground, refusing to give up, he replies calmly, "Because I choose to."

Our human free will makes us more powerful than we can imagine. If we understand that narcissistic entitlement strengthens our fears, it is incumbent upon each of us to learn how to inoculate our feelings of entitlement. Entitlement is a parasitic virus that feeds on our fears and insecurities while fueling our extremes. With The Personality Color Matrix technology, we cannot only treat the root of our individual dis-*ease*, but we can boost our collective immunity to fear's poison and reclaim our power. We are on the verge of a paradigm shift. I hope you can see it.

Life can be heaven. Life can be hell. You choose. You have all the power.

> *"Our goal is to create a beloved community*
> *and this will require a qualitative change in our souls*
> *as well as a quantitative change in our lives."*
> – Martin Luther King, Jr.

GLOSSARY

1. Green - Yellow - Compassion is the glue that seals the cusp between green and yellow color personality tendencies. Both colors *care* and long to be of *service*. People with strong yellow tendencies care about serving the individuals they love. The compassion they feel is personal. Their desire to relate and connect with others motivates them to be of service. Individuals with strong green personality tendencies care about groups of people. The compassion they feel is more communal (even global). Their desire to serve a higher purpose motivates them to join causes and movements to create a more fair and just society (or world). Because of their compassionate nature, individuals with strong yellow and green personality tendencies value warmth over strength. They prefer to think with their heart. The key lesson for this combination is to see the value and wisdom of strength.

2. Blue - Green - Individuals with strong green and blue personality tendencies love to solve problems and are characterized by their **Openness**. That means they are both open to new ideas, mostly from individuals that they deem to be credible or virtuous. While individuals with strong blue tendencies focus on solving detailed problems, individuals with strong green tendencies take action to solve global problems or issues in their communities. Blue and green color tendencies are both deeply devoted to things that they commit to. They both love to read about subjects that fascinate them and travel the world to explore and discover. In their extreme, their openness transforms into dismissiveness. The key lesson for this combination is to remain open to seeing the value and wisdom in perspectives that they may ideologically or factually disagree with. These are new opportunities to explore other interpretations of reality and understanding.

3. Red - Green - In addition to being complementary colors, green tendencies and red tendencies share a Personality Color Chord centered around **Honor**. They respect those who live honorably and stand up for their beliefs. While individuals with strong green personality tendencies find fulfillment in belonging to groups, individuals with strong red personality tendencies find fulfillment in leading groups. In either case, both green and red color personality tendencies take pride in who they are, where they come from, and what they believe. In a centered state, this translates to a sense of patriotic nationalism reminiscent of the competitive (yet united and collaborative) spirit of the Olympic Games or International Sports. However, in its extreme, this sense of Nationalism can quickly transform into a bullying and exclusionary Supremacy Identity. The key lesson for this combination is to be humble, mindful, and respectful of others, seeing them as an extension of yourself.

4. Green - Purple - Adherence best describes the Personality Color Chord between Purple and Green tendencies. Both of these colors value and respect politeness. They both believe that there are rules to civility that should be followed. Both are disciplined and demonstrate a sense of responsibility. They set high standards for themselves and others. Both personality tendencies are also adept at seeing the big picture, delegating, mediating, and leading others effectively through education and training. They prefer structure and order and exhibit a strong sense of integrity and fairness in their actions. In our culture, this quality is commonly referred to as "political correctness." At its extreme, such strict adherence to a regulatory or ethical code of conduct becomes stringent and policing. The key lesson for this combination is to discover and define yourself as an individual outside of your career or group identity.

5. Orange - Green - The Personality Color Chord connecting green and orange color tendencies is defined by **Inspiration**. Both color personality tendencies focus on "what can be," embracing possibilities, and dreaming about the future. Individuals with strong green or orange tendencies approach life with creativity, pronoia, and optimism. Both value relationships and are often seen as warm, engaging, and encouraging. While those with strong green personalities are known for their empathy and integrity, those with strong orange personality tendencies bring energy and enthusiasm into interactions. Combined, these colors emphasize connecting with others and fostering human potential. However, in their extreme, their naivety can lead them to be led astray or taken advantage of, and their idealism or fanaticism can quickly transform into withdrawn escapism. The key lesson for this combination is to approach life with pragmatism.

6. Red - Yellow - Steadfastness defines the Personality Color Chord between red and yellow color tendencies. In their center, individuals with strong red personality tendencies and yellow personality tendencies are loyal and committed to the end. Both colors are devoted to serving and defending people, projects, or principles entrusted to their care. They can also be highly driven in their respective areas of interest. While individuals with strong yellow personality tendencies are motivated by a desire to serve and be supportive, especially valuing relationships, individuals with strong red personality tendencies are often motivated by the pursuit of success and challenges. Despite these differences, both types are reliable and willing to go the extra mile to achieve their objectives, whether it be to serve others or meet a challenge head-on. Combined, these colors emphasize creating safety to support and protect what they care about. In their extreme, individuals with strong red and yellow personality tendencies can become emotionally volatile, possessive, and blameful. The key lesson for this combination is to learn to release personal grudges and take accountability for past or present aggressive or passive-aggressive transgressions.

7. Blue - Yellow - Introspectiveness defines the Personality Color Chord between Yellow and Blue tendencies. In their centers, both of these color personality tendencies are extremely thoughtful. However, what they dwell on can be quite different. While individuals with strong yellow tendencies tend to overthink relationships and become immobilized, individuals with strong blue tendencies tend to overthink global problems and procrastinate in an attempt to perfect projects. Both value stability and consistency in their environments. They strive to maintain harmony, albeit in different ways—yellows through nurturing relationships and avoiding conflict, and blues through precision and accuracy. Both color personality tendencies appreciate a sense of structure and can be detail-oriented. Individuals with strong yellow personality tendencies ensure that people's needs are accommodated in a supportive manner, and individuals with strong blues tendencies focus on getting things right. In its extreme, this introspective nature transforms into a paralyzing state of rumination over past or present failures. The key lesson for this combination is to stop beating themselves up and let go of whatever negative thoughts are immobilizing them, replacing them with thoughts that are positive and self-affirming.

8. Purple - Yellow - In addition to being complementary colors, yellow and purple personality tendencies share a Personality Color Chord centered around **Service & Mediation**. Individuals with strong yellow and purple personality tendencies both demonstrate responsibility and dedication to their tasks and relationships. Yellow tendencies focus on supporting people and fostering intimacy and trust, while purple tendencies are more task-oriented but still value trust and effective communication. Both yellow and purple personality tendencies aim to create positive outcomes and can be very reliable. Neither try to make waves. They would much prefer to make peace and move on toward being of service to their family at home or their colleagues and clients at work. At its extreme, this dedication to serving and helping others can result in self-neglect. In a professional context, this can result in burnout and exhaustion. In a personal context, the result is a feeling of disconnection and resentment towards loved ones or feeling so overextended and overwhelmed attending to others that we fail to make proper time to care for ourselves. The key lesson for this combination is to take care of yourself in order to better serve others.

9. Yellow - Orange - Sociability is the glue that seals the cusp between orange and yellow color personality tendencies. Both colors prioritize communication and have a people-oriented approach. They thrive in social settings and value relationships and connections with others. Yellow personalities focus on serving and supporting others, often putting people's needs first, while orange personalities bring energy, enthusiasm, and a sense of fun to their interactions. In their centers, they are also willing to extend the most grace whenever others around them miss the mark. While individuals with strong yellow personality tendencies are naturally sympathetic to other people's feelings, individuals with strong orange personality tendencies can relate to times when they have fallen flat on their faces and respond with compassion and encouragement when others fail. Combined, orange and yellow personality tendencies can be very engaging and charismatic, making them effective at building trust and maintaining relationships. In their extreme, they can believe themselves to be deserving of special treatment that accommodates their hypersensitivity, anxiety disorders, or inability to focus, show up on time, or complete mundane tasks. We refer to this entitled mindset in which one's "specialness" makes them an exception to the rule, *"exceptionalism."* (Although there is nothing exceptional about it). The key lesson for this combination is to declare self-autonomy and not lean or rely on others for support.

10. Purple - Orange - The Personality Color Chord between orange and purple color tendencies is defined by **Maximization**, the desire to get the most out of what you have time to access. While individuals with strong purple personality tendencies are determined to maximize productivity and efficiency, individuals with strong orange personality tendencies are determined to maximize their time to play and have the most fun possible. This dichotomy epitomizes the motto, "Work hard. Play hard." These colors also share the capability to engage and motivate others. Purple and orange tendencies combine to create a driven, energetic, and adaptable quick-thinker, adept at navigating social and professional environments to achieve their goals. In their extreme, individuals with both strong purple and orange tendencies struggle with moderation. Their desire to maximize results leads them to exemplify binge-like behavior that can become harmful. In a professional context, their tunnel vision can transform them into workaholics. In a personal context, their desire to escape can derail their productivity or capacity to manage their responsibilities effectively. The key lesson for this combination is to exercise balance.

11. Blue - Orange - In addition to being complimentary colors, orange and blue personality tendencies share a Personality Color Chord centered around **Cleverness**. Individuals with strong blue and orange personality tendencies both have a knack for creativity. While blue personalities are detail-oriented and craft intricate and immersive worlds and stories, individuals with strong orange personalities showcase dynamic and energetic performative creativity. Both color tendencies can be inventive and imaginative in how they communicate, tell stories, and explore new ideas and possibilities. While individuals with strong blue tendencies rely on their intellect, individuals with strong orange tendencies rely on their wit and sense of humor. In their extreme, this cleverness can result in procrastination and acrimony. Their sharp words can leave wounds that are impossible to fully heal. The key lesson for this combination is to stay humble and learn to refrain from saying things publicly that jeopardize their relationships and careers.

12. Purple - Red - Leadership is the glue that seals the cusp between red and purple personality tendencies. Both color personality tendencies love to lead. They both value time, hard work, individual effort, and getting things done. Individuals with strong purple and red personality tendencies share a focus on results and achievement. Both red and purple personality tendencies are driven and determined, often setting high standards for themselves and those around them. In addition, they value taking responsibility and would prefer to be respected rather than liked. They possess a strong sense of self-confidence and are not afraid to take charge to achieve their goals. While people with strong purple personality tendencies emphasize efficiency and strategic planning, red personalities are more straightforward in their approach. Both value competence and are often seen as leaders who can effectively guide others towards success. In their extreme, individuals with strong purple and red personality tendencies transform from leaders to fascist dictators, censorial bullies, and tyrannical autocrats, imposing their arrogant and prideful will or agenda upon others. The key lesson for this combination is to learn the wisdom of compassion. There are more effective ways to lead people than with forceful strength. Learning to channel warmth motivates others to follow naturally.

13. Orange - Red - Confidence is the glue that seals the cusp between red and orange personality tendencies. Both red and orange personality tendencies have strong personalities and are highly individualistic. Both like to get their way. Neither likes to be told what to do. Individuals with strong orange and red personality tendencies both exhibit a high level of energy and drive. They are action-oriented and enjoy taking on new challenges in dynamic environments. Both types are natural leaders, though their styles differ: individuals with strong orange personalities lead with charisma and enthusiasm, while individuals with strong red personalities lead with assuredness and assertiveness. They are both motivated by results and can be quite persuasive when pursuing their goals. Additionally, they embrace taking risks and can adapt quickly to change. In their extreme, they can be self-absorbed and inconsiderate. The key lesson for this combination is to tell the truth as often as possible, or at least not lie.

14. Red - Blue - The Personality Color Chord connecting red and blue color tendencies is defined by **Expertise & Intensity.** Individuals with strong red and blue personality tendencies share a focus on achieving results and a strong sense of determination. Both types value precision and reliability, though they express these qualities differently. Red personalities are decisive and direct, often prioritizing action and quick decision-making. Blue personalities, on the other hand, are detail-oriented and meticulous, ensuring that outcomes meet high standards. Both appreciate competence and efficiency and are dedicated to completing tasks successfully. They rely on their intelligence and analytical skills to navigate challenges. In their extreme, this expertise can transform into arrogance and demeaning haughtiness. The key lesson for this combination is to be mindful of others' feelings and sensitivities and learn to advise without being too critical or condescending.

15. Blue - Purple - Practicality is the glue that seals the cusp between blue and purple personality tendencies. Both purple and blue personality tendencies love order, education, and structure. Relying on their heads for guidance, they both value logic, forethought, discipline, and pragmatic thinking. Individuals with strong blue and purple personality tendencies share a focus on detail and a commitment to quality outcomes. Both types value information and are keen observers, using their analytical skills to solve problems effectively. Blue personalities emphasize accuracy and precision, while purple personalities prioritize efficiency and organization. Despite their different motivations, both types have a tendency to be thorough in their work, ensuring that all relevant details are considered. They strive for excellence and are often respected for their reliability and competence. In their extreme, their practical nature transforms into a hypercritical or censorial need to control information and be right. The key lesson for this combination is to learn to be flexible and provide space for warmth, compassion, and creativity to flourish.

ABOUT THE AUTHORS

In 2008, Dawn L. Billings was selected by *O, the Oprah Magazine,* and The White House Project as one of the nation's 80 emerging women leaders and chosen as one of 15 "Women of Achievement" by the Cobb County YWCA.

Dawn is the founder and executive director of the Relationship Help Resort in Arizona, where she offers relationship healing intensives for couples looking for ways to strengthen their marriages and rebuild their broken relationships. Dawn is a personality and relationship expert who specializes in entitlement issues that are currently plaguing our society.

Dawn is the author and architect of the acclaimed relationship personality test PrimaryColorsPersonality.com and the founder and CEO of the informative RelationshipHelp.com programs. She is the author of the RelationshipHelpatHome.com curriculum, an online relationship-building program that can be enjoyed at your convenience in the comfort of your own home.

Corbin B. Billings is an award-winning filmmaker, author, motivational speaker, and co-creator of The Personality Color Matrix, an online digital personality assessment technology that helps individuals hack their personalities and upgrade their understanding by recognizing the six core constructs of human behavioral tendencies.

An innovator, trendsetter, and unifier by nature, Corbin is dedicated to finding cutting-edge techniques to help people understand one another, communicate with respect and dignity, and navigate from a state of divisive extreme discontent to one of centered gratitude.

Email: connect@thecolormatrix.com. Phone: 310-237-2567.

THANK YOU FOR READING OUR BOOK!

Thank you for purchasing a copy of our book! We're thrilled to have you join our growing community of centered relationship seekers on this journey of self-discovery and understanding. As a token of our sincere appreciation, we're excited to offer you the opportunity to take the full online six-test series for **FREE**.

These tests are designed to provide deep insights into your personality and help you navigate life's challenges with greater clarity.
Scan the QR Code and use code: ReconnectNow

We appreciate your interest in our book and value your feedback as it helps us improve future versions. We would appreciate it if you could leave your invaluable review on Amazon.com with your feedback. Thank you!

www.ingramcontent.com/pod-product-compliance
Lightning Source LLC
Chambersburg PA
CBHW050242010526
44107CB00032B/1385/J